LAKES SPORT & SLATE

Peter Sterling
Dan Robinson

Limestone:
 Les Ainsworth, Nick Wharton

Slate:
 Paddy Cave, John Holden, Misha Nepogodiev, Steve Scott

Micro-Granite:
 Colin Downer, Bill Young

Sandstone:
 Chris Fisher, Paul Jennings, Ron Kenyon

Contributors:
 Al Davis, Brian Davison, Rick Graham, Craig Matheson, Al Phizacklea, Keith Phizacklea, Alan Steele

Artwork:
 Al Davis, Peter Sterling

Maps:
 Don Sargeant

Photo Research:
 John Holden, Steve Scott, Peter Sterling

Editor:
 Steve Scott

LAKES SPORT & SLATE

WARNING

Climbing is a dangerous activity that carries a risk of injury or death. You climb at your own risk. You are the sole judge of conditions. You take responsibility for your own actions.

The information in this guide is derived from a number of sources. While every effort is made to check its accuracy please do not presume that any of the material in this book is accurate. Neither the publisher nor anyone involved in the publication of this book can be held responsible for omissions, mistakes, nor held liable for any personal or third party injuries or damage, howsoever caused, arising from its use.

A catalogue record for this book is available from the British Library.

ISBN 978-0-85028-063-0

Designed by Wired Guides
Layout by Peter Sterling

Maps redrawn by permission of Ordnance Survey
© Crown copyright and database rights 2020 OS 100012930

Published by Wired Guides and The Fell and Rock Climbing Club of the English Lake District Limited - Industrial and Provident Societies Reg. 30506 R

© The Fell and Rock Climbing Club of the English Lake District Limited
FRCC Guides 2020

Dreaming of Red Rocks F7a+ (page 263) Liam Lonsdale — Keith Sharples

FRCC

The Lake District is a fantastic compact mountainous area in the north west of England containing so much and attracting so many with its scenery, culture and huge range of activities. Scattered amongst these fells is a stunning collection of crags with routes for everyone. This guidebook gives a selection of sports routes and detailed slate coverage. Coupled with its sister book **Lake District Rock**, which focuses on traditional climbing, it will keep most people happy for a lifetime.

Lakes Sport & Slate documents climbing the four rock types where fixed protection climbing is prolific in the Lakes: Limestone; Slate; Micro-Granite; and Sandstone.

The Fell and Rock Climbing Club (FRCC) has been producing rock climbing guides to the Lake District since 1922. These authoritative guides are produced by an energetic and enthusiastic group of climbers who know the area better than anyone, and this guide brings together that knowledge in a comprehensive selection of the best climbs on offer.

Whilst the FRCC has its origins in the Lake District, its membership is now spread throughout the United Kingdom with activities covering many aspects of "fell and rock". The club offers an extensive meets programme and a collection of well-situated huts and cottages principally in the Lake District, but also in Scotland. The Club has a long history and remains very active, ever open to new members who don't necessarily need to be climbing high 'E' numbers – a keen interest in the fells, whether for rock climbing, walking, mountaineering, ski touring or fell running is our shared enjoyment. Take a look at the **Fell and Rock Climbing Club** website: www.frcc.co.uk

I have had the pleasure of being involved with FRCC guidebook production for many years and it is always exciting as a new one nears publication. I would like to thank the guidebook team for their work and their commitment to making this project happen. As you flick through its pages I am sure you will want to get out and climb these Lake District crags – not only those you may have been to before, but also others which may have been off the "crag radar". I hope this guide will inspire you to get out and enjoy these magnificent crags and challenging routes!

Ron Kenyon – Guidebook Secretary FRCC

Pete Whillance, FA of *Life in the Fast Lane* (E5), Hodge Close (page 126) — Ed Cleasby

CONTENTS

INTRODUCTION
Lakes Sport & Slate	2
FRCC	4
We Are Wired	8
Using this Guidebook	10
Grades	11
Access & Conservation	12
Crag Guide	14
Top Routes	18
Acknowledgements	20
Editorial	22
Useful Information	23
Cumbria Bolt Fund	24
FRCC Guides	26
History of Lakes Sport & Slate Climbing	28
Geology Notes	34

LIMESTONE 36
Chapel Head Scar	38
Mill Side Scar	58
Scout Scar	60
Humphrey Head	72
Warton Main Quarry	80
Barrow Scout Cove	90

SLATE 92
Slate Quarrying Historical	94
Saddlestone Quarry	98
High Blue Quarry	100
Hodge Close Quarry	104
Parrock Quarry	136
The Works	140
Bakestone Quarry	150
Moss Rigg Quarry	152
Tilberthwaite Quarry	156
Runestone Quarry	170
Cathedral Quarry	180
Common Wood Quarry	192
Thrang Quarry	196
Dalt Quarry	198

MICRO-GRANITE 204
Micro-Granite Quarrying Historical	207
Bramcrag Quarry	208

SANDSTONE 254
St Bees Head	256
Coudy Rocks	274

INDEX 282

Up Town F6c (page 50) Yan Preston — 📷 Nick Wharton

WE ARE WIRED

In terms of guidebooks, Britain is one of the richest countries in the world. Since the word Go, activists and clubs combined to record the efforts of the day, meticulously noting the pioneering ascents of explorers so that those who came after could follow in their footsteps and marvel at their achievements. This all began back in 1909 in Snowdonia when JM Archer Thomson & AW Andrews wrote the first complete guidebook to the mountain crag of Lliwedd.

For over a century the clubs have maintained this incredible record of first ascents. These have been chronicled and revised to give climbers the most up-to-date and accurate account of climbing in Britain. These organisations have undertaken the gargantuan task of publishing definitive guidebooks to put this knowledge into the hands of climbers. This work has depended on volunteers, climbers who are committed to contributing something invaluable to the rest of us, putting something back into the world they love.

Wired is a new concept that brings these clubs together. Under this banner, the voluntary guidebook producers share their collective knowledge, skill and enthusiasm to take the information they have spent so long creating and use it in new and creative ways.

www.wired-guides.com

Wired Guides are published by a co-operative of UK definitive guidebook publishers including: the **British Mountaineering Council**, **The Climbers' Club**, the **Fell & Rock Climbing Club** of the English Lake District, the **Northumbrian Mountaineering Club**, the **Scottish Mountaineering Club**, and the **Yorkshire Mountaineering Club**. Wired guidebooks aim to document the whole of the UK describing the very best – world-class – rock climbing these beautiful green islands have to offer.

The **Wired Guides** collaborators:

The **Fell & Rock Climbing Club** has been producing guidebooks and documenting climbing in the Lake District National Park and Cumbria since 1922.
www.frcc.co.uk

 The **BMC** first became involved in publishing Peak District guidebooks in 1972 and has had a continued role ever since. Today it produces definitive guides to the gritstone and limestone crags of the Peak District and Lancashire. With gritstone guides to Stanage, Burbage, Millstone and Beyond, Froggatt, Over The Moors, The Roaches and Lancashire as well as Peak Limestone, it maintains the definitive record of over a century of climbing in this great area.
www.thebmc.co.uk

The **Climbers' Club** published the world's first ever guidebook in 1909 and is today still one of the largest definitive guidebook publishers with guidebooks covering Snowdonia, Pembroke, the South West and South of England. The club has eight huts in: Scotland, the Lake District, the Peak District, Cornwall, Pembroke, and Snowdonia. Club membership is open to all experienced climbers.
www.climbers-club.co.uk

 The **Northumbrian Mountaineering Club** documents the climbing and bouldering in Northumberland.
thenmc.org.uk

 The **Scottish Mountaineering Club** founded in 1889 has recorded new routes in its annual journal since 1890. It now publishes a range of climbers' guidebooks covering the whole of Scotland, as well as scramblers' and hillwalkers' guides. All profit from SMC guidebooks goes to the Scottish Mountaineering Trust, a registered charity providing grants to support the Scottish mountains and the communities who enjoy them.
www.smc.org.uk

 The **Yorkshire Mountaineering Club** publishes definitive guidebooks documenting Yorkshire's gritstone and limestone.
www.theymc.org.uk

USING THIS GUIDEBOOK

CHARACTER
The district offers a superbly varied climbing experience with roadside, high mountain, sport and bouldering venues. The complex geology presents amazingly varied rock, with granites, volcanic ashes and lavas, slate, limestone and sandstone all represented. The whole district forms a dome with radial drainage creating deep valleys, like the spokes of a wheel, with England's highest mountain, Scafell Pike, in the centre. You will generally be climbing in a spectacular mountain setting or amongst trees and bracken in a beautiful valley.

CONDITIONS
Year round climbing can be enjoyed; the maritime air is generally mild and can be wet. In the spring, summer and autumn wet weather generally moves through quickly followed by a day or two of cooler showery conditions before the next weather front. When high pressure prevails, long stable periods of dry warm weather can be enjoyed, sometimes for several weeks.

LOGISTICS
The North West of England has superb air, rail and road links making it easy to reach. The stunning lake and mountain scenery and huge range of activities makes this a very popular tourist destination. With so many attractions it gets very busy in holiday periods with congested roads around the main centres – Ambleside and Keswick.

www.visitcumbria.com/tourist-information-centres/

Fly: Edinburgh, Glasgow, Liverpool, Manchester, and Newcastle, all approx. 2hrs drive.

Train: Windermere and Penrith

Moving Around
A car is easiest. However, it is feasible by bus. These run throughout the district in summer, but are less frequent out of season.

Please don't threaten access; park considerately.

www.lakedistrict.gov.uk/visiting/plan-your-visit

MAPS
- BMC Harveys 1:40,000 Lake District
- Harveys Super Walker 1:25,000
- OS Explorer 1:25,000 OL4, OL5, OL6 and OL7
- OS Landranger Sheet 90

A compass is useful.

WEATHER
All year venue – check the forecast. MWIS and the Met Office offer reliable forecasts.

www.mwis.org.uk

www.metoffice.gov.uk

www.lakedistrictweatherline.co.uk

Midges: Aren't generally a problem, but can be a nuisance late May to early September.

LAYOUT
This book is laid out based on the four main sport climbing rock types: limestone, slate, micro-granite, and sandstone. See area map inside front cover.

Crag Guide
The crag guide (page 14) is a useful tool for choosing where to climb. It gives an indication of the character of the crag and the range of grades available.

Icons
See inside rear cover flap for an iconography key.

Gear
A comprehensive rack is required for the trad climbs. Quickdraws and a full weight rope for sport climbs. Some sport routes require a 70m rope; an indication of rope length and number of quickdraws is given for most sport climbing venues.

Bouldering
www.LakesBloc.com

Corrections, New Routes, etc.
www.frcc.co.uk

THE ROCK, THE ROUTES, & THE FIXED GEAR
Check everything. The routes described are a record of what's available. Yet, while finalising the guide several rockfalls have altered things. All quarries are unstable and rockfall occurs on natural crags. Some of the fixed abseil points may look OK, but there is a lot of rubbish around.

You cannot presume that any bolts, pegs, fixed gear or even the line itself is secure. You must use your judgment and if you are in any doubt, back things up or back-off. All mountain crags are bolt free and should stay that way. These are not outdoor climbing walls. Stay alert and don't drop your guard.

GRADES

Trad climbs use British grades and sport climbs use French grades. Grade ranges are colour coded – Green, Blue, Red and Black (see inside rear cover flap for grade colouring). To make choosing routes quick and easy these are shown in the text and on the topos.

UK Adjectival and Technical Grade	French Grade
	1
Moderate	2
	2+
Difficult	3-
	3
Very Difficult	3+
Mild Severe	4
Hard	4+
Mild Very Severe 4a / 4c	5
Very Severe 4a / 4c	5+
Hard Very Severe 4c / 5b	6a
5a / E1 / 5c	6a+
5b / E2 / 6a	6b
5c / E3 / 6a	6b+
6a / E4 / 6b	6c
6a / E5 / 6c	7a
	7a+
6b / E6 / 6c	7b
	7b+
6c / E7 / 7a	7c
	7c+
6c / E8 / 7a	8a
	8a+
7a / E9 / 7b	8b
	8b+
	8c
	8c+

ACCESS & CONSERVATION

BIRD RESTRICTIONS
Bird restrictions are agreed each January with climbers represented by the FRCC and BMC. The agreements are published by late January with updates posted through the spring and early summer and can be found at www.thebmc.co.uk/modules/RAD/ or on the FRCC website www.frcc.co.uk. Many crags contain nesting sites and are protected by law. Crags where there are likely to be restrictions are indicated with this bird icon – 🐦 Not all of the crags are signed and restrictions will normally be lifted if birds are not nesting.

ABSEILING FROM TREES
Pulling your ropes after abseiling directly from trees damages the bark and eventually the tree will die. Often there are established abseil points which have fixed gear that protects the trees; please use them. If there is no fixed gear then you should place your own sling around the tree and be prepared to leave it in place.

PROTECTED SITES
Many of the crags and their environs in this guidebook are protected sites: they may fall within a Site of Special Scientific Interest (SSSI), a Nature Reserve, a Bird Sanctuary, or have other protected status. If you cause damage, which could include disturbing animals, birds, plants, or geology you may find you are criminally liable and some type of enforcement action may follow. Heavy gardening is frowned upon and likely to be illegal. If you are unsure; check the status.

QR CODES
Two QR codes are used in this book. Use of QR codes is now common, intuitive, and easy; just point the camera of most smart-phones at the code and the phone will automatically present an option to navigate to the coded location.

Alternatively, for those without smart-phones, the map illustrations and GPS co-ordinates given may be used in place of the QR code.

Parking
The parking location (or most popular location) for each crag is given with:

Access
Up-to-date access details, restrictions, etc. for most crags may be easily checked on the BMC Regional Access Database (RAD) with:

 **CRAG CODE**
www.thebmc.co.uk

Access	Check the Regional Access Database (RAD) on www.thebmc.co.uk for the latest access information
Parking	Park carefully – avoid gateways and driveways
Footpaths	Keep to established paths – leave gates as you find them
Risk	Climbing can be dangerous – accept the risks and be aware of other people around you
Respect	Groups and individuals – respect the rock, local climbing ethics and other people
Wildlife	Do not disturb livestock, wildlife or cliff vegetation; respect seasonal bird nesting restrictions
Dogs	Keep dogs under control at all times; don't let your dog chase sheep or disturb wildlife
Litter	'Leave no trace' – take all litter home with you
Toilets	Don't make a mess – bury your waste
Economy	Do everything you can to support the rural economy – shop locally

BMC Participation Statement — Climbing, hill walking and mountaineering are activities with a danger of personal injury or death. Participants in these activities should be aware of and accept these risks and be responsible for their own actions and involvement.

#BelayBetter / BELAYING

Spotting the climber at the start of the route

Be alert and mobile for the first points:

= GRIGRI / REVERSO / VERSO

Primary belaying position

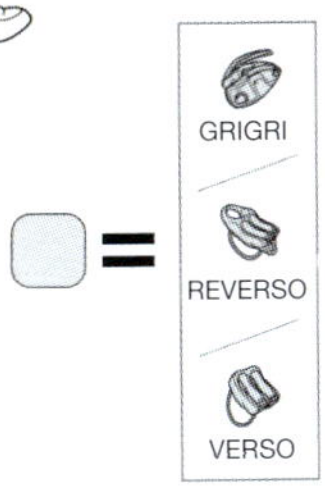

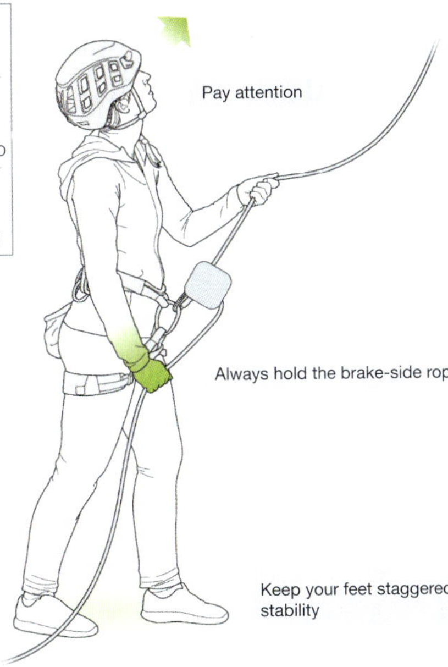

Pay attention

Always hold the brake-side rope

Keep your feet staggered for stability

Remember that before using your equipment, you must have read and understood the supplied Instructions for Use.

Access the inaccessible®

CRAG GUIDE

	Crag	Page	Style	← F4+	F5 - F6a+	F6b - F6c+	F7a →	Routes
Limestone	Chapel Head Scar	38			2	29	40	71
	Mill Side Scar	58			2	5	6	13
	Scout Scar	60		6	10	14	15	45
	Humphrey Head	72			7	8	15	30
	Warton Main Quarry	80		3	19	4	3	29
	Barrow Scout Cove	90		6	2	3	3	14
Slate	Saddlestone Quarry	98				2	2	4
	High Blue Quarry	100		1	2	8		11
	Hodge Close Quarry	104		1	18	35	54	108
	Parrock Quarry	136		1	7	9	10	27
	The Works	140						24
	Bakestone Quarry	150						10
	Moss Rigg Quarry	152				2	1	3
	Tilberthwaite Quarry	156		2	14	23	14	53
	Runestone Quarry	170		2	23	13	2	40
	Cathedral Quarry	180				15	14	29
	Common Wood Quarry	192		1	9	8	3	21
	Thrang Quarry	196				1	4	5
	Dalt Quarry	198		1	16	7	2	26
Micro-Granite	Bramcrag Quarry	208		2	99	85	4	190
Sandstone	St Bees Head	256		5	19	31	29	84
	Coudy Rocks	274			8	10	12	30

← HS | VS - HVS | E1 - E3 | E4 →

Approach	Aspect	Altitude	Notes	Page	
15mn	SW	70m	Perfect, clean, and hard; a venue of national significance.	38	Limestone
15mn	SE	100m	Relatively small crag, with sound rock and good climbing.	58	
10mn	W	170m	Great climbing and views - sea to mountain; a wide range of grades minutes from Kendal.	60	
2mn	W	10m	Climbing by the seaside with endless westerly views over Morecambe Bay.	72	
5mn	S	70m	First acquaintance can be deceptive; some of the best routes in Lancashire!	80	
8mn	SW	20m	A small but entertaining summer evening venue.	90	
55mn	N	540m	An impressive venue, but has aged fixed equipment and is a long uphill walk.	98	Slate
30mn	SW	380m	A fine sunny option for an evening or short day.	100	
5mn	SW	170m	The focus of Lakeland slate climbing in an incredible hole in the ground.	104	
10mn	NW	180m	Easily accessed pleasant slate climbing.	136	
10mn	-	180m	One of the UK's dry tooling crucibles; not to be missed by those with the tools and biceps.	140	
15mn	-	180m	A minor dry tooling venue.	150	
25mn	NW	180m	Esoterica at its adventurous best.	152	
5mn	NW	220m	Easy approach and a wide range of styles and grades.	156	
25mn	W & E	250m	Recent bolting activities should ensure the popularity of this wonderfully located venue.	170	
10mn	NW	150m	An awesome ecclesiastical hole of high quality slate.	180	
15mn	S	150m	Duddon's sports crag; a collector's piece, currently with antiquated fixed equipment.	192	
5mn	S	160m	Langdale's sports crag; overhanging tests.	196	
20mn	S & N	120m	Borrowdale's sports crag; don't get excited, can be surprisingly pleasant when midge free.	198	
10mn	W	200m	A unique very high quality and fun venue for all with an open and sunny outlook.	208	Micro-Granite
20mn	W	5m	Absorbing seaside location with sport for all, or just sunbathe and dream of paradise.	256	Sandstone
3mn	S	160m	An idyllic setting at the heart of Appleby near to the River Eden and bathed in sunshine.	274	

Sky F6b+ (page 125) Anna Taylor — 📷 Jonathan Doyle

17

Limestone

Slate

Micro-Granite

Sandstone

FUN & GAMES

TOP ROUTES

We've picked out the following routes from this guidebook to highlight what some might think of as the best of the climbs described on each of the four rock types. They are highlighted throughout the book with:

This serves (at least) two purposes: to save you the effort; and to provide a seed for many debates about perceived route quality. Do make sure not to let us know what you think!

EASTER EGGS

And finally, to help with rainy day entertainment, which does happen now and then in the Lakes, there are a few gargoyles hidden in the book. Again, when you find them, do make sure you don't let us know about it. ☺

	Route	Crag	Grade	Page
LIMESTONE	Good Medicine	Scout Scar	5+	66
	Born Free	Scout Scar	6a	66
	Gravy Bones	Warton	6b+	84
	A Fistful of Steroids	Scout Scar	6b+	68
	Born to Run	Scout Scar	6c	66
	Interstellar Overdrive	Chapel Head	6c	44
	Cadillac	Millside	6c+	59
	Ivy League	Scout Scar	7a+	68
	The Route of All Evil Direct	Chapel Head	7b	50
	Wargames	Chapel Head	7b	51
	The Firing Squad	Humphrey Head	7b	74
	Super DuPont	Chapel Head	7b+	54
	Phantom Zone	Chapel Head	7b+	44
	Prime Evil	Chapel Head	7c+	54
	The Torture Garden	Warton	E6	86
SLATE	Behind the Lines	Hodge Close	HVS	129
	Kick Off	Tilberthwaite	HVS	160
	Mad Alice	Hodge Close	6a+	134
	Night of the Hot Pies	Cathedral	E1	187
	Big Mirror	Hodge Close	E2	127
	Treacle Slab	Tilberthwaite	E3	169
	Darklands	Cathedral	6b	189
	Joie de Vivre	Hodge Close	6b+	116
	Sky	Hodge Close	6b+	125
	Anvil Arête	Tilberthwaite	E3	162
	Limited Edition	Hodge Close	E4	127
	Malice in Wonderland	Hodge Close	E4	129
	The Main Event	Hodge Close	E5	116
	First Night Nerves	Hodge Close	E5	116
	Ten Years After	Hodge Close	E5	126
	Basillica	Cathedral	7a	190
	Rebel Alliance	G-Spot	7b	113
	Stage Fright	Hodge Close	E6	125
MICRO-GRANITE	Blencathra Badger	Bramcrag Quarry	5c	235
	Captain Pugwash Revisited	Bramcrag Quarry	6a	251
	The Sunshine Gang	Bramcrag Quarry	6a+	224
	The Charcoal Burner	Bramcrag Quarry	6b	219
	The Mission	Bramcrag Quarry	6b	222
	Coup-de-Grace	Bramcrag Quarry	6b+	224
	Dancing in the Danger Zone	Bramcrag Quarry	6b+	217
	Skywalker	Bramcrag Quarry	6b+	247
	Tipton Slasher	Bramcrag Quarry	6b+	229
	The Aphasic Syndrome	Bramcrag Quarry	6c	240
	The Hurt Locker	Bramcrag Quarry	6c	212
SANDSTONE	Fisherman's Friend	St Bees	5	265
	Andy's Route	St Bees	6b	262
	The Apiarist	St Bees	6b+	258
	Nectarine	St Bees	6c+	258
	Swarm	St Bees	7a	258
	Dreaming of Red Rocks	St Bees	7a+	263
	Song to the Siren	St Bees	7a+	268
	Sink the Bismark	St Bees	7b+	271
	Sea of Sand	St Bees	7c	271

ACKNOWLEDGEMENTS

Often, I hear people say 'you are lucky to live in the Lake District'. This is erroneous. I am not lucky. It is a carefully engineered choice to live in what I feel to be one of the most beautiful areas I know. With the care put in to producing this book I hope that some of my love and enthusiasm for this area comes across.

With my hopes said, it is still true that initially I felt like an imposter receiving the lead baton from Dan Robinson for the first ever Wired (and FRCC) guidebook whose main theme would be so narrowly focused. Certainly, Dan deserves recognition for his part in helping conceive the idea of a guidebook focusing on sport and slate climbing in the Lakes. However, my feeling of relative inadequacy stems from the question, what have I ever done on slate? But all modern guidebook workers owe a massive debt, going back over a century, to every volunteer involved in club published guidebooks. Their efforts, carefully recording adventures on our crags, are the foundation of all guidebooks. Creating a guidebook script is relatively easy really. It relies on this massive team of volunteer contributors that stretches from current activists back through time to the very first person to bother writing about their adventures so others could follow. Some authors are, I'm sure, motivated to write for reasons of vanity and others to support commercial interests. But the overwhelming majority are simply being altruistic in their desire to share the magic of climbing. Therein lies the common ground of my comfort receiving that baton. I trust I've done it justice and you find the book to be useful and as innovative as it was conceived to be.

This is not a book of selected routes like other Wired guidebooks that came before. It is a definitive book for a specific set of climbing styles - sport and slate climbing in the Lakes plus conveniently nearby crags in Cumbria and Lancashire. This scope and the requirements of contemporary climbers have led to an expansion of technologies used in the book's production: the dedicated use of an electronic database for collaborative recording of route details; QR codes for parking and other internet resources; aerial photography; etc.

Given then that this undertaking is the work of a huge team, in the tradition of any acknowledgment piece I want to pay tribute to a number of key people: Steve Scott for pushing me forward; Al Davis for having endless attention to detail; Ron Kenyon for his never ending commitment; the whole of the FRCC Guidebook Committee for their progressive and open minded approach; David Simmonite for his photographic skills; Don Sargeant for yet more world-class mapping; Colin Downer and Bill Young for creating what is now one of the area's most popular venues, Bramcrag Quarry; numerous contributors of content and critical feedback including Les Ainsworth, Andy Barr, Dave Cronshaw, Jonathan Doyle, Chris Fisher, Rick Graham, John Holden, John Kettle, Craig Matheson, Misha Nepogodiev, Al Phizacklea, Keith Phizacklea, Keith Sanders, Alan Steele, and Nick Wharton.

Oh, and we must not forget the advertisers who have helped make this venture happen. Please thank them with your custom.

The Lakeland Climbing Foundation, and Jeremy Wilson, deserve a special call out for their generous support of the Cumbria Bolt Fund. Without this support many routes would not exist and more would have much poorer quality fixed equipment. Please help make this charity, which helps disabled children, young people, and adults experience the great outdoors, an even larger success by making use of Kendal Wall.

Lastly, every volunteer has friends and family that also play a part in directly supporting the production efforts or indirectly support by supporting these volunteers. Thank you all!

Peter Sterling
March 2020

Diagram base image credits:
(LA) Les Ainsworth; (MB) Max Biden;
(BB) Ben Bush; (AD) Al Davis; (NG) Neil Gresham;
(PJ) Paul Jennings; (RK) Ron Kenyon;
(AP) Al Phizacklea; (AS) Alan Steele;
(PS) Peter Sterling; (BY) Bill Young;
(NW) Nick Wharton.

KENDAL WALL
INDOOR ROCK CLIMBING IN THE LAKE DISTRICT

Largest Climbing Centre in the country:

- Over 200 lead routes, up to 25m
- Over 500m^2 of bouldering
- Trad placement, aid and dry tooling facility
- Europe's first indoor Via Ferrata
- Full range of instruction, including NICAS
- Dedicated training room
- Conference facility, shop & cafe

Whether you are a novice or expert we have something for everyone.

Size Does Matter
The tallest wall in England

info@kendalwall.co.uk

01539 721766

www.kendalwall.co.uk

Skyline — Europe's first indoor Via Ferrata

KENDAL CRAZY CLIMB

Join us for a brand new and completely bonkers vertical climbing experience!

It's fun, it's wacky, it's CRAZY!

Absolutely no experience required
Age 5 years - Adults

EDITORIAL

To suggest that the Lakes is the epicentre of sport climbing in the North of England would be something of a bold over-statement. But don't dismiss the climbing here; it's better than you may think… Alan James believed the 'new wave' sweeping the country was worth sharing. He recruited Andy Hyslop and Paul Cornforth and FAX 04 THE LAKES was the outcome. In the intervening 26 years no single guidebook has been published that covers much the same ground; it's time that was sorted…

Ironically it was the eradication of aid that created the sports climbs when leading climbers realised that the *in-situ* gear was the protection needed to push grades. Let's be clear, a sport route is fully equipped; 1979 was the year Jeff Lamb red-pointed *Trilogy* on **Raven Crag** Langdale, protected by clipping the fifteen pegs left in place by Graham West twenty years earlier and over in Borrowdale Ron Fawcett climbed *Hell's Wall* in similar style. Strapped to a flimsy tree, Ed Cleasby opened up the highest part of **Chapel Head**; the transition from tree to rock was secured by a bolt; the route was *Android*; the tree is gone.

Here in the Lakes an enviably strong predisposition against fixed gear exists; something of our heritage would be lost if bolts supported progress. With huge improvements in protection, a consensus emerged that bolts would not be placed in mountain rock.

Some routes retained the nails. *Hell's Wall* typifies this genre. Originally climbed by Syd Clark and Brian Henderson in 1964 as a winter project, today the climb still bristles with iron, is frequently worked and is given a French grade. Routes here are generally climbed on pre-placed gear, fixed or otherwise, truly sport climbing garnished with a traditional reticence to change.

With new lines in the mountains at a premium, activists who had sun-rocked explored the untapped potential of the limestone outcrops and slate quarries. Finding gear very difficult to place in the compact and steep rock, bolting started on the fringes. In 1984, with no reliable battery drills, Al Phizacklea took a generator to **Humphrey Head** and placed thirteen in one day. The route that emerged, *The Firing Squad*, aptly summarises the tense situation. 1986 was pivotal. **Hodge Close** was considered the hub of radical, bold and technical climbing. The meagre three bolts Paul Carling placed to produce *Limited Edition* caused quite a stir. Some ignored the clamour and retorted with the hammer of the drill. At **St Bees** Al Phizacklea and Andy Jones brokered an access agreement which opened the door for development of **Apiary Wall** and **Scabby Back**; a similar consensus was reached at **Chapel Head**. By 1990 the uneasy silence was palpable and a local area BMC agreement about what could be bolted, and what should not, was reached. Hand-drawn topos publicised the climbs and sales funded equipment through the South Lakes Bolt Fund. Almost immediately teams moved in to **Bramcrag Quarry**, which being in private ownership, development was unfettered by opinion. Colin Downer gained access and, since 2009, has single-mindedly directed the creation of the most popular sport venue in the Lakes.

Thirty years ago much of the specialist gear was not freely available or was too expensive; in response climbers developed their own. A draughtsman, Al Phizacklea designed and fabricated hangers for use with proprietary bolts; John Adams sourced high-quality stainless steel rod to manufacture staples in his machine shop and a precise drilling jig was designed for their placement. When tested the rock failed before the staples!

Dry tooling has its aficionados and the disused overhanging slate caverns near **Hodge Close** present perfect venues for building technique and strength. In just a few years **The Works** has become a venue of national importance.

The BMC Lakes Area and the Cumbria Bolt Fund are inextricably linked. Recent constitutional changes recognised the status of many of the quarries and outcrops as sports venues; the green light for much of the preparatory work for this guide. Despite these agreements some historical challenges have been lost to bolts; *Moonchild*, *Sky* and *Darklands* being examples. However, leading local climbers are supporting the preservation of heritage lines such as *Stage Fright* and *Life in the Fast Lane*.

The crags in this guide have undergone a similar evolution. Once the compromise of poor bolts, rusty pegs and minimalist gear meant that you either climbed with what was there, or not. Over the years poor or badly placed gear has resulted in many accidents. The Cumbria Bolt Fund, with support from local climbers, is rectifying this situation - but don't make the mistake of thinking that sport means safe or mundane; there are many adventures to be found in these pages.

Steve Scott, April 2020

USEFUL INFORMATION

CLIMBING WALLS

Ambleside
Ambleside Climbing Wall (Adventure Peaks)
Climbing wall and bouldering area available to anyone. Location 101 Lake Road, Ambleside.
☎ 015394 33794
www.adventurepeaks.com

Barrow in Furness
Park Leisure Centre
Good access and low cost, but very limited lead climbing and a cramped bouldering area. Excellent other facilities.
☎ 01229 871146
www.barrowbc.gov.uk

Carlisle
Eden Rock
With over 800sqm of climbing surface this is one of the largest dedicated bouldering walls in the UK. Excellent facility for all abilities and ages.
☎ 01228 522127
www.edenrockclimbing.com

Cockermouth
Leisure Centre
Varied bouldering with natural stonework and Bendcrete. Low cost and good access in the town's leisure centre.
☎ 01900 823596
www.allerdale.gov.uk

Egremont
Wyndham Sports Centre
A good facility located in the centre of Egremont on the west coast, only half an hour from Wasdale Head. Bouldering, leading walls, and a huge roof. Unfortunately no longer open to the public except on a club booking basis.
☎ 01946 820356

Kendal
The Lakeland Climbing Centre
A magnificent indoor climbing facility with excellent bouldering and leading. Includes a very impressive 23 metre main wall and a huge roof. Located on the Lake District Business Park, across the A6 from Morrison's supermarket. Changing and shower facilities.
☎ 01539 721766
www.kendalwall.co.uk

Keswick
Keswick Climbing Wall and Activity Centre
Located to the east of Keswick near the Castlerigg Stone Circle. Bright, airy climbing wall and bouldering wall with a stunning view of Helvellyn out of the main barn doors.
☎ 017687 72000
www.keswickclimbingwall.co.uk

King Kong Climbing Centre
Various lead walls, large bouldering area, training room, cave experience, kids adventure play area and cafe. In central Keswick.
☎ 017687 79959
www.kingkongclimbingcentre.com

Penrith
Penrith Leisure Centre – Eden Climbing Wall
An excellent leading wall adjoining the town's swimming pool and leisure centre.
☎ 01768 863450
www.northcountryleisure.org.uk/eden/penrith-leisure-centre

CONTACTS

BMC - British Mountaineering Council
☎ 0161 445 6111
www.thebmc.co.uk

FRCC - Fell & Rock Climbing Club
www.frcc.co.uk

Lake District National Park Authority
☎ 01539 724555
www.lake-district.gov.uk

Cumbria Tourism
☎ 01539 8222 222
www.golakes.co.uk

Cumbria Bolt Fund
Details of the condition and age of routes re-equipped by the CBF can be found on the CBF website
www.cumbriaboltfund.co.uk

CUMBRIA BOLT FUND

From a modest and tormented start, bolt protected climbing in the Lake District notoriously and controversially developed slowly before the style was finally embraced. The quality of this early equipment, and the bolting, was variable. Bolts are susceptible to corrosion stress or fatigue and do fail. By 2005 it was realised nationally that many bolts which had been in place for more than 20 years were in a dangerous state and in need of replacement.

BMC BETTER BOLTS CAMPAIGN
As a consequence of the 2007 BMC Better Bolts Campaign the Cumbria Bolt Fund (CBF) was set up to co-ordinate the replacement of bolts throughout the Cumbria. Since then many bolts have been replaced, yet there are still more needing attention. Upgrading old bolts to modern standards, providing bolts for new routes, and ensuring we maintain and follow the locally agreed and accepted ethics is the core ethos behind the CBF.

QUALITY ASSURANCE & TRAINING
The placement of bolts conforms to current best practice. This includes placing bolts that are appropriate to rock type and location, all in high-grade stainless steel with modern anchors.

The CBF uses standardised training methods and we have produced a set of training and instructional videos which can be viewed on the CBF website.

CBF RE-EQUIPPED ROUTES
A comprehensive list of re-equipped routes can be found on our website.

THERE IS A COST
The bolts, equipment and resin are expensive, with CBF expenditure to date being over £13,000. In addition to the support from the BMC, funds and equipment have been contributed by the FRCC, Lakeland Climbing Foundation, professional outdoor users, local climbing clubs, Rockfax, Needlesports, Wilf's Cafe, Edelrid, personal donations, and from collection boxes around the area.

To donate and help fund the bolting - follow the link to our website or scan the QR code.

THE BOLTS DON'T GO IN ON THEIR OWN
The CBF has an ongoing commitment to re-equip routes in Cumbria. Much still remains to be done and there is plenty of scope for new sport routes. This guidebook highlights what Cumbria has to offer. By co-ordinating future bolting the CBF can maintain standards of equipment and training at what is an internationally acceptable level.

Please get in touch if you would like to help.

Dan Robinson, Ron Kenyon
CBF Trustees

http://www.cumbriaboltfund.co.uk
https://www.thebmc.co.uk/bolts-advice-guides
https://www.thebmc.co.uk/cumbrian-bolt-fund

Rusty! Would you trust your life to it?

Were we ever really happy with this?

Stainless steel bolts used by the CBF

Bolt replacement work at **St Bees** — 📷 BEN BARDEN

Lower-offs used by the CBF

Laddered access at **Thrang Quarry**

CBF "Cowstail" lower-off

FRCC GUIDES

FRCC Guides publishes a series of rock climbing guide books to the Lake District.

The climbing is extremely varied, with high and remote mountain crags, easy to access lower level crags in the valleys, quarries and impressive sandstone sea cliffs. The rock is tremendously varied too: volcanic rocks predominate – basalt, andesite, rhyolite, tuffs and pyroclastic ashes; there are granite intrusions; micro-granite, slate, limestone and sandstone are all represented.

Loosely based on the valleys that radiate from the hub of the District, our nine volume comprehensive series provides detailed information about the climbing, access and approaches, area and crag maps, and other useful information.

There are two selective volumes published as **Wired Guides** – **LAKE DISTRICT ROCK** includes the best crags and climbs across the whole District; bolted sport venues are the focus of **LAKES SPORT & SLATE**, which also includes all of the climbing on slate.

Clear photo-diagrams are used to indicate the routes, with detailed mapping, OS grid reference crag location and, in the most recent guides, QR codes to parking and access restrictions.

LAKE DISTRICT ROCK
The award winning selective guidebook to Lakeland rock climbing.
ISBN: 978-0-85028-057-9

LAKES SPORT & SLATE
Sport and Lakes slate climbing.
ISBN: 978-0-85028-063-0

Buttermere & St Bees
North eastern Lakeland and the sunny sandstone cliffs of St Bees.
ISBN: 978-0-85028-048-7

Borrowdale
This popular valley offers a lifetime of superb roadside cragging.
ISBN: 978-0-85028-058-6

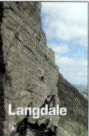

Langdale
Some of the most varied, enjoyable and popular climbing in the Lake District.
ISBN: 978-0-85028-054-8

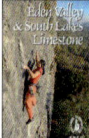

Eden Valley & South Lakes Limestone
North, East and South Cumbria outwith the Lake District.
ISBN: 978-0-85028-052-4

Gable & Pillar
The traditional home of Lakeland climbing.
ISBN: 978-0-85028-047-0

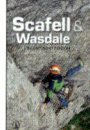

Scafell & Wasdale
Coinciding with the centenary of the first ascent of the *Central Buttress*.
ISBN: 978-0-85028-055-5

Duddon & Wrynose
Tranquil and friendly outcrops above trees and bracken in this ever popular valley.
ISBN: 978-0-85028-064-7

Dow & Eskdale
Accessible and majestic mountain crags.
ISBN: 978-1-8380054-0-5

Eastern Crags
From Thirlmere north to Carrock Fell and south to Kendal, east to Patterdale and beyond.
ISBN: 978-0-85028-051-1

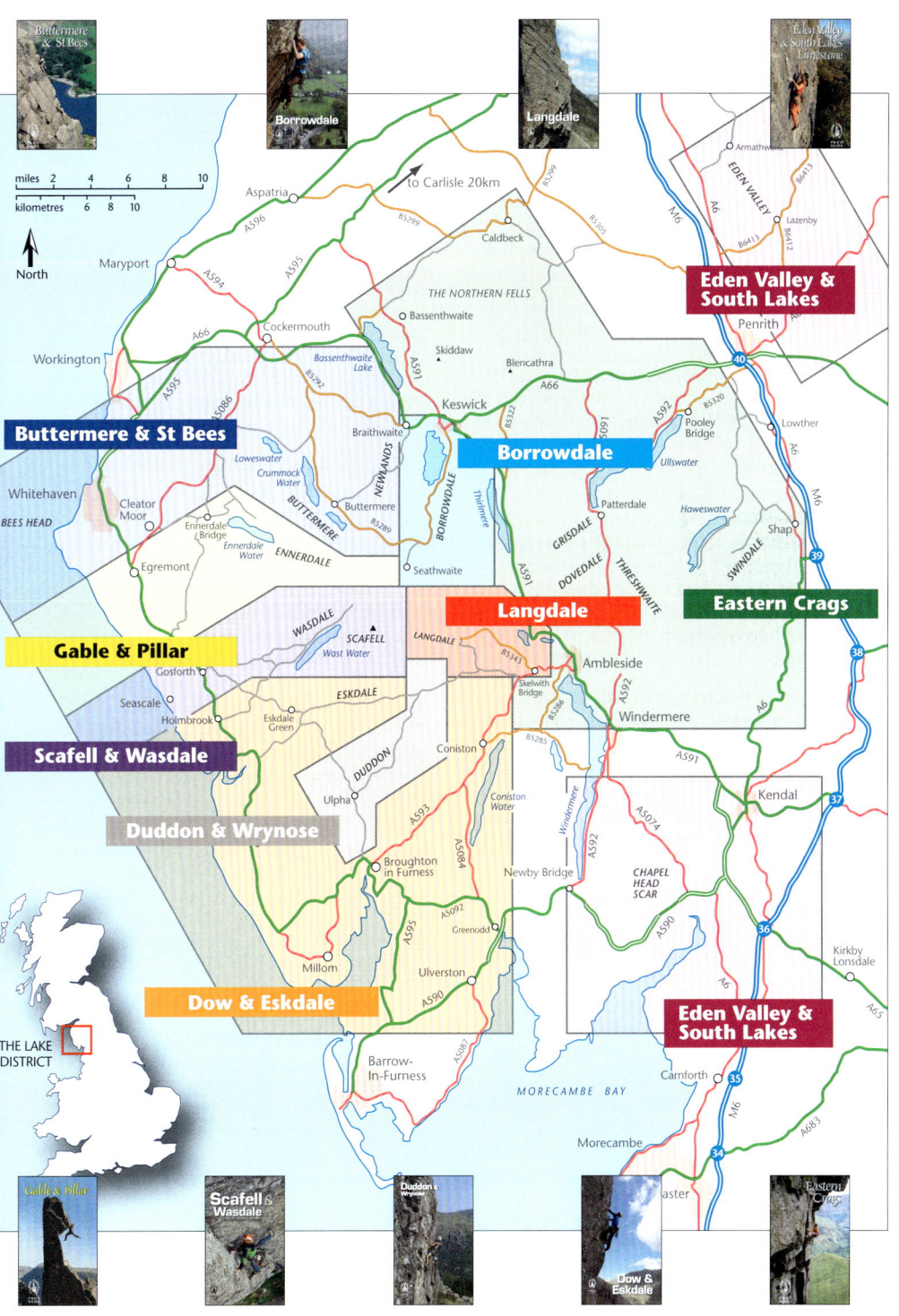

HISTORY OF LAKES SPORT & SLATE CLIMBING

LIMESTONE

Climbing on the limestone scars and in local quarries began in the 60s, exploits being largely unrecorded. Les Ainsworth enthusiastically set about exploring and recording developments on the crags of the North West. Many routes were of doubtful quality and there were unresolved access agreements, but the potential was huge. The steep, compact, featureless limestone favoured fixed gear; threads and pegs were accepted but unreliable, yet bolts were considered unethical, hindering development.

At **Chapel Head Scar** Les Ainsworth and Dave Cronshaw picked the obvious easier natural lines. Word soon spread; Ron Fawcett climbed *Moonchild*; Pete Livesey matched Fawcett with *Lunatic* and local, Ed Cleasby, added *Cyborg*. A significant breakthrough came in 1979 when Cleasby found a devious way up Great Buttress creating *Android*, placing a bolt to secure the transition from a flimsy tree to rock. Gary Gibson, renowned for monopolizing development, paid a flying visit spurring the locals into a frenzy of activity. Al Phizacklea completed a long-standing project to produce *Wargames* – probably still the best route on the crag and originally protected by drilled threads; Paul Cornforth did the decent thing and placed a proper bolt to protect the crux of *Perverse Pépère*, heralding a new wave of development.

In 1992 Dave Birkett, with pessimistic foresight, climbed the alternative access route onto Great Buttress ready *For When the Tree Falls*! Gaps continued to be filled and by 2016 the unbolted leftovers were equipped and unfinished projects completed converting the crag into one of the most significant and comprehensively equipped sports venues in the North West.

Over the road at **Humphrey Head** Mick Goff led the early work in the late '60s. Many of these early developments have been lost under vegetation. Some do still exist subsequently cleaned of aid, *Triggerfinger* being one of the best. A new era dawned in 1984 when Al Phizacklea and Rob Knight turned up armed with a bolt gun to produce *The Firing Squad*, at that time considered an act of desecration attracting widespread derision. After the furore had died down, Al returned to add top belays and new routes were created. Having heard (as was rumoured at the time) the noise of the drill from the bar of The Golden Rule in Ambleside, Paul Cornforth arrived to add *Humphrey Hymen*. A later surge of activity culminated with John Dunne freeing the aid route out of Edgar's Arch. Towards the end of the '90s Les Ainsworth and Dave Cronshaw, eschewing the logical step of placing bolts and preferring to dice with death, developed Forgotten Walls. A big clean up was arranged by the CBF in 2016 with comprehensive re-bolting.

At **Scout Scar** it was a similar story with local developments going unrecorded. *Ivy League* was aided and *Born Free* created by Frank Booth. By the mid '70s the old aid routes were climbed free and new routes began appearing. As on other crags the drill was brought into use; the leading architect was Jim Bird. After a long period of stagnation, in 2014, the Allan's created *Douglas*, which despite looking like a meandering climb has a burly finish. The CBF collaborating with the guidebook team stepped in and, with funds donated by both the CBF and the Lakeland Climbing Foundation, the untapped potential for easier and mid-grade climbs was realised.

Millside Scar was first explored when Dave Cronshaw and Les Ainsworth, tails between their legs, took a stroll round from White Scar. They succeeded on the obvious line, the striking *Pioneer's Cave*. *Cadillac* by Ed Cleasby and Al Phizacklea in 1982 was a significant ascent; the bolts you clip today were a later addition.

At **Warton**, until 2010 when Les Ainsworth bolted his own routes on the sunny **Terrace Wall**, the climbing was trad with an esoteric appeal; many visitors scuttled away without even roping-up. Other bolts have appeared since and in 2015 Keith Phizacklea snuck in *Gravy Bones* on the far left of the **Main Wall**. With this guide in preparation the plans to upgrade old bolts and dispense with the ironmongery on agreed lines are being realised.

SLATE

Rising standards during the 1970s gave those with vision and talent the confidence to attempt what were once futuristic lines in unlikely venues. The search for new ground was competitive and at a high pitch when, in 1980, perhaps the most significant development took place. At this time teams were distinctly territorial; the Lakes was polarised North and South. Despite South Lakes climbers being aware of the impressive walls around **Hodge Close Quarry** it was a Carlisle team who began abseiling, excavating and gardening; the soaring peg-scarred crack of *Stiff Little Fingers* was the first route to fall. Easy access to fast-drying rock was a compulsive draw, as was the potential for absorbing, substantial routes on the impressive west-facing **Main Wall**. The team expanded and swarmed over the crag revealing its potential, and revelling in its virginity, routes fell quickly. The Carlisle team took an Easter break; Ed Cleasby and Rob Matheson "woke up" and, with Al Phizacklea helping, six more new lines were developed. On their return and surprised at the pace, the two teams worked side-by-side cleaning lines with mutual respect in a congenially competitive atmosphere. Rob Matheson had cleaned a line where the only solution to the complete lack of protection seemed to be a bolt. Pete Whillance was offered the lead, subject to the same strict no bolt ethic adopted by Rob. Pete led the pitch one evening producing the sketchy *Life in the Fast Lane*. The quality of the routes produced during this phase is undisputed, yet the acquired taste of doubtful rock in an uninspiring hole left others cold. When Whillance led *Stage Fright*, his last contribution, the peak of this scary smearing was probably reached. At E6 6b this climb epitomises the unphased determination and technical excellence demonstrated by the then leading protagonist of this style of climbing.

After Whillance left the area it seemed that only exceptional climbers who had the ability to remain cool in the most serious situations would develop the quarries further. Strong opinions were expressed amongst some of the locals that a radical new approach to protection was required. Parallel development of the Welsh slate scene – where bolts were used for protection – seemed a tempting option, but the strong ethical stance of bolt-free slate that was maintained during development of **Hodge Close Quarry** deterred the wannabees. In 1986, Paul Carling profanely flew in the face of tradition placing three bolts for his ascent of *Limited Edition*. The result was a superb and very popular route – it seemed that everybody wanted to climb it while the bolts remained in place. Most local climbers waited to see whether these would be chopped, yet John Daly and Keith Phizacklea jumped at the opportunity. The following winter saw this pair cleaning and climbing around twenty routes at **Tilberthwaite Quarry**, then only used for top-rope practice and easy soloing. The interest in local quarries spread to **Cathedral Quarry** where Roger Brookes and Jim Cooper added three lines, including *Night of the Hot Pies*, a pointer to the potential. The superb line of *Darklands* was climbed and across in **Tilberthwaite Quarry**, Paul Ingham climbed a desperate steep pillar to give *Megabyte* at E6 6c.

Unsurprisingly, the focal point of this slate boom became **Hodge Close**, where Al Phizacklea placed several large bolts with an electric generator and drill to create a number of routes. In the true tradition of non-competitive sport, Al and Steve Hubbard raced to the quarry to beat a 'rival' team of Paul Carling and Glenn Sutcliffe for the prized girdle traverse resulting in the 'score-draw' of two traverses climbed on the same day; probably a unique event in climbing history! Rick Graham with Al Phizacklea eventually claimed the best and most sustained route on the wall with *First Night Nerves*, a superb line protected by six bolts.

With the now widespread acceptance of bolts, the blank walls that remained became the focus, bringing an inevitable rise in technical standards. New additions at **Hodge** pushed the technique of friction climbing firmly into the 6c category. However, the introduction of cordless drills was what really supported development. Bolts could be placed with little effort, drastically cutting the work involved in cleaning and preparing new routes. Activity spread to the previously untouched friable areas of slate, where quality was sometimes sacrificed for quantity.

By the late-80s short technical pitches on established cliffs and new outcrops were de-rigeur and the routes on slate followed this vein. Retro-bolting dragged **Parrock Quarry** out of obscurity; at this once popular evening venue many lines have now fallen down or are buried under moss and lichen. One of the best quarries to mature from this activity was **Cathedral** and over at **Hodge**, Andy Hyslop created an area which remained dry even during downpours; ironically **The All-weather Gym** is now considered a danger zone.

1987 witnessed a radical step in new route creation; this began in **Hodge Close** when matchsticks were chipped up a blank, overhanging wall on the opposite side of the pool creating a desperate edgy problem. *Curtain Call* was enhanced the following spring.

History of Lakes Sport & Slate Climbing

"It is hoped that this will be an isolated case – what will remain to challenge the future generations of climbers if we selfishly chisel the 'last great problems' that still exist?"

This plea, concluding the historical section of the 1988 guide, appeared too late to prevent further acts of chipping. The most serious was at **Cathedral Quarry**, where a steep, holdless wall was drilled and chipped to create a venue for a climbing competition. Reaction was swift; all of the blatantly chipped holds were cemented up. The point was made, yet the cement was gradually removed. Impatience distorts ethics and four short years later, routes such as *Michael Angelo*, *Pigs Against the Wall*, *Major Misdemeanor* and *The Shining* all utilized chiselled holds.

Paul Ross and Denis Byrne-Peare sneaked in and grabbed one of the most stunning lines on slate; *Titanic Arête*. The only other 'off-comer' was Dave Pegg, who red-pointed *Command Performance* at **Hodge**. The quest for unclimbed rock led to the discovery of two new quarries in 1991. Mick Miller imaginatively initiated the development of Betsy Crag Quarry (**Runestone Quarry**) and in the Coppermines Valley, Rascal How (**Blue Quarry**) had several additions; where, as bolts were expensive, imaginative drilling was employed to create nut placements.

Several issues dogged the quarry climbing fraternity in the early '90s. The first was the mystery of the disappearing hangers, apparently stolen at random. This idiotic action was countered by using bonded staples of stainless steel. A more insidious threat came from rave parties which attracted large groups to the **Hodge Close** area. Chaotic attempts to prevent these gatherings culminated in the destruction of Peatfield Quarry, a Machiavellian triumph for the quarry operator, an ominous loss to the climbing world.

The climbing at **Dalt Quarry** was developed by Alastair Nicol, in 1991/92, as part of a Geography O Level project, whilst at Keswick School, entitled "Recreational use of cleaved volcanic ash".

1992 started with some hard routes appearing in **Parrock Quarry**. *The Groove*, an enigmatic route soon gained a reputation for fun – especially for those watching the proceedings! **Hodge Close** continued to be the centre of development, despite the illusion that there was little unclimbed rock left. One section of the quarry to attract attention was the overhanging wall above the pool where Paul Cornforth climbed the audacious line of *Pigs Against the Wall*, the first E7 in the area. High on the flanks of the Old Man of Coniston, the massive collapsed cavern at **Saddlestone**

Quarry provided some impressive challenges; the very steep arête taken by *The Shining* stands out. Another impressive line, *Basilica* in **Cathedral**, was completed linking *Barbi Junior* to *The Cruel Sea*, providing an excellent strenuous exercise. In the 1994 guide Al Phizacklea wrote: "How ironic… that the historical section… started and finished with those deplorable chipped holds."

The pace has slowed and the rock changes. In **Hodge** *Carpe Diem*, bolted in 2009 on newly cleaned rock, was popular; a recent rockfall has smashed the lower hangers and altered the start. Stuart Wood and B Scroggs climbed *The Big Link* giving a huge, very bold and tenuous traverse across the main wall seemingly protected by a tiny sapling – an equally exciting journey for both leader and second.

Dry tooling has developed globally and, after some scouting around the Tilberthwaite area, local technicians developed **The Works**. As the quality emerged, initial objections from other climbers abated and a huge spread of routes is on offer. Another aspect of the diverse climbing world is Deep Water Soloing, bringing to mind sun-kissed crags with blue water. In 2018 Neil Gresham developed **The G-Spot** at **Hodge Close** - warm weather is recommended as the water is deep and cold.

The Cumbria Bolt Fund was formed in 2007 with the objective of improving the bolts in the area. Production of this guide inspired a burst of activity, in particular at **Scout Scar** and **Runestone Quarry**. The publication of this guide showcases the best of the slate and the possibilities for the future. When you climb here remember these crags are unnatural, created by explosives. Extensive areas can be loose, unstable and do just fall down. Rock falls are inevitable and often they're huge. Just take a walk up to **Moss Rigg Quarry**.

Let There be Light M10+ (page 146) Matt Foot — 📷 JONATHAN DOYLE

MICRO-GRANITE
Bramcrag Quarry

In January 1991, at the BMC Lakes Area meeting, the controversial decision to support bolting of quarried rock was agreed. Attendance was poor; amongst them were Al Phizacklea, John Holden and Ron Kenyon. Curiosity had taken Phizacklea into the huge quarry seeking out new routes. Mildly impressed, he suggested an exploratory visit to mukka Holden in March, following the green light given at the Area meeting. This visit resulted in two excellent routes, *Marine's Slab* and *Barrow Boys' Day Out*. The latter was named as a riposte to Paul Ross who had ventured south the previous year to steal the plum line of *Titanic Arête* at **Moss Rigg Quarry** and the provocatively named groove of *Borrowdale Lads' Day Out*. Phizacklea also produced *Blencathra Badger* as a further taunt, named after Paul's champion terrier.

Then, as now, preparation was a problem, particularly accessing a suitable position to drill a lower-off. Phizacklea and Holden returned in April and, having bushwhacked to the top of the quarry through the protective gorse, managed to drill anchors for minimal cleaning. Five excellent routes were created including *Eastern Promise*, originally climbed as a trad route, and *Coup d'Etat*; they had a superb day. There was a limit of two bolts placed on the other routes dictated by impoverishment and the ethics of the time. Hangers were not freely available (or cheap) so, using his draughtsman skills, Al created drawings for the fabrication of 'suspension hangers' by the machine shop at Vickers shipyard, with black mastic applied to prevent corrosion.

New Dad Ron Kenyon climbed *Nappyrash* in the lower quarry, ground-up on trad gear with no prior cleaning - a very bold undertaking. Then seemingly tirelessly added eight further routes throughout the quarry in this same bold style. He returned to add bolts but, given the technology of the time, this was not a simple task. Friends were enlisted to help carry an 40kg generator into the lower quarry to aid drilling. Long leads were taken from the generator up the face of the lower quarry and into the upper. The one exception to the minimalist bolting was *Farewell to Adventure*, the only true sports route from this period. Climbers repeating the existing routes were spooked by the bold nature of the climbing and the worrying state of the rock. The fusillades of stones triggered by the resident family of goats which roamed the scree above the quarry at that time didn't add encouragement.

In 2009, inspired by the photo in the 1992 FRCC guide, Colin Downer repeated *Eastern Promise*. Lowering off he noticed the prominent groove in the centre of Main Wall; *Bobby Dazzler* was cleaned and climbed. The following year, Downer returned to complete the excellent *History Boys*. The obvious south-facing wall to the far left became the next target. *Michelangelo* was prepared but, due to cruciate ligament damage, the line was handed to Mike Norbury.

Surgery ruled Downer out the following year but a seed had been sown. In 2012, he began exploring the quarry in earnest. Early recruits in this work were Luke Jones and Cam Fowler and then Bill Young became second-in-command and navvy in the laborious preparation work. In the next eight years, buttress after buttress was cleaned and developed creating over 130 new routes and retro-bolting existing lines. As each new buttress was developed, the initial problem was accessing a suitable lower-off position to facilitate cleaning and bolting. Downer employed every trick in the book, including long-dormant aid-climbing techniques. Lonely days were spent dangling from ropes preparing routes to make them climbable with many epics. The groove of *Hurt Locker* took seven days to prepare.

The black groove on **Grand Wall** had frequently attracted Downer's attention, but the capping roofs left him out in space unable to reach the rock to bolt a lower-off. A direct approach from below left his belayer in mortal danger. The problem was finally solved by climbing the slab to the right (*Heaven Can Wait*). With Bill Young patiently belaying for many hours safely out of the line of fire, Downer aided leftwards across the yellow wall cleaning blocks as he went. After eight days work, *The Mission* was completed.

At this time Downer was living on the slopes of Blencathra with line of sight to the quarry. A powerful telescope allowed him to focus on activity; he would turn up when friends were climbing. Self-funded initially, as work increased this became untenable and generous contributions were provided by the local clubs. Retro-bolting and cleaning of existing routes continued and, encouraged by first ascentionists and recognising that some excellent routes were being neglected, the remaining unbolted lines succumbed to the drill

SANDSTONE
St Bees

WP Haskett Smith records climbing on the rotten sandstone of **St Bees** in the nineteenth century by the local vicar. Seventy years later in 1964, Chris Bonington and Dave Johnston made the first known ascent on the main cliff, up the pinnacle known as *Lawson's Leap*; the details are unrecorded. Joe Wilson and Ged Cowan made the first recorded route; *MMT* on the South Head in 1968. The foot and mouth epidemic of 1967/8 forced climbers to travel, scouring the country for accessible rock. From the Peak, Keith Myhill and Tom Proctor came up, Tony Wilmot made the long drive from Bristol and, to check the claims out, Ken Wilson looked in – most didn't come back! Brian Smith was roped in and with Bill Young, Mike Burbage, Bob Bennett and other locals a wave of idiosyncratic activity began, particularly on the North Head. Media claims of a new Gogarth were slightly misplaced – yet adventures were had and in 1969 a guide was produced by Ian Angell claiming there was potential for 14,000 climbs!

In the early '80s activity at **St Bees** began to pick up again, though records of the climbs are somewhat hazy. During this period a group of local climbers explored the boulders climbing most of the mid-grade problems. **Scabby Back** was explored and more routes followed, all of them with natural protection and the occasional peg. The intention of returning resulted in these climbs being unpublicised. In the Autumn of 1989, when Andy Jones, Al Phizacklea and Rick Graham returned from the bolted sandstone cliffs of Rheinpfalz in Germany, the true potential of **St Bees** was realised. An initial trial to hand drill a couple of bolts for top roping proved successful and within a month a dozen routes on **Apiary Wall** had been bolted. In September 1990 an access agreement ushered in the next wave of interest. A few unbolted routes were climbed, the most impressive being Dougie Hall's very bold *Run Wild, Run Free*. Many of the original climbs from the early '80s were retro-bolted, sometimes in the mistaken belief that they were new routes. This period of intense development lasted from 1989 to 1994 with *Nectarine*, *The Apiarist*, *Virgin Queen*, *Andy's Route*, and *Dreaming of Red Rocks* being some of the highlights.

Another lull followed with only a handful of new climbs. The most significant, in terms of difficulty, was *I Wish I Was* from David Birkett in 1998; although only a short pitch this provided the first F8a of the headland. This period also saw the addition of the brilliant *Promenade Crack* by Keefe Murphy.

The bouldering boom has brought many activists to the superb blocks below **Apiary Wall** and the **Main Cliff**. Since problems weren't recorded in the '80s and '90s when the likes of Hall, Birkett, Dave Hinton, Al Wilson and Pete Strong were all active, it is hard to say how much really is new. One thing is for sure; these boulders provide excellent problems on superb rock in a most beautiful location.

Alan Steele, Keith Phizacklea and P Ibbinson headed north with their drills in 2010 and developed the **Fleswick Bay** area - a bit of a longer walk but plenty of stars to go for. A little later **Siren Wall** was developed – the abseil approach giving an element of commitment! It is unlikely that this is the end of the story – on the reckoning of 1970 there are still about 13,900 routes left to go. Many obvious lines and challenges are still there for the taking; it just needs someone with the vision to take **St Bees** forward again.

Coudy Rocks

Mauled by climbers over the years, including local lad Leo Houlding, the potential as a sport venue wasn't realised until 2009. Following a recce the previous March, a group including Ron and Michael Kenyon, Dan Robinson and Eric Parker, a drill, some bolts and severe doubts as to the suitability of the rock, began work. With bolts in place and after some refreshment at the Royal Oak, the routes started to flow. A number of equipped lines remain as open projects. The news of this guide stimulated more activity and there are now 32 routes – many more than originally expected.

The crag is on land belonging to Harold Bainbridge, a great chap for allowing us to climb and walk across his land; we should remember to respect his benevolence.

GEOLOGY NOTES

LIMESTONE

Limestone consists of white and grey carbonate sedimentary rocks of Early Carboniferous age, typically 350-320 million years old and in gross terms up to 1000m in thickness. These rocks form a ring around the Lake District with some large escarpments; other exposures are significant quarried holes. The limestones were deposited in a tropical sea when the UK was located on the Equator. Corals, bryozoa and shelly fossils are common. There are occasional small reefs or bioherms and the main sequences are biological limestones formed from oozes, limestone clays, marls and shell beds. Many of these units have been subsequently re-crystallised after burial and take on a sugary, hard, brittle or crystalline texture. Varied composition leads to varying rates of polish.

Limestones are usually compact with limited joints or fractures, offering climbers few placements for natural gear, hence the bolting solution. Karst effects from glacial melt-waters have created some fluted and pocketed areas by solution processes on vertical faces. Relatively recent carbonate precipitation results in tufa streaks, for example at **Chapel Head Scar**. Some units can be pocketed or fractured in places and calcite or quartz veining is common, occasionally with sandy patches. There are numerous karstified limestone pavements around the Lake District with typical clint and gryke geometries, but these are restricted to bedding plane outcrops on escarpment tops, not climbable cliff faces.

Quarries were often dug for ease where the limestone was brittle and broken, so these can be more fragmented than some natural faces. The natural faces are often slow to dry with some seepage where porous with higher water retention.

SLATE

Slate is technically a metamorphic rock, but also volcanic here in the Lake District. The clue is in the name, those flat things on the roof, or huge flat slates used occasionally in pub floors, or in drystone walls or fences for example in the Coniston area. Why are they flat? Because they have cleavage allowing them to be split by hand. Why do they have cleavage? Because the rocks are fine-grained muds, ashes and volcanic tuffs that, during tectonic compression, rapidly developed cleavage.

The Lake District slates are about 450 million years old (Late Ordovician) and they were deposited as a result of the massive volcanic episode that occurred due to a plate collision and closure of the Iapetus ocean. This resulted in the outpouring of several thousand metres of lava, volcanic ash and volcanic ejecta collectively known as pyroclastics.

Some of these rocks were deposited in lakes that formed as the Lake District volcanic centre collapsed due to post-eruptive thermal subsidence. The collapse formed a huge caldera. Some formed as subaerial ash-fall deposits. The finer-grained rock types took cleavage better than the coarse lavas, volcanic intrusives or coarse tuffs. The finer rocks became the slates due to alignment of clay and other silicate minerals in response to the pressure-related cleavage development.

The fine-grained units were metamorphosed by heat and pressure during the Caledonian mountain-building between 400 and 395 million years ago. The original rocks were relatively (and still are today) flat-bedded or only gently dipping. The cleavage that developed has a strong vertical or inclined geometry at odds with the bedding, hence slate quarries have dominant vertical lines that cross the original bedding.

Some of these rocks have great beauty, for example the cross bedding or ripple marks and slump structures created during lake sedimentation. Other units show flow-banding as a result of high-temperature and violent gas-rich volcanic activity. See the slate floor in the Newfield Inn at Duddon for the best example, or the bar top in the Scafell Hotel in Borrowdale, or some of the stones set aside at Honister Quarry.

Slate therefore, from a climber's perception, is normally quick-drying, very fine-grained, smooth volcanic ash or tuff. Metamorphism was not intense, but it varied from place to place and some holds are brittle, snapping easily, whereas others are tougher as at **Hodge Close**. Holds are on the soft side and become rapidly polished at **Tilberthwaite**. Many original slate routes were done in trad style with limited natural gear plus the occasional peg or bolt e.g. *Ten Years After* or *Stinky Dinks*. However, since most slate cracks had a habit of widening overnight sometimes with spectacular rock collapses, bolting of slate has become the norm to reduce the risks and increase the scope for climbing. Nevertheless, slate is inherently risky due to the constant expansion of cracks created by the quarried voids, especially where trees are present (e.g. *Malice*) and large collapses occur on a regular basis. No doubt earthquakes along the Coniston fault contribute to this process.

MICRO-GRANITE

Bramcrag Quarry is within the surface outcrop of the Threlkeld micro-granite, one of several granites across the area that were intruded from 450-400 million years ago, the Shap, Ennerdale, Eskdale and Skiddaw granites being the others. The underlying Lake District granite batholith (from where all these intrusions were sourced) is estimated from gravity surveys to be 3-4 km beneath surface in the area of the quarry.

The Skiddaw and Shap granites are the most recent of these granites (ca. 400 mya.), with the Threlkeld micro-granite being formed ca. 450-440 mya. just after the Carrock, Eskdale and Ennerdale intrusions. This period coincided with the final stages of Borrowdale Volcanic activity in the Lake District and it is likely that the Threlkeld intrusion is roughly contemporaneous with the late stage ignimbrites (volcanic tuffs) of the Borrowdale Volcanic Series. It is these rocks that form most of the Lake District climbing crags.

The micro-granite was intruded in the form of a sub-horizontal sheet or laccolith. The intrusion penetrated the contact between the underlying and older Skiddaw slate group, and the younger Borrowdale Volcanic Group above. So in the **Lower Quarry**, the micro-granite sits beside dark grey Skiddaw slates (partially metamorphosed by the intrusion and visible at the south end of the lower quarry). This contact with the Skiddaw slate is about ten paces from where the path crosses the outlet stream. In the upper quarry, the highest and wildest **Grand Wall** area is overlain by Borrowdale group volcanic rocks.

The micro-granite is light to medium-coloured, hard and quite smooth, with a fairly complex mineralogy and alteration products. The main mineral constituents are plagioclase feldspar, subordinate alkali feldspar, garnet, quartz, zircon, sericite and apatite.

There are frequent earth tremors in the area due to the active north-south Coniston fault that runs up St. John's in the Vale. The most recent earthquakes have been at Grasmere and on High Rigg (Dec 18th, 2016 and March 6th, 2018). The High Rigg tremor and the recent Castle Rock collapse were very close to Bramcrag Quarry. These earthquakes are thought to have a major impact on rock collapse on some of the local crags, so with the quarried nature of Bramcrag, extreme caution should be taken.

SANDSTONE

After the end of the Carboniferous limestone, gritstone and coal measure deposition came the Hercynian or Variscan mountain-building phase (300-280 ma.) caused by another major continental collision (between Laurussia and Gondwana). Permian and Triassic sandstone deposition ensued.

These sandstones were deposited in fault-bounded inter-montane basins when the area was geographically located as the Sahara Desert is today under the full influence of trade winds and desert sedimentary environments.

Think red sandpaper, sometimes hard, sometimes soft, sometimes Permian 275 million years old, sometimes Triassic, 250-230 million years old.

Appleby's **Coudy Rocks** are of Permian age (Penrith Sandstone 275 ma.).

The **St Bees** sandstones are of Triassic age (Sherwood sandstone formation 250 ma.)

Hence the Eden Valley Permian rocks are often wind-blown desert sandstones that are in effect fossilised sand dunes, showing large scale cross-bedding. The hardness of the sandstones depends on the degree of cementation by quartz overgrowths on the rounded sand grains. The redness derives from a coating of iron oxide; the harder units are cemented with quartz that fills the pore spaces or occasionally rarer minerals like anhydrite.

Later Triassic units as at St Bees are often alluvial braided river deposits as the climate evolved away from arid desert conditions. The St Bees sandstone is somewhat harder than the Penrith sandstone with more abundant jointing and less wind influence during deposition.

Climbing on sandstone is a tough challenge due to the rounded nature or lack of good positive holds. The absence of cracks for natural protection has created the opportunity for bolting these blank faces.

As these are often very porous rocks, seepage from bedding planes can occur long after the rain has stopped.

Dave Bodecott

LIMESTONE

A Fistful of Steroids F6b+ (page 68) Justin Shiels — 📷 Ben Bush

Crags
- **CHAPEL HEAD SCAR** — Page 38
- **MILL SIDE SCAR** — Page 58
- **SCOUT SCAR** — Page 60
- **HUMPHREY HEAD** — Page 72
- **WARTON MAIN QUARRY** — Page 80
- **BARROW SCOUT SCAR** — Page 90

Limestone

CHAPEL HEAD SCAR
OS Grid Ref: SD 443 862
Altitude: 70m

War Hero F7a (page 47) Rachel Somerville — David Simmonite

CHAPEL HEAD SCAR

With perfect, smooth, compact limestone and rough tufa formations, **Chapel Head Scar** is a brilliant destination. This impressively steep crag overlooking the quiet wooded Witherslack valley is recognised as a climbing venue of national importance and is often in condition. Some areas suffer from seepage after prolonged rain yet it enjoys the sun in the afternoon and evening. Midges can be troublesome; of more concern are the ticks, the whole area is infested. The crag is situated in the National Park, a Nature Reserve and SSSI and climbers enjoy a good relationship with the Rangers. Selfishly disregarding the few rules could ruin this for everyone and you must respect the access restrictions:

- No climbing left of **Central Gully Wall**.
- Use only marked paths.
- No gardening.
- Trees are protected and must not be damaged.
- Use the lower-offs - do not top-out from any route.
- Do not leave any litter whatsoever - finger tape, banana skins, orange peel, chalk wrappers, etc.
- Go before you go.

There is usually a restriction from 1st March to 30th June to protect nesting peregrines. Please check the BMC RAD for updates.

Approach: M6 J36 - A590 Witherslack. Cross a cattle grid (shop and pub on left) then follow the road through the village; after about 5km reach Witherslack Hall. On a rising left-hand bend turn right and park on the right. The crag can be seen across fields above the woods to the east. Head towards it on a broad path, passing through gates and into woods. After 200m take the first path on the left crossing scree to arrive at **Moonchild Buttress**.

42 | Limestone

Central Gully Wall
A handful of short enjoyable easier routes at the furthest left end of the accessible part of the crag, right of the vegetated Central Gully.

① Cool Your Jets Mum 12m F6c+
The smooth wall just right of the gully is hard, then trend right to a belay.
S Halford 1992

② Le Flange en Decomposition 15m F6b+
You can think up your own translation, but do not get the wrong impression of this worthwhile short route. Climb the shallow groove, step left and climb to the belay passing an overlap.
A Phizacklea, S Hubbard 1986

③ Gully Wall 16m F6b
Climb the groove of *Le Flange en Decomposition* to the bulge then move right up a shallow groove to a belay.
W Lounds, P Sanson 1977

④ Johnny No Mates F6c+
Climb the smooth groove to the right to reach the *Gully Wall* traverse.
J Adams

⑤ Gully Wall Direct F6c ★
Starting just right of the smooth groove, take a rising line up steep ground on fingery sidepulls until *Gully Wall* is reached at the end of its traverse right.
D Bates 1985

⑥ Winter Pincher 15m F6b+
Climb the stubborn shallow hanging groove.
T Walkington, D Bates 1985

⑦ Oddbods 15m F6b+
The next short groove.
D Bates, T Walkington 1985

⑧ Strongbow 15m F6b
The third hanging groove.
I Greenwood, A Phizacklea 1979

⑨ Comedy Show 15m F6b
The fourth and last groove on this wall.
D Bates, T Walkington 1985

Eraser Head F7b+ (page 50) Ian Cooksey — Nick Wharton

Moonchild Buttress

Steep climbing on solid clean rock with some of the best routes on the crag. This section lies immediately above the point at which the path arrives at the cliff.

10 Burkini 10m F5b
A short line left of the ash tree.
C Matheson 2016

11 Yashmak F6c
Start just right of the ash tree.

12 Heinous Penis 21m F6c
Some might think it's soft at the grade. From the white patch climb the smooth rib through a bulge to the wall above. Shares a lower-off with *Yashmak*.
A Phizacklea, P Ingham 1986

13 Starshine F6b
Located 2m left of the *Interstellar Overdrive* start. Technical start up the broken crack system.
L Ainsworth, D Cronshaw 1974

14 Jelly Head 25m F7a ★
A left-hand finish to *Interstellar Overdrive*. Climb over the roof on the upper wall leftwards then up.
J Bird, A Tilney 1991

TOP 15 Interstellar Overdrive 24m F6c ★★★
A great route, one of the best lower end sports routes on the crag. Start a few metres left of the slanting groove/ramp of *Sun God*. Climb the pocketed lower wall up a vague groove until the angle eases. Clamber over a dead yew tree and up to the roof, then move right into the hanging groove. Follow this with increasing difficulty to the top.
D Cronshaw, D Knighton 1979

16 Sun God 25m F6a+ ★★
A good warm up following the prominent flake-line that separates the slabby wall of *Interstellar Overdrive* and the steeper *Zantom Phone*. Follow the flake to the dead yew tree then continue up the groove and bulging flake behind.
D Cronshaw, L Ainsworth 1974

Perhaps the best way up this wall is to start up *Sun God*, then join *Cement Head* and finish up *Interstellar Overdrive*, F6c+.

17 Cement Head 25m F7a+ ★★
Although this is only really half a route (the top half!), it does climb over superb rock.
J Bird 1989

18 Combat Plumber 25m F7a ★
A entertaining combination that allows easier access to the top of *Phantom Zone*. From the ledge below the Interstellar tree, step out right as for *Cement Head* but keep going until beneath the upper groove of *Phantom Zone*. Climb the thin wall to the overlap then step right to climb the groove.

19 Zantom Phone 25m F7c+ ★★
Thin fingery climbing up the steep clean wall right of the groove of *Sun God*. Start below the wall and make hard moves, including a mono, to eventually reach *Cement Head*, finish up this.
P Ingham 1986

TOP 20 Phantom Zone 25m F7b+ ★★★
Brilliant! From the toe of the buttress, just left of where the approach path reaches the crag, make a hard rock-over to a good tufa on the right. Move up and initially left then back right over steepening ground, to get through the bulge and into a vague groove. At the top of this is a small ledge offering a brief respite. Continue up the thin wall to gain and climb the smooth groove above to reach a belay on the left.
P Ingham 1986

21 Stan Pulsar 25m F7b+ ★
Make the rock-over to reach the tufa on *Phantom Zone* then swing steeply right and pull up onto a small ledge at the foot of a groove. Climb the groove to a step left onto a ledge. Move back right and up to a hanging flake/groove. Climb this and the crack to a lower-off.
S Hubbard 1986

22 Surfing with the Alien 25m F8a ★
Even more steep and fingery than its neighbours! This route gains and then climbs the rib to the right of *Phantom Zone*. Start where the path meets the crag. Climb the thin wall and steep rib to a lower-off just below a ledge.
J Gaskins 1992

23 Moonchild 24m F6c+ ★★
This significant route in the early development of the crag takes the striking groove. E4 5c in old money! Steeply to a scoop on the right. Pull up and left into another scoop then straight up, climbing the flake. Finish up and left at the yew tree. Alternatively, step left at the second scoop and climb a crack to a lower-off.
R Fawcett, A Evans, D Parker 1974

24 Bleep and Booster 27m F6c ★★
The shallow groove to the left of *Moonchild*. Climb *Moonchild* to a good hold then move left to reach better holds at the bottom of the groove. Or make hard moves up and left from the start of *Moonchild* F7a. Step up and right to something of a rest before pressing on up the groove until stopped by the capping bulge. Pass this on its left then head right to gain entry to the next groove. At the top of this stand up beneath the left side of the prominent prow to reach the lower-off on its left.
S Hubbard, A Mitchell 1985

Moonchild Buttress | **Chapel Head Scar** | 45

46 Limestone

⑳	Phantom Zone	F7b+ ★★★
㉓	Moonchild	F6c+ ★★
㉔	Bleep and Booster	F6c ★★
㉕	War of the Worlds	F6c+ ★★
㉖	62 West Wallaby Street	F7a+ ★
㉗	War Hero	F7a ★★
㉘	Tricky Prick Ears	F7b ★★★
㉙	Maboulisme Merveilleux	F7c+ ★★
㉚	Not the Full Shilling	F8a ★★★

Moonchild Buttress | **Chapel Head Scar** | 47

Limestone

25 **War of the Worlds** 37m F6c+ ★★
A long route that winds its way up and left across the buttress, taking in a lot of excellent climbing along the way. Tie a knot in the end of the rope! Climb *Moonchild* into the groove and swing left into *Bleep and Booster*; keep traversing left to the groove of *Stan Pulsar*. Go up this to the resting place on the left. When you are ready, step down then head up and left above *Phantom Zone*, then up to the right-hand end of the roof, just left of the widest groove. Pull right into the groove and follow it to the belay up on the left. Finishing up *Stan Pulsar* is **War of the Pulsars** F7a.
R Fawcett 1978

26 **62 West Wallaby Street** 27m F7a+ ★
The residents of this famous address would probably find some ingenious way of getting to the top; you'll probably need to rely on power and technique! Tackles the steep wall to the right of the *Moonchild* groove. Climb the wall and steep bulge on small but positive holds to reach a good ledge. Trend rightwards to join *War Hero*.
K Phizacklea 1997

27 **War Hero** 26m F7a ★★
A great route. Start by the first rock step. Climb straight up the wall to a shallow corner at 6m. Head leftwards over a bulge before climbing up and right to gain, first a small ledge, then up again to a larger ledge with the remains of a tree stump. Continue up the wall to the left of the corner on fantastic rock.
Photo page 38.
S Whittall, K Phizacklea, A Phizacklea 1997

28 **Tricky Prick Ears** 27m F7b ★★★
A tremendous route with a lot of climbing. Start a couple of metres up the slope by the second rock step below a shallow blank groove. Climb the groove to reach the long flake (sometimes a bit damp). Make a difficult move (crux) out left and up to easier ground. Move up and right, over the next bulge, to reach a resting position on the left (adjust your cap). When you are ready, move up and right across the steep white wall to reach the overhanging groove. Make hard moves to enter and then follow this groove to the top. Awesome!
P Cornforth 1988

A variety of link-ups are possible **62 War Trick** F7b, **War Trick** F7b+, **Tricky War** F7b, **Tricky Lunatic** F7a, **Luna Prick** F7a+, etc!

29 **Lunatic** 25m F6c ★
Climb the slim groove and flake/crack. Then continue to a ledge. Traverse right to the corner and the top.

30 **Maboulisme Merveilleux** 16m F7c+ ★★
A spectacular route up incredibly steep rock way out there above Great Gully. It can be slow to dry but once it is, there are no excuses left; you just have to do it. Start at a ledge with a bolt belay some way up the gully. From the ledge traverse left across the gully, take a deep breath and fire yourself up the big holds. Keep heading outwards to a hard move on the lip. Pull over and finish more easily up and left.
P Cornforth 1986

31 **Not the Full Shilling** 18m F8a ★★★
Climbs the overhanging wall to the right of *Maboulisme Merveilleux*.
Photo this page.
C Matheson 10.2016

Not the Full Shilling F8a Craig Matheson — MATHESON COL.

Limestone

Route of All Evil Wall
A solid wall of compact rock with an amazing headwall.

32 The Route of All Evil 30m F7a+ ★★
A meandering route (consider using twin ropes) up this excellent wall. Start at the foot of the corner/groove on the left; climb this with a step right onto a small ledge. Move back into the right-trending groove and climb up the centre of the wall to reach a large break. Go up to another break which is then followed leftwards to a reasonable rest. Step back right then finish up a shallow scoop in the left side of the headwall.
G Smith, A Phizacklea 1983

The Route of All Evil Direct 26m F7b ★★★
Perhaps the most popular, and rope-drag free, way to experience the best bits of *The Route of All Evil* is the left-most line of bolts joining the top and bottom with the middle of *Eraser Head*.

33 Eraser Head 25m F7b+ ★★★
Start up the initial corner/groove, pull across to the left-most line of bolts to the final headwall. Moves right gain the central bolt line to finish up the superb smooth pocketed rock; the original finish to *The Route of All Evil*, known at the time as **True Path**.
Photo page 43.
J Bird 1991

34 Cyborg 21m E2 5c ★
Can just be done on bolts as a very sporting sport route! Start up the corner/groove and step right onto the ledge as for *The Route of All Evil* (or start as for *Mid-Air Collision* and climb direct to the ledge). Continue traversing right then move up to a tufa pillar with an excellent natural thread on the left. Go up the pillar and the wall above to a small sapling and ledge with a lower-off up and right.
E Cleasby, M Lynch 1975

35 Mid-Air Collision 25m F7b ★★★
Start up the thin wall right of the groove, briefly joining the groove then leaving it where it curves right at jugs. Quest over bulges to thin moves rightwards gain the capping roof and lower-off.
A Hyslop 1991

A popular variation of *Mid-Air Collision* is to finish moving left in to the top of *Eraser Head*.

36 Omega Factor 18m F6c ★
A steep direct start to *Cyborg*. Start below and climb a white groove with an open niche containing a holly tree. Leave the niche (crux) then move steeply up and left to reach a good flake. Climb back right and up to join *Cyborg*, where the bolts run out! Continue to its ledge and lower-off.
D Knighton, D Cronshaw 1979

37 The Borg 25m F7a+ ★★
Start up *Omega Factor*, climbing the crux moves of this before traversing left to the groove of *The Route of All Evil*. Follow this to the break then head right to climb the arête right of *Mid-Air Collision*.
I Cooksey, K Phizacklea 2011

Rubble Wall

38 Betty Rubble 25m F6c ★★
The left-hand bolted line to a hanging groove.
C Matheson 30.07.2017

39 Barney Rubble 25m F6c ★★
The far right line of bolts. Finish spectacularly on an exposed arête.
C Matheson 2015

Great Buttress
At first vertical, then becoming steeper as it continues rightwards, eventually becoming quite undercut. The rock on the main part of the buttress is fantastic with tufa pillars to help in places!

40 Sad But True 27m F6c+
Good climbing up the wall left of the yew tree, though the rock becomes rather brittle in the upper section. Start as for *Half-Life*.
S Whitall, K Phhizacklea 1996

41 Half-Life 27m F6b+ ★
Start up the right-facing corner/flake directly below the large yew, the Up Town Tree, growing 5m up the crag. The tree prevents a good view of the wall above - the climb is better than might be expected. Climb the corner and tree then onto the wall to a horizontal break. Move left and up into an open groove over some nice crozzly tufa. Go up the groove, then up and right to make an awkward move to stand below the steep upper bulge, joining *Up Town*. Move up and right into another groove with a lower-off at the top.
E Cleasby, I Postlethwaite 1977

42 Up Town 27m F6c ★★
An even better companion to *Half-Life* with possibly the best small tufa formation on the crag. Climb the right-facing corner/flake directly below the large yew tree as far as the horizontal break then move right and up, heading for the fabulous stalactite like tufa. You can climb *Witherslack Alice* to this point. Go up the tufa and the groove above until a very delicate puzzling move gains a standing position below the steeper upper bulge (*Half-Life* comes in from the left). Move up and right into another groove.
Photo page 7.
G Gibson 1984

Great Buttress | **Chapel Head Scar** | 51

43 Witherslack Alice 26m F6c+
Takes a line starting right of the Up Town Tree. Fingery start (clipstick recommended) up to and through the break to the right of the tree. Follow the easier shallow corner to where the rock steepens again, gain holds in the horizontal break and move up and right to good finishing holds. Or finish moving left in to *Up Town* at the same grade.
A Towse, P Short, D Short 2004

44 Shades of Mediocrity 20m F7a ★
Start 6m right of the tree at the left-hand of two tufa stumps. Stand up on the tufa then climb up, moving left at a small overlap. Continue, then drift back right over some excellent clean rock to a bolt belay.
S Wood 1992

45 Gilbert Cardigan 20m F7a+ ★
Take a more direct line, this time moving slightly right then back left to a lower-off.
K Phizacklea 1992

46 Guloot Kalagna 21m F7c ★
Hard and fingery climbing. Start 4m right of the tufa stumps beneath a tufa fin. Climb up to an overlap and over the bulge into the large scoop. Use tufas to climb the next bulge then up the steep thin top wall.
P Cornforth 1991

47 Electric Warrior 21m F7b ★★★
A superb route with big moves on fat tufas. Start behind the ex-holly tree beneath a fat tufa that looks like a Rice Krispie cake. Climb the rough flutings until a big move up and right allows access to a small ledge from where the lower-off is reached.
A Mitchell 1986

48 Agent Provocateur F7c+ ★
Extends *Electric Warrior*.
A Mitchell, P Cornforth 1987

49 Calling Mr Hall 21m F8a ★★
Start at the other side of the ex-holly from *Electric Warrior*. Climb up to an undercut in the fluting then make a series of hard moves through the bulge to gain a thin groove. Go up this and then the awkward bulge to finish.
P Cornforth 1990

TOP 50 Wargames 24m F7b ★★★
Probably the best route on the crag! Steep to start but on good holds then more delicate in the upper half. Start at a short smooth lower wall, sometimes wet but don't let that put you off. Power up and outwards using tufas, side pulls and pockets (not necessarily in that order) until you are forced into a big move right on undercuts to the base of the hanging groove. Go up the groove and onto the small ledge on the left. Draw breath, then climb the wall all the way to the overlap at its top. Overcome this then trend rightwards on good holds to reach the lower-off. Fantastic!
A Phizacklea 1985

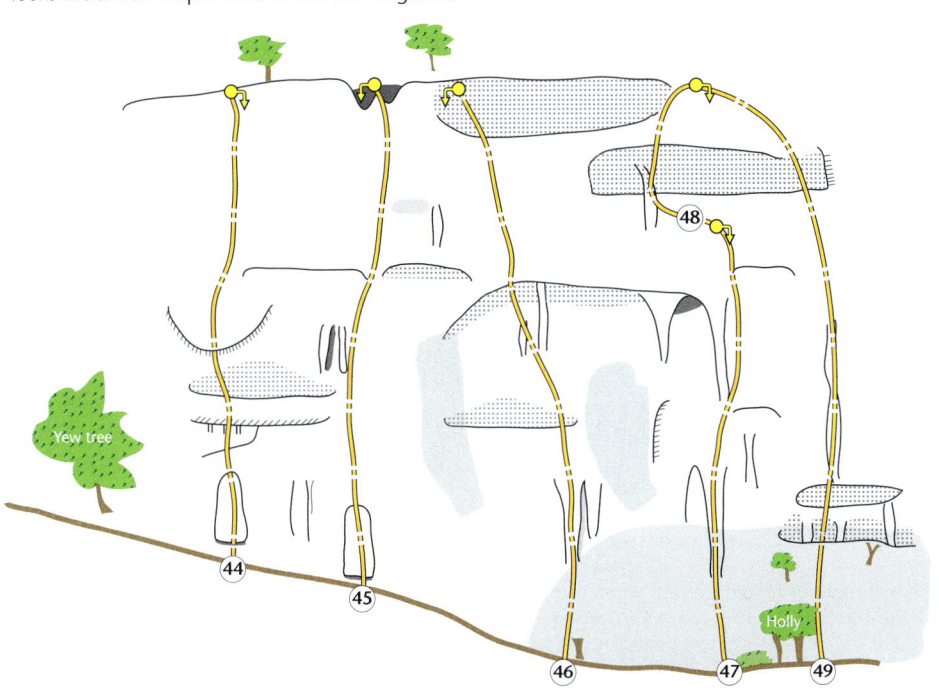

Limestone

49	Calling Mr Hall	F8a ★★
50	Wargames	F7b ★★★
51	More Games	F7c ★
52	Stretchy Perineum	F7b+ ★★
53	Perverted Start	F7b+ ★
54	For When The Tree Goes	F7b+ ★
55	Perverse Pépère	F7b+ ★★
56	Song for Europe	F7b+ ★★★
57	La Mangoustine Scatouflange	F7b+ ★★★
58	Super DuPont	F7b+ ★★★

Limestone

51 More Games 9m F7c ★
Start beneath the left end of the bulging roof at 5m and climb up and leftwards to reach the base of the hanging groove; then follow the bolts. It is possible to join *Wargames* at the lip and reduce the overall grade to **F7b+**.
D Birkett 1992

52 Stretchy Perineum 10m F7b+ ★★
Climbs the right side of the bulging overhang, providing an excellent direct start to *Perverse Pépère*. Start at the large tufa stump 'stuck' onto the wall. Gain the top of the tufa then move up and left past tufa flutings to achieve an awkward position beneath the right side of the roof. Make hard moves through the roof, past a short crack, and up the wall to reach a ledge. Finish up *Perverse Pépère*.
P Cornforth 1987

53 Perverted Start 12m F7b+ ★
A slightly harder right-hand variation from *Stretchy Perineum* moving to the flutings before climbing straight up and slightly right, with a hard fingery move to join *Perverse Pépère*. Finish up this or, if you are feeling stronger, *Song For Europe*.
P Ingham 1986

54 For When The Tree Goes F7b+ ★
Remember the Android tree? In the middle of **Great Buttress** a tall dismal-looking ash tree grew from the base of the crag supported by a length of rope. It should have been treated with the respect and care that we give to gnarly oldtimers that have given such good service. Sadly, now gone.
D Birkett 1992

55 Perverse Pépère 25m F7b+ ★★
Excellent. Climb steeply into the scoop. Traverse left and up to the next ledge. Take a deep breath and climb straight up with a big move to reach a massive hold. Continue up to climb the flake and step right to the lower-off.
P Cornforth, P McVey, A Phizacklea !985

56 Song for Europe 23m F7b+ ★★★
A magnificent route out of the top of the large scoop. Climb steeply into the scoop and from its top right continue up excellent tufas, through a small roof and the wall above, to reach a right-trending line up the top wall. Go straight up to the lower-off on *Perverse Pépère*.
P Cornforth 1989

57 La Mangoustine 22m F7b+ ★★★
  Scatouflange
A great route providing fingery climbing, Go steeply into the scoop then move up and right to stand on a small ledge beneath the steep wall. A few finger-searing moves eventually lead to a tufa fluting. Follow this up and right until the lower-off is reached at the left end of the large roof. The Flange Finish continues to the lower-off above the overhang to the right.
P Cornforth 1986

58 Super DuPont 22m F7b+ ★★★
Climb the wall using various tufa fins to a small triangular overhang. Make a hard boulder problem move to stand on top of the overhang then continue up into the broad scoop above. At the top of the scoop, where the rock steepens, make an initial move up into the right-trending groove, then pull out left to reach a ledge. Climb straight up from here, eventually reaching the lower-off at the left end of the large roof (as for *La Mangoustine Scatouflange*).
P Cornforth 1985

59 Super Duper DuPont 24m F7c ★★★
Start as for *Super DuPont*. Make a boulder problem start up into the scoop and climb up to the right-trending groove but this time follow the groove past large tufa side-pulls until it is possible to climb straight up the steep grey wall, with a precarious mantelshelf move to get established on the top wall. Finish up and right at a chain at the right end of the large overhang.
P Cornforth 1986

60 Prime Evil 24m F7c+ ★★★
Amazing climbing up a steep wall made entirely of Rice Krispies – beware of finger tendons going 'Snap, Crackle and Pop!' Start as for *Super DuPont*, but head up and right using the tufa flutings and tiny crozzly finger edges to get established on the rough grey wall. Climb the wall on the small holds to reach a vague scoop up on the right, then climb the bulging wall above to the overhang. Hard moves over this gain the headwall which is followed to the chain at the right end of the large overhang (as for *Super Duper DuPont*).
A Mitchell, S Sutton 1988

61 Unrighteous Doctors 24m F7c+ ★★★
A fantastic route that provides a counter-diagonal to *Super Duper DuPont*. Start at the tufa just left of the yew tree. Climb the wall on superb tufas, pockets and crozzly holds, heading leftwards higher up, to eventually reach a junction with *Super Duper DuPont* at the top of that route's right-trending groove. Pull up and left onto the upper wall and follow this to the break in the middle of the large overhang. Pull through the overhang at this point and up to a lower-off. Magnificent!
Photo opposite.
D Birkett 1991

62 Doctor Evil 24m F7c+ ★★★
The hardest part of *Unrighteous Doctors* followed by the hardest part of *Prime Evil* was always going to be a hard sustained route.
J Freeman 2011

Unrighteous Doctors F7c+ (opposite) Andy Mitchell — 📷 Nick Wharton

Great Buttress | **Chapel Head Scar** | 57

63 Tufa King Hard 11m F6c ★★
Not that hard! Start just right of the yew. Climb parallel tufas then continue up the right-trending groove on big holds until a pull up and left through the bulge, plus one tougher move on smaller holds, gains the lower-off.
A Burnell 1992

64 Tufa King Far Finish 15m F8a ★★
The extension finish to *Tufa King Hard*.
C Matheson 23.10.2016

65 Driller Killer 30m F7a+ ★
To the right of the tufa pillars of *Tufa King Hard* is a small overlap at about 3m. Climb up to and over this then up the scooped wall behind to reach good tufas below the next overlap. Traverse left at this level, across *Tufa King Hard*, to reach a ledge behind the yew tree. Make hard moves up and left through the bulges to reach easier ground.
P Ingham, P Cornforth 1985

66 Videodrome 26m F7c ★
A harder variation finish to *Driller Killer*. From the ledge behind the yew tree, step back right and make even harder moves up through the bulges.
P Ingham 1987

67 Warm Push 8m F6b+
At the base of the wall, in its centre, is the left side of an 'archway'. Follow this to stand on a large hold, then the white streak to the overlap; lower-off up and right.
M Greenbank 1986

68 Reefer Madness 9m F6c+
Climb small but perfectly formed tufas where the right side of the 'archway' should be. Go straight up the wall heading left at the top to the same lower-off as *Warm Push*.
I Vickers, D Cronshaw 1991

69 Doctor's Dilemma 7m F6c+
Start at the right side of the wall by a triangular niche at head height. Make a few hard moves up the short smooth wall to the overlap. Then either traverse left to the lower-off of the previous two routes (doubles the length of the route!) or thread the bolt.
J Bird 1992

There are two traverses of the **Great Buttress**.

70 Cosmic Dancer F7b ★★
A 'sporty' left to right girdle, it may be wise to take a rack.
1 F7b 24m Climb *Electric Warrior* and continue right past *Wargames* into *La Mangoustine Scatouflange* to take a hanging belay on its traverse.
2 F7a 14m Continue the traverse of *La Mangoustine Scatouflange* and cross *Super DuPont* with finger searing moves. Move up to the roof and traverse below it to reach the *Super Duper DuPont* lower-off.
1986

71 Le Grand Traverse 85m F7c ★★
A pumpy right to left traverse. Start up *Driller Killer* and follow this to the point it goes right. Here swing left to gain a traversing line and follow this strenuously all the way to *Wargames* to finish up this route.
1994

MILL SIDE SCAR

OS Grid Ref: SD 450 845
Altitude: 100m

Small, sound and good. The crag emerges like a ship's prow above the trees at the south western tip of the Whitbarrow escarpment. *Cadillac* stands proud as the 'big tick', and although tamed by the bolts, is still a challenge.

Approach: Park immediately after crossing the cattle grid from the A590 on to the Mill Side road. Continue on foot into Mill Side and take the steep lane on the right by the phone box. Where the track levels, pass a path on the left (Beck Head) continuing for a few hundred metres to a path on the left rising through woodland. Follow this and after 200m take a less obvious path left over scree to the crag.

Map on page 40.

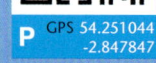

50m rope

10 quick draws

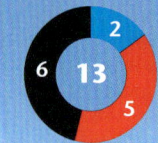

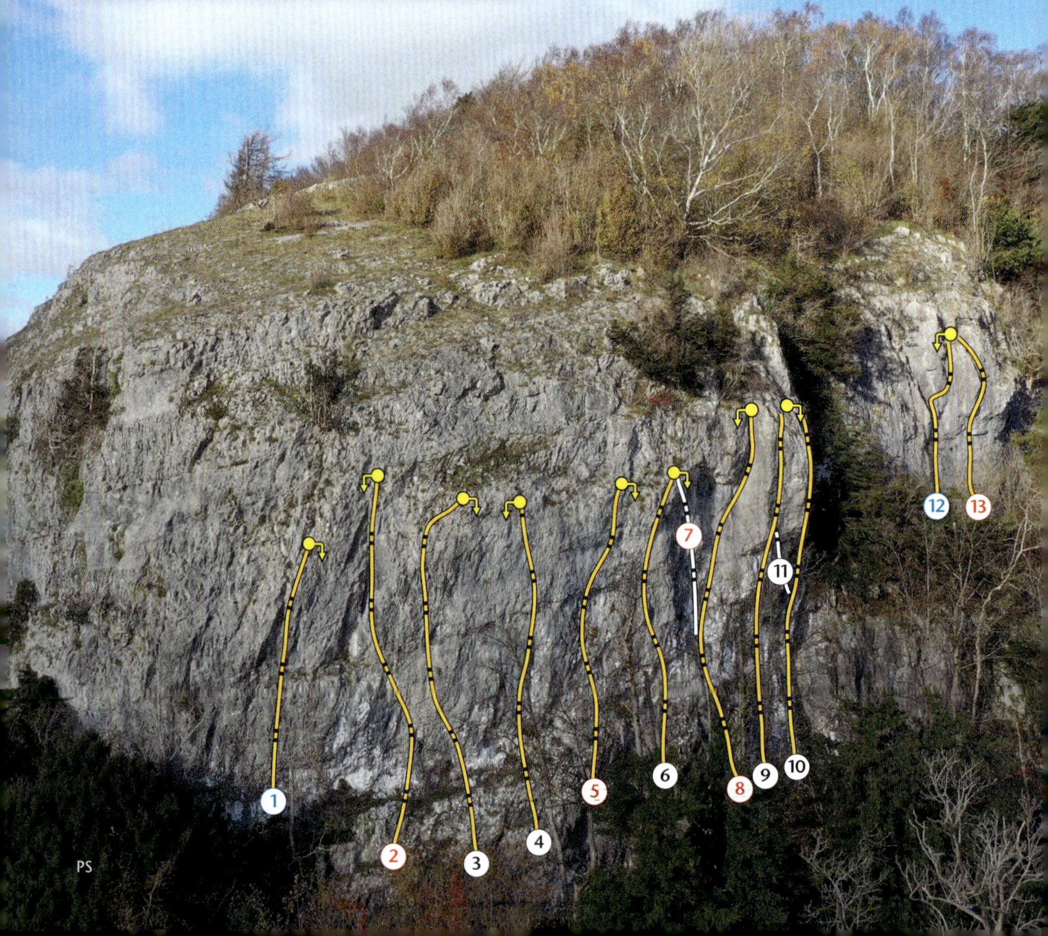

Mill Side Scar

① **Proton** 8m F6a ★
The left-hand line of bolts starting from a higher ledge. The bulging wall and grooves.
K Phizacklea 01.1995

② **Pathfinder** 18m F6b+ ★
The scruffy lower wall and a hard bulging section guard the enjoyable top groove.
A Evans, D Parker 1974

③ **The Green Route** 20m F7c
Good initially but marred by a tough unpleasant finish on poor rock. Left of a white lichen patch, continue left of a small cave and over bulges to the final wall using a pair of sharp artificial crimps.
K Phizacklea 1995

④ **Firebird** 20m F7a+ ★★
Left of the large white patch of lichen, climb the lower wall to the ledge by a small low cave. Enter a short thin groove and climb the wall above.
J Daly, K Phizacklea 01.1995

⑤ **Mustang** 21m F6b ★★
Rears up impressively just left of the pedestal. Cross the break to a small niche then left, passing a small tree, to break up and right to reach ledges below the tough top wall.
R Graham, E Rogers 28.06.1991

⑥ **Integrali** 22m F7a+ † ★★
Climb easily up the right-hand side of the short pedestal to the break. Crank the bulge to reach the thin right-leaning yellow corner. Up this to a lower-off on the right.
D Donnini, K Phizacklea 02.1995

⑦ **Camaro** F6c+
Follow *Cadillac* to the ledge. Move left and pull steeply up the blunt rib until a step right gains a ledge and pockets. Breathe in and make a series of long pulls to finish at the *Integrali* lower-off.
J Kettle 12.06.2018

TOP ⑧ **Cadillac** 24m F6c ★★★
Committing technical climbing; top quality. Climb the line of bolts to the left side of the pinnacle to a ledge. Take the rightwards trending grooveline on flakes and edges. After good footwork on the immaculate smooth wall, climb the hanging grove to finish.
Photo this page.
E Cleasby, A Phizacklea 12.04.1982

⑨ **Countach** 23m F7b ★★
Power up the bulges, grooves and cracks. Excellent. The second bulging crack can be avoided to the right (peg) at F7a+.
P Ingham, P Botterill March 1985

⑩ **Straight-8** 19m F8a ★★
Start up the wall right of *Countach* to the cave below the roof. Move right and climb the bulge direct via a tough sequence to an independent belay.
J Freeman 29.04.2014

⑪ **Straight Tach** F7a+ ★★
Link up - *Straight-8* into *Countach*.
D Eastham 24.09.2016

Upper Right Tier

An area of clean solid rock sporting two short routes reached by scrambling up from back along the approach path. Or climb the first section of **Pioneers' Cave** (HS) to reach the ledge.

⑫ **Fossil Groove** 9m F6a
The left-hand line.
I Greenwood 1982

⑬ **Fossil Crack** 12m F6b
The more technical right-hand line. Span to reach the bottom of the hanging crack.
I Greenwood 1982

Cadillac F6c Dan Robinson — Nick Wharton

SCOUT SCAR
OS Grid Ref: SD 486 915
Altitude: 170m

Born Again F6a+ (page 66) Chris Shiels — Keith Sanders

Scout Scar | 61

Limestone

SCOUT SCAR

Pumpy or technical - or both. The popular routes are clean and sound. Some of the easier or less-travelled routes require care. The potential was realised in the 1980s and the crag has been re-equipped a couple of times, with the most recent wave of development in the easier grades being completed by **Cumbria Bolt Fund** volunteers supported by the generosity of the **Lakeland Climbing Foundation**. Only a 5 minute drive from Kendal with a 10 minute walk from the car, the crag can get busy, especially in the late afternoon. The vista across the Lyth Valley is expansive and sitting on the top watching the sunset after an evening of climbing is sublime.

Approach: From Kendal town centre head up Beast Banks towards Underbarrow and cross over the A591. Follow the road uphill towards a mast. As soon as the road starts to descend, park in a disused quarry on the right. Cross the road, pass through a gate and walk south along the top of the scar passing a shelter, the Mushroom. Some 300m past this drop down to the west and locate a path in a nick in the scar and go steeply down, crossing a fence, into the trees. The climbs are to the left.

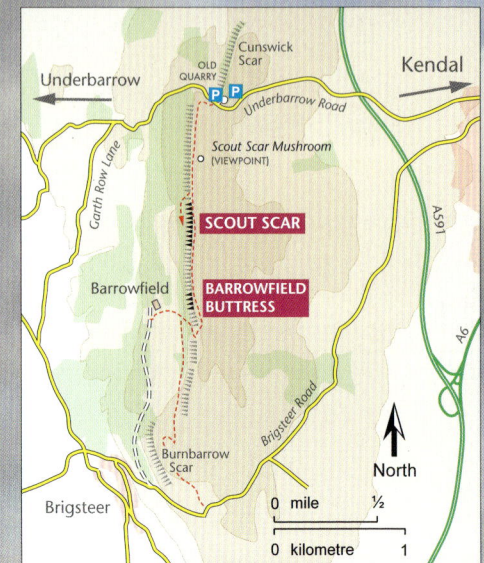

From P on Underbarrow Rd

Scout Scar 63

RAD Scout Scar

GPS 54.324599 -2.787685

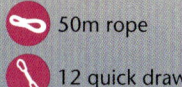
50m rope
12 quick draws

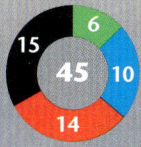
6
15
45
10
14

Limestone

Slate

KENDAL

Micro-Granite

Barrowfield
250m beyond wall
Page 71

Central
Page 66

Remainer
Page 64

Undercut
Page 64

Far Right
Page 71

Sandstone

Ivy League
Page 68

Limestone

Remainer Buttress
Offers a pleasant set of easier routes. Slightly hidden behind the large yew trees up left of **Undercut Buttress**.

1 Corbyn 11m F4 ★
On the far left a decision was made, finally, to unearth the line that starts up the vague corner.
P Sterling 9.12.2019

2 Swinson 9m F4+
Straight up to the *Johnson* lower-off.
D Robinson, P Sterling 9.12.2019

3 Johnson 9m F4+
Unsure of 'straight up', this line lies to the right before trending left to a shared lower-off.
P Sterling 9.12.2019

4 Farage 8m F5+ ★
The far right, well as far right as you can go in 2019, passes a small overlap before the lower-off.
P Sterling 9.12.2019

Undercut Buttress
The first substantial section of crag reached along the cliff-base path, it has a large overhang at the left side and a series of overlaps. The climbing here is short but fierce.

Left of *Scarfoot Wall* is a scramble, **Descent Route** M, that passes (and uses) the large beech tree with care.

5 Scarfoot Wall 8m F4+
Climbs the centre of the wall to the left of *Scarfoot Chimney* to a lower-off over to the right.
N Wharton 02.2020

6 Scarfoot Chimney 8m F3
Climbs the obvious chimney to a lower-off shared with *Scarfoot Wall*.
Pre-history, CBF 2020

7 Mr T 11m F6a+ ★★
Start behind the large ash tree at the left end of the buttress. Climb the short wall leading to the arête. Continue up the left side of this to a lower-off.
N Wharton 02.2020

8 Sheepwrecked 11m F6b ★
Start as for *Mr T* behind the tree. Climb the short wall before moving rightwards then up the centre of the wall to a lower-off.
N Wharton 02.2020

Undercut Buttress Scout Scar

⑨ **Feral** 11m F6c ★
Start 2m right of the tree below a groove. Make hard moves on undercuts and sidepulls to get established on the wall. Move up into the groove and a ledge; then move up and left again to join *Sheepwrecked*. Follow this to the top.
N Wharton 02.2020

⑩ **9½ Weeks** 12m F7a ★
Pass two overlaps to enter and climb the groove above. Climb either left or right at the second overlap; it's bolted for each direction. Solid.
J Bird 18.05.1987

⑪ **First Blood** 14m F7a+ ★
Boulder the roof at its widest point on undercuts and head for a good hold. Excellent powerful climbing.
P Carling, M Glaister 13.11.1985

⑫ **Sylvester Straits** 12m F7c ★
Another powerful climb. Battle your way up using strength and finesse.
J Bird, C Lewis 23.08.1986

⑬ **Meet the Wife** 12m F7b+ ★★
Three stacked gymnastic boulder problems. Warm up before you try this one!
M Lardener 14.08.1991

⑭ **Telegraph Road** 15m F7a ★★
The easiest route breaching the eponymous undercut, and probably the best. Tough moves up the vague, steep depression lead to a square flake and so on to the top.
P Carling, M Glaister 23.04.1986

Limestone

Central Area

Continuing right of **Undercut Buttress** is the deep vegetated Red Rock Gully. A few routes, some trad, start on the walls slightly up the gully, and to the right of the gully a tree arches over the path.

⑮ **Douglas** 13m F6b ★
Starts left of *Bornville* a little way up the overgrown gully. Follow the initial wall and groove before moving left to a scoop and fine wall to the top.
Photo opposite.
C Allen, R Allen 1.07.2014

TOP ⑯ **Good Medicine** 20m F5+ ★★
Start below the cleaned slab right of Red Rock Gully. Pass a crux bulge at one third height.
S Halford, K Jaques 02.2020

⑰ **Bornville** 12m F6a
A hard start gains the line of bolts rising leftwards across the clean area of rock to a lower-off below the prow and dodgy-looking groove.
S Halford 1993

⑱ **Born Again** 26m F6a+ ★★
A really good route providing a relatively easy way up the largest part of the crag.
Photo page 60.
J Bird 1992

TOP ⑲ **Born Free** 26m F6a ★★★
Climb to and pass the right end of the overlap; then trend left up a vague groove before a traverse right to the base of the corner/crack. Lower-off at the top of the tower. Or, for an all bolted trip, avoid the corner/crack and stay left to the *Born Again* lower-off

TOP ⑳ **Born to Run** 25m F6c ★★★
A great technical route using small pockets and fingery holds.
J Bird, D Seddon 11.03.1985

㉑	A Fistful of Steroids	F6b+ ★★★
㉒	Ropearse	F6b
㉓	Beers for Fears	F7a+ ★
㉔	Crimes of Passion	F7a ★★
㉕	Grave New World	F7b ★★
㉖	Kathleen's Nightmare	F7a ★

Douglas F6b (opposite) Garry Lister — 📷 Ron Kenyon

Limestone

21 A Fistful of Steroids 24m F6b+ ★★★
Whilst drug-induced rippling muscles may help power you through the initial bulge, the rest of this excellent route requires style and finesse. Fantastic.
Photo page 36.
J Bird 21.05.1986

22 Ropearse 16m F6b
Climb the wall and flake to the right of the bulge to a ledge and the wall above trending slightly rightwards.
S Halford 4.08.1991

23 Beers for Fears 16m F7a+ ★
Climb flakey rock through the bulges on holds which have since disappeared.
D Seddon 19.07.1986

24 Crimes of Passion 15m F7a ★★
A varied, technical and sustained route up the centre of the wall; the initial section is nails.
J Bird, F Booth 17.6.1986

25 Grave New World 13m F7b ★★
Climb the wall to the bulge, pull over this and up to the chain.
Photo opposite.
D Seddon, J Bird 21.05.1986

26 Kathleen's Nightmare 13m F7a ★
Follow the arête; find a kneebar to unlock the lower section. A clipstick is wise should you fail to unlock this section or indeed right up to the third clip! Make a hard move at half-height to reach a sidepull.
N Conway 1986

Ivy League Buttress

Round the arête is a corner and a cave at ground level.

27 Kathleen 16m F6b+
A worthwhile route up the hanging corner and wall on the right. Pass the tree stumps then move on to the right wall.
P Short, A Towse 1984

28 Bar Six 16m F7b
Strenuous. Boulder out from the back of the cave directly through the roof to the obvious large hold on *Spectral Wizard*.
N Conway 4.04.1987

29 Spectral Wizard 16m F7b ★★
One for boulders; power and heel hook your way over the lip with difficulty (**V5**) to gain a hard reach left into a good sidepull. Continue to the top much more easily.
J Bird, N Conway 4.07.1986

30 Ivy League 16m F7a+ ★★★
Routes like this make any visit worthwhile. Climb the line of pockets and continue up to a small bulge. Overcome this using smears and undercuts then feel the burn in the top groove.
T Walkington 1982

31 A Vision of Things Gone Wild 16m F7b+ ★★
Another fierce route and coveted flash. Visualise up and right over two bulges to the small overhang. Burst left through this and then straight up.
T Mitchell, D Bates 20.05.1986

32 Idle Times 15m F7a ★
Where the ground starts to rise, a vague groove leads to a square-cut overlap; over this and up the wall and short corner.
D Bates 19.05.1986

33 Leather Pets 16m F6c+ ★
A good red point on this steep tricky wall.
A Hyslop 21.04.1991

Ivy League Buttress **Scout Scar**

Limestone

Grave New World **F7b** (opposite) Ruth Hardy — 📷 Ron Kenyon

Ivy League Buttress

26	Kathleen's Nightmare	F7a ★
27	Kathleen	F6b+
28	Bar Six	F7b
29	Spectral Wizard	F7a+ ★★
30	Ivy League	F7a+ ★★★
31	A Vision of Things Gone Wild	F7b+ ★★
32	Idle Times	F7a ★
33	Leather Pets	F6c+ ★

Far Right Buttress

34	Broken Zipper	HS
35	Crossed Loraine	F5+ ★★
36	Poetry in Motion	F6b+
37	Poetry in Commotion	F7b ★
38	High Heels	F6c+ ☆
39	Out of the Ice Project	
40	Scout Post	F6c

Barrowfield Buttress | **Scout Scar** | 71

Far Right Buttress

The lower wall is good solid rock. Up and right is an overlap at half-height.

Thanks to CBF volunteers this wall began its transformation from traditional obscurity into a modern sports venue in 2019.

Approach: Right of *Ivy League Buttress* on the normal approach path.

An abseil station is anticipated at top belay of *Broken Zipper*.

㉞ **Broken Zipper**   26m   HS
Incomplete retro-bolting of a vegetated traditional climb. Climb the right-hand side of the crumbling zipper. It is possible to top out and belay while enjoy the stunning views of the Lakes.

㉟ **Crossed Lorraine**   14m   F5+   ★★
Climb the curved hanging groove to the lower-off.
CBF 2019

㊱ **Poetry in Motion**   14m   F6b+   ★
Left of the vague rib in the middle of the face.
A Tilney, CBF, S McCabe 1991

㊲ **Poetry in Commotion**   14m   F7b   ★
A rising leftwards traverse on good rock to join *Poetry in Motion*.
J Bird 14.05.1986

㊳ **High Heels**   16m   F6c+   ☆☆
Climb the groove of *Icicle* for 3m before stepping left and pulling through the small overhang and heading direct to the lower-off.
CBF, S Melville 02.06.2020

㊴ **Out of the Ice**   Project
Start up the groove, **Icicle** HVS, then move right towards the good rock; enjoy this before moving right at the top to the lower-off of *Scout Post*.
CBF, D Robinson 4.12.2019

㊵ **Scout Post**   15m   F6c
Boulder off the ground into the easier wall to the right of the corner.
C Allen, R Allen 30.11.2014

Barrowfield Buttress

This completely separate buttress lies further along the scar to the south, directly above Barrowfield Farm. It is reached in a few minutes along the top of the scar. Descend the steep ground where the scar fades into the hillside then traverse a short way back underneath the scar until you locate the bolted lines.

① **Wheelbarrow**   18m   F6c+   †
Climb the clean wall starting left of a blocky overhang.
C Allen 2020

② **Toirdealbach**   18m   F6b   †
Right of *Wheelbarrow*, past the loose gully, is an overhung corner. Climb direct passing the overhang on the right; then the groove above.
M Liptrot 1986; CBF, C Allen 2020

The next routes are back towards the approach.

③ **Blue Screw**   18m   F6c+   ★
A solid route up the middle of the wall.
P Carling, S Wilson 13.12.1986

④ **Crumblefoot**   18m   F6a+
Climb the right-hand side of the wall to an area of broken rock.
G Sutcliffe, P Carling 7.12.1986

HUMPHREY HEAD

OS Grid Ref: SD 390 740
Altitude: 10m

Humphrey Head is a small headland that protrudes south into Morecambe Bay, west of Grange-over-Sands. It is technically a sea-cliff, but it is blessed with a large flat base on the edge of the Bay that is ideal for picnics, barbecues, etc. Offering better weather due to its outlying sea-level position it is a lovely venue, well worth travelling to for its best climbs. Although not as popular as it once was, recently there has been work to rejuvenate and re-equip the crag bringing routes back into condition.

Approach: Easily reached by driving through Grange-over-Sands to Allithwaite. Just after the end of the village there is a signposted turn to the left. Follow the narrow road, turning left after the level-crossing, until the road ends at the beach.

There is usually a restriction on climbing from 1st March to 30th June to protect nesting birds. Please check the BMC RAD for updates.

RAD Humphrey

P GPS 54.158392 -2.935279

 50m rope

 10 quick draws

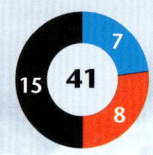

15 | 41 | 7 | 8

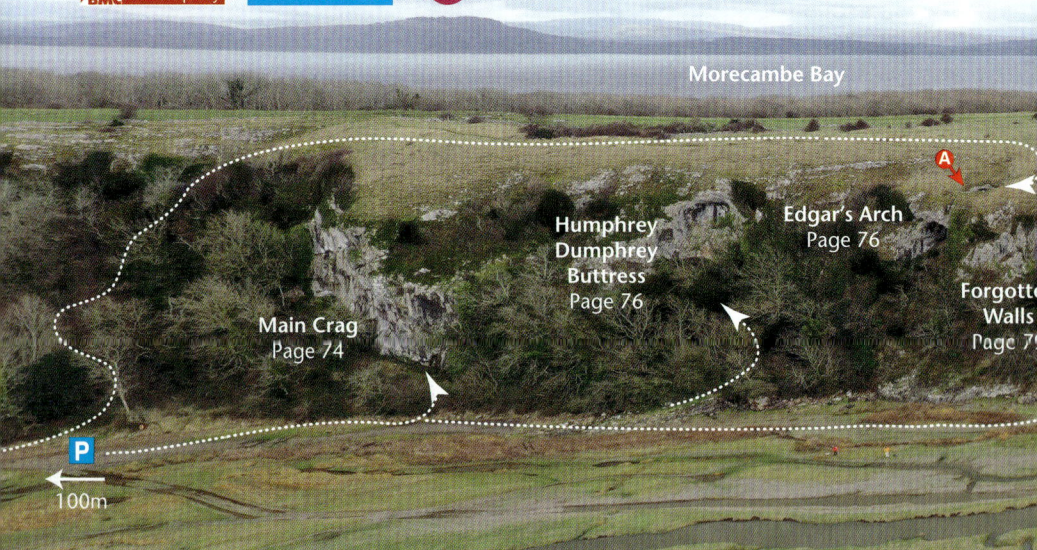

Morecambe Bay

Main Crag — Page 74
Humphrey Dumphrey Buttress — Page 76
Edgar's Arch — Page 76
Forgotten Walls — Page 7?

100m

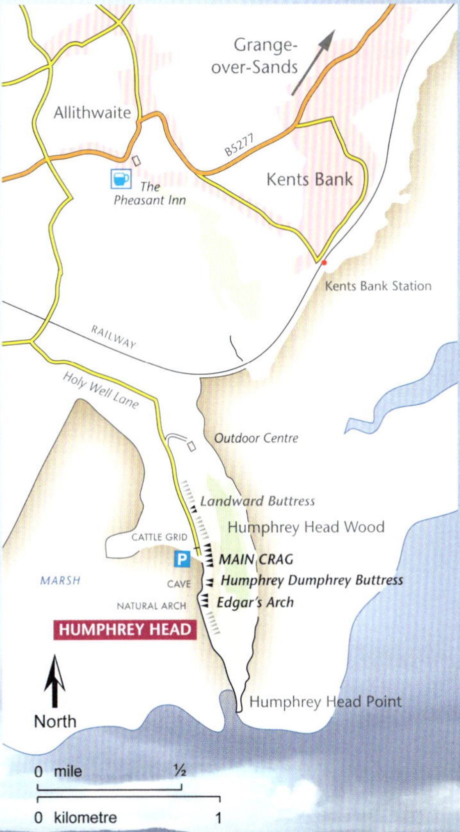

Humphrey Head | 73

Limestone

Slate

Micro-Granite

Sandstone

Map labels:
- Grange-over-Sands
- Allithwaite
- B5277
- Kents Bank
- The Pheasant Inn
- Kents Bank Station
- RAILWAY
- Holy Well Lane
- Outdoor Centre
- Landward Buttress
- Humphrey Head Wood
- CATTLE GRID
- MARSH
- P (parking)
- CAVE
- MAIN CRAG
- Humphrey Dumphrey Buttress
- NATURAL ARCH
- Edgar's Arch
- HUMPHREY HEAD
- Humphrey Head Point
- North
- 0 mile ½
- 0 kilometre 1

Bouldering
The Wolf Hole

PS

Limestone

Main Crag

The most significant and largest wall with a handful of good-quality entertaining mid-grade climbs.

The first routes start from a higher ledge.

① Sniffin' the Saddle Direct　21m　F6a+
Start towards the left end of the ledge. Climb the bulging wall past a bolt then up and right to reach a good flake on *Sniffin' the Saddle*. Finish up this.
R Graham May 1991

② 3-2-1　20m　E2 5b
Start in the middle of the ledge below a left-facing corner. Climb the corner and the one above then move left and follow a shallow groove to a bolt belay.
E Rogers, K Forsythe 04.1989

③ Sniffing the Saddle　18m　F6a+　★
Take the left-facing corner to reach a shallow niche on the right. Up to a ledge; then go left, use the flake, and finish on sharp pockets and a good hold.
A Phizacklea, J Topping 07.09.1986

④ Fusion　17m　F6c
Follow *Sniffing the Saddle* to the ledge then climb the thin crack in the headwall.

⑤ Trigger Finger　F6c　★★
Right from the scoop to a tufa pillar and then left with a cruxy section below the upper wall.

⑥ Shot by Both Sides　8m　F7a　★
From the right climb to the overlap where fingery moves lead to a pocket.
J Topping A Phizackles 06.09.1986

TOP ⑦ The Firing Squad　19m　F7b　★★
Probably the best route here! Start down and right of the ledge a few metres right of the large tree. Climb the steep fingery wall to a small ledge. Continue in the same line past a long reach to gain a ledge and easier climbing (briefly) before attacking the desperate shallow crack and hard finishing move.
A Phizacklea R Knight 09.05.1984

⑧ Hammerlock　22m　E4 5c
Halfway along the *Virility* gangway is a very dodgy left-trending groove - this has been climbed.
M Goff 1968

RK

(9) **Virility**   24m   E1 5b
Start at the base of the steep wall, right of the upper ledge, where a right-trending gangway starts. Follow the gangway to a niche at its end. Step up and right around the arête and climb the none-too-solid wall to a bolt belay out right.
K Woods, AH Greenbank 1966

(10) **Live Rounds**   20m   F7a+   ★
A direct line crossing the gangway. Start just left of where the path arrives at the base of the wall.
R Graham L Steer 31.03.1989

(11) **Shooting the Load**   20m   F7a   ★
Short lived and cruxy. Climb directly to the niche, then continue above, trending left to finish as for *Live Rounds*.

A good hybrid, **Humphrey Cushion** F7a+ ★★ climbs *Shooting the Load* then heads left at half-height to join *Live Rounds*.
R Graham L Steer 31.03.1989

(12) **Coup de Grace**   16m   F7b+   ★★
The wall with a crux at the top. No cliches.

(13) **Humphrey Hymen**   16m   F7b+   ★★
(Met a Sly Man)
A hard steep fingery route up the grey wall.
P Cornforth 07.09.1986

(14) **Stymen**   16m   F6c   ★
An obvious feature round to the right is a sentry box several metres up the wall. Start left of the sentry box and climb the wall to a scoop then up the wall above.
R Graham May 1991

(15) **Noda**   16m   E1 5a
Climb up into the sentry box then, using a suspect flake on the left, move up and right into a short groove. Climb this and the crack above. All a bit loose.
M Goff, J Duff 20.10.1967

(16) **Pork Pie**   16m   F6a+   ★
Enjoyable climbing through the sentry box to moves up and right, then straight up the wall.
Photo this page.
R Graham May 1991

(17) **Humphrey Bogart**   16m   F7a+   ★
Several metres right of the sentry box, surmount an overlap just above head height and climb the technical scooped wall above.
K Forsythe 1991

(18) **Sunflake**   15m   HVS 5a
At the right-hand end of the wall a large flake can be seen at the top.
 Climb up to, then up the flake - a bit overgrown in the lower section.
AH Greenbank 1968-ish

Pork Pie F6a+ (this page) Katy Forrester — RON KENYON

Limestone

Humphrey Dumphrey Buttress

From the beach a large clean rocky depression can be seen in the hillside 40m right of the Main Crag. Down and left of this, the following routes lie above a deep cave with a central pillar.

Approach: This area is reached by a path starting down and right of the depression.

19 Humphrey Dumphrey   8m   F6a   ★
The bolt line just left of the cave.
I Greenwood 07.09.1992

20 Englebert Humphreding   8m   F7b
A one move wonder! The central bolt line above the cave, starting just right of the pillar.
I Greenwood 29.03.1994

21 Mr Self-Destruct   12m   F7b
The snappy right-hand bolt line, just right of the cave.
J Gaskins 08.07.1997

Edgar's Arch

Further right again is a large blow hole which has created a large rock arch - this provides some steep climbing. It can be reached by a dodgy path from the beach - it is much easier, especially when the ground is wet and slippy, to walk along the top and either use a bolt located 8m northeast of the hole to abseil in, or scramble down (rope sometimes *in-situ*) into the roofless cave behind the arch.

22 Mindfields   15m   F7a+   ★★
Start underneath the arch and climb past two bolts to the roof. Follow the line of pockets running up and right beneath the roof to reach the deep hole on *Slightly Shoddy*, then up the overhanging wall above.
J Gaskins 27.05.1998

23 Head Like a Hole   15m   F8b+
As for *Mindfields* to the roof, but where that route goes right, take a line of bolts across the roof following a vague V-groove and heading for a hole in the inner arch and a lower-off.
J Gaskins 07.08.2004

24 Hollow Lands   12m   F6c   ★
Start inside the cave and climb the steep wall past a couple of bolts to a peg. Move up and left over the roof then step left to a large hole and finish at the lower-off above.
M Radtke, J Metcalfe 25.11.1989

25 Slightly Shoddy   11m   F7a
Not so much of the Slightly! Start in the corner on the back wall of the cave. Climb the rounded tufa pillar to reach the deep hole then up the overhanging wall above.
A Hyslop 16.04.1991

26 Back to the Future   11m   F7c+   ★
Climbs underneath the arch from the inside to the outside. Start just right of the crack and head up to a bolt then right, following a line of holds underneath the arch, along a prominent flake/crack to a hanging flake on the lip. Now change direction and start climbing up (instead of down) to reach the top.
Photo page 78.
A Hyslop, J Hyslop A2 1977

27 Direct Variation   F7c+
Climb straight up where *Back to the Future* goes right and finish at the lower-off of *Head Like a Hole*. The bolts currently do not have hangers and it's described as poor, which gives you two reasons not to try it.
J Gaskins 2005

Edgar's Arch | **Humphrey Head**

Limestone

Back to the Future F7c+ (page 76) Chris Smith — 📷 Nina Stirup

Forgotten Walls

Right again is a clean area of rock with a large right-facing corner in its centre and a grassy ledge below.

28 Adela 18m F6c
Climb the deep corner and step left onto the ledge. Climb up past a bolt to the horizontal break. Continue up, then left, using pockets to reach a thin diagonal crack on the left. Step up to a good jug then make a long step back right to finish.
D Cronshaw, L Ainsworth 20.09.1997

29 January 22m F6a ★
The easy right-facing corner then up the depression on lovely bubbly rock.
I Greenwood, A Widowson Jan 1981

30 Where Bolters Fear to Tread 23m F6a ★
The arête and short slab.
D Cronshaw, L Ainsworth 19.09.1997

WARTON MAIN QUARRY

OS Grid Ref: SD 491 724
Altitude: 70m

Crunchy Kibble F7a (page 86) Nick Wharton — David Simmonite

Limestone

WARTON MAIN QUARRY

Some people come to Warton only once and swear they will never go back; others love its sunny, long adventure-filled dubiousness.

There is much loose rock in places and so the quarry can seem daunting on first acquaintance. However, for those who make the effort to get to know the place, they are rewarded with some of the best routes in Lancashire, especially if the sun is shining.

Beware, the car parking area is known as an opportunity spot for thieves; leave nothing in your car.

Approach: The quarry dominates the hillside above Warton and its entrance is about 1km past the George Washington pub on Crag Road from Warton to Silverdale. **Main Wall** is reached by passing the access sign on the gate and crossing the quarry floor. **Terrace Wall** is most easily accessed using the normal **descent** from **Main Wall**: Use the path from the south west corner of the car park to ascend the hill around the main quarry. After leaving the woods continue to a pasture above the west side of the quarry with views across Morecambe Bay. Just before another stile follow a fence rightwards to its corner and enter another wooded area at a small post stile. From here a prickly trod leads east along the edge of the main quarry, care needed. At its end a roped scramble down accesses the terrace.

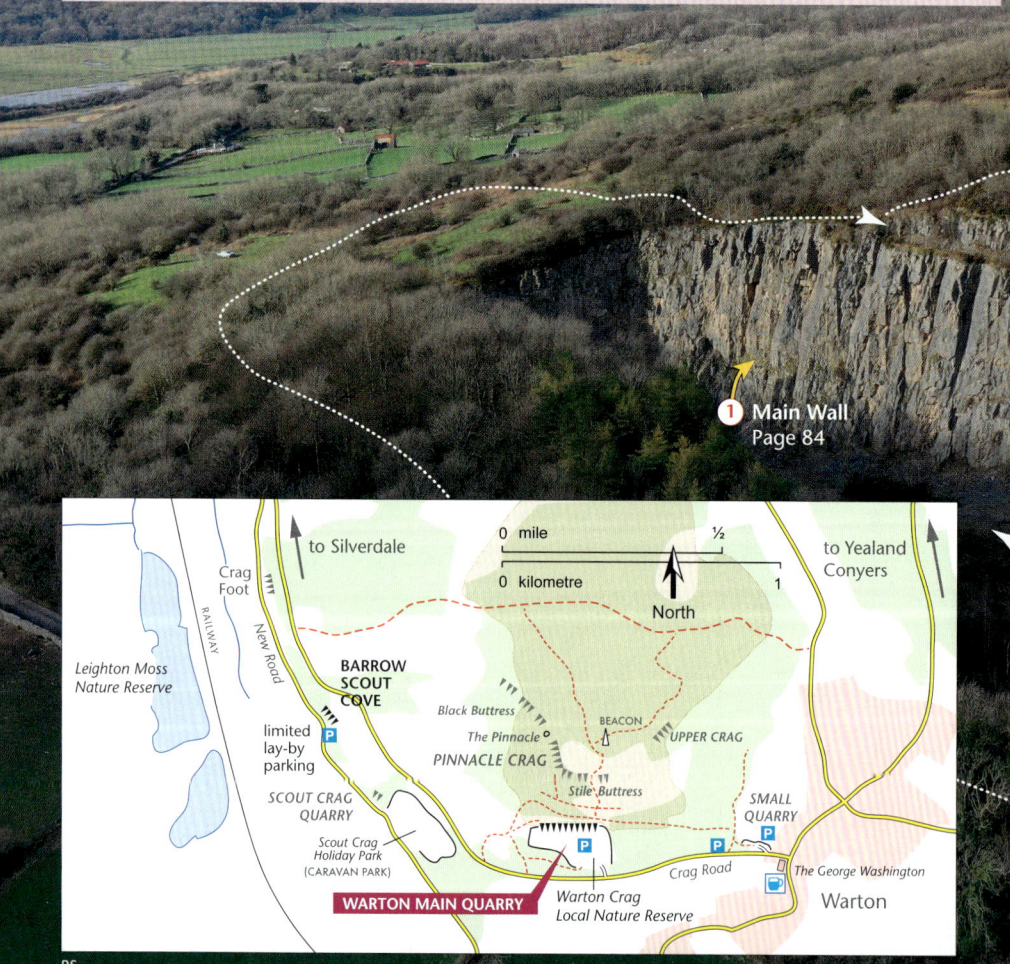

1 Main Wall
Page 84

Warton Main Quarry

Access: The quarry is a Local Nature Reserve and a Site of Special Scientific Interest (SSSI) so there are some restrictions on climbing in order to protect the wildlife. **There are climbing restrictions throughout the quarry to protect nesting birds from February 1st to the end of June.** Notices in the quarry provide the latest information on any climbing restrictions and the Silverdale Area of Outstanding Natural Beauty team monitor the situation very closely so that these restrictions do not remain any longer than is necessary. Check the BMC RAD for updates.

The quarry floor below **Main Wall** provides an excellent habitat for many small orchids which can be easily damaged underfoot. The pools also provide essential habitat for newts and other pond-life. Climbers are asked to keep away from these areas from early April to the end of June and to watch where you walk at all times.

60m rope
14 quick draws

3 4
4
30
19

Limestone
Slate
Micro-Granite
Sandstone

Terrace Wall
Page 88

Modern Wall
Page 85

End Walls
Page 86

RAD Warton Main Quarry
GPS 54.144769 -2.780249

Main Wall

① Gravy Bones 50m F6b+ ★★★

Towards the far left corner of the quarry from the car parking a large hidden slab can be found, the right edge of which is home to the classic trad route **Deceptive Bends** E1 5b. Left again is a large slab that does not reach the quarry floor. This is the main objective of this brilliant long sports route. There is no lower-off; belay from trees back from the quarry rim.
1 15m Climb the cracked wall hidden behind the trees. Move right at the 4th bolt onto the rib. Cautiously cross unstable ground to belay on a small tree.
2 40m The interesting slab passing a couple of overlaps. Take care with the rock after the final bolt.

With careful rope work it is possible to ascend in one long and absorbing pitch.
K Phizacklea 2015

Modern Wall

1 **The Year of the Cat** 34m E2 5a
S Parr 1976

2 **Celestial Cyclone** 25m E3 5c
D Bates 1986

3 **Zero Tolerance** 26m F6a+ ★
A worrying start soon reaches a slight rib. After surmounting this, continue up the steep slab with a small overhang near the top. The lower-off is above.
N Siddiqui, R Siddiqui 1998

4 **21st Century Schizoid Man** 25m E3 5b
B Davison, A Richardson 1999

5 **Modern Times** 26m HVS 5a ★
Bold, one bolt and one peg.
S Parr, S Lund 1975

Limestone

End Walls - Left

⑥ Crunchy Kibble 30m F7a ★★
Avoids the poor rock and upper crack of the trad route **Oddballs** E4 5c. Climb to the overlap, tricky to pass, then follow bolts to the overhang which is passed to the right and so to the top.
Photo page 80.
K Phizacklea 2015

⑦ The Torture Garden 30m E6 6b ★★★
D Bates, T Walkington 1987

⑧ Mighty Fly 30m E5 6b ★★★
D Bates, T Walkington 1985

End Walls - Right

9 **Moonshine** 22m F6a ★★
A delicate route with only two bolts, but they are where it matters. From the top of a vague fluting make delicate moves to a small ledge. Continue with a slight step left towards the top. Belays well back.

BOLT FUND DEVELOPMENT

Cumbria Bolt Fund volunteers are planning to renew the fixed equipment, pegs, old bolts, etc., on the following routes bringing them up to more modern (some might say "sport" climbing) standards when the 2020 restrictions for nesting birds have ended. We hope that this will create a range of routes from approximately F6a through F7a.

1 The Year of the Cat
2 Celestial Cyclone
4 21st Century Schizoid Man
5 Modern Times
7 The Torture Garden
8 Mighty Fly

Limestone

Terrace Wall

Fantastic views and lots of sun with a good selection of intermediate sport climbing on solid rock, which tends to dry out quickly, so it is often in condition when other nearby areas are still wet.

① **Plastic Wall** 11m F4
The groove, then left onto a blunt arête. No lower-off.
L Ainsworth, D Cronshaw 2008

② **Sam's Day** 14m F4
Through a nick in the overhang to a ledge. Step left and up to another ledge and finish. No lower-off.
L Ainsworth, D Cronshaw 2008

③ **Blinkered** 15m F6c † ☆
The wall left of *Off the Sneck*; absolutely no use of the wide crack of **Bus Pass** (VS 5a) on the left or bridging into *Off the Sneck* at this grade.
P Sterling 30.09.2019

④ **Off the Sneck** 15m F4
The corner.
D Cronshaw, L Ainsworth 2008

⑤ **No Line** 15m F5+
D Cronshaw, L Ainsworth 2008

A nice **F6a** combination can be made by climbing the start of *No Line* and finishing direct in to the top of *Breakthrough*.

⑥ **Breakthrough** 15m F6b
Tricky moves on to the rounded rib.
D Cronshaw, L Ainsworth 2007

⑦ **Star Wars** 36m F5+ ★★
May feel like a **HVS**. Start up *Breakthrough* to a sloping ledge, then a rising traverse rightwards to *Red Bush*. Finish here or continue, with fewer lines (bolts) to cross to *Close Encounters*.
J Cooper

⑧ **Return of the Jedi** 15m F5+ ★
D Cronshaw, L Ainsworth 2006

⑨ **Star Trek** 16m F6a ★★
L Ainsworth, D Cronshaw 2006

⑩ **Ray of Hope** 17m F6a

⑪ **Middle Way** 17m F6a

⑫ **Red Bush** 19m F6a ★
10, 11 & 12 D Cronshaw, L Ainsworth

⑬ **Forphil** 17m F6a ★
J O'Neill, J Calver 2008

The right-hand end of **Terrace Wall** is also referred to as **The Playground**. Don't step off!

⑭ **Riding on Air** 22m F5 ★
A traverse of **The Playground** to the lower-off of *Walking on Sunshine*.
J Cooper 1986

⑮ **Polo** 22m F4 ★
J Cooper

⑯ **Close Encounters** 12m F5

⑰ **Misplaced** 12m F6a
D Cronshaw, L Ainsworth 2006

⑱ **Walking on Sunshine** 13m F5 ★
J Cooper 1986
Photo opposite.

⑲ **Melting Point** 12m F5 ★
L Ainsworth, D Cronshaw 2006

⑳ **Boiling Point** 12m F5
D Cronshaw, L Ainsworth 2206

Walking on Sunshine F5 (opposite) Peter Sterling — David Simmonite

BARROW SCOUT COVE

OS Grid Ref: SD 481 724
Altitude: 20m

Sleeping Sickness F6a+ (opposite) Dave Cronshaw — Roger Vickers

Barrow Scout Cove

With a lovely outlook across Morecambe Bay this is a small and compact sunny venue for those short on time.

The small cave right of *Pincher* is a 12,000 year old Palaeolithic scheduled site. In order to preserve it, climbers have been asked not to either climb or venture farther right than *Pincher*.

Approach: Use the small lay-by on the east side of New Road about 600m north of South Crag Holiday Park. The crag is reached quickly by a short overgrown path directly above the parking.

① **Fuel My Fire**   8m   F7a+
Through the roof.
J Gaskins 1999

② **Serial Thrilla**   8m   F7b+   ★
The roof at its widest point.
J Gaskins

③ **The Perfect Drug**   F6c
Start behind the hazels.
J Gaskins 1999

④ **Their Law**   8m   F7a
Start at the staple between two grooves. Follow the left groove through the roof.
J Gaskins 1999

⑤ **Like a Dick Only Smaller**   10m   F6a+   ★
From *Their Law* to a bolt above the initial bulge. Then reach a jug on the right and power across the roof to a tree belay.
N Siddiqui, J Gaskins 1998

⑥ **Sleeping Sickness**   10m   F6a+   ★
Immediately right of *Their Law* finishing on jugs.
Photo opposite.
D Cronshaw, I Vickers 1990

⑦ **TV Fan**   8m   F4
Above the fallen tree.
J Gaskins 2003

⑧ **Picture This**   8m   F4
2m right of *TV Fan* at a slightly higher level.
J Gaskins 2003

⑨ **The Modern World**   8m   F3
The weakness between two roofs.
J Gaskins 2003

⑩ **Modern Man**   8m   F3
The right-hand roof at its narrowest.
J Gaskins 2003

⑪ **Scouse**   8m   F4
From the rock step climb to the left of a small overhang.
C Hodge 1985

⑫ **Pincher**   8m   F4
To the right of a niche at 3m.
L Ainsworth, D Cronshaw 1996

FAR CRAG FOOT
Approach: Approximately 200m north along New Road from the **Barrow Scout Cove** lay-by and 80m south of **Crag Foot**, which is visible from the road, directly opposite a transformer power-line pole, a short dirt scramble directly from the road reaches the base of this small buttress.

The Gray Race   9m   F6b
Ten in 2010   9m   F6a   ★

SLATE

Limited Edition E4 6a (page 127) Ed Booth — 📷 David Simmonite

Crags
- **SADDLESTONE QUARRY**   Page 98
- **HIGH BLUE QUARRY**   Page 100
- **HODGE CLOSE QUARRY**   Page 104
- **PARROCK QUARRY**   Page 136
- **THE WORKS**   Page 140
- **BAKESTONE QUARRY**   Page 150
- **MOSS RIGG QUARRY**   Page 152
- **TILBERTHWAITE QUARRY**   Page 156
- **RUNESTONE QUARRY**   Page 170
- **CATHEDRAL QUARRY**   Page 180
- **COMMON WOOD QUARRY**   Page 192
- **THRANG QUARRY**   Page 196
- **DALT QUARRY**   Page 198

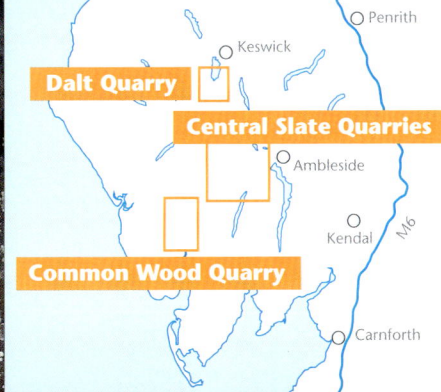

HISTORICAL

HIGH BLUE QUARRY

Blue Quarries are situated behind the terrace of cottages known as Miner's Row. There are three separate quarries, High, Middle and Low which all worked the light-green slate band. An access road zigzags up the hillside, serving each quarry.

On the High Blue quarry bank, are the remains of an upper pier of an aerial flight which was used to carry slate clog from the upper workings down to the Coppermines valley for processing. It was constructed in the 1920s by the Mandall Company. They also installed a slate saw in the valley to process the blocks.

All that remains of the aerial flight is the upper slate pillar. From here, the operator could control the rate of descent of the cradle of slate block on its journey down to the valley.

The quarries closed at the onset of the Second World War, and quarrymen not required for military duty transferred to the Old Man workings.

PARROCK QUARRY

The Parrock workings were established in the late 18th century when a tunnel was driven from lower down the hillside to intersect the light green slate band below Wyth Bank.

At least six separate 'companies of men' were involved in working Parrock agreeing a 'bargain' with the leaseholder to work a particular chamber. Each company was assigned a location for tipping the slate below the entrance to the tunnel which resulted in the well-known and historic 'Parrock finger tips' being created, one tip for each company.

Eventually, in 1898, it was decided to 'open top' the large Parrock close head. This was always an extremely dangerous operation and on this occasion a large quantity of slate fell to the chamber floor as the roof was being removed. It buried a Cornish quarryman, James Bond. His body wasn't located for 5 weeks despite a team constantly searching for his remains.

At the end of the 19th century, a long powered incline up to the rim of the quarry was installed. A steam winder was placed at the head of the incline and flatbed trucks of slate clog were hauled out of the quarry to be processed at High Parrock Tip. This incline was also used to remove slate from Hodge Close Quarry. Today, much of the track bed and masonry still survives. This was one of the longest inclined railways operating in the district at that time.

HODGE CLOSE QUARRY

When fully operational, the vast pit of Hodge Close was nearly twice its present depth to the water level but constant rock falls over the years have reduced the apparent depth significantly. During its working life, pumps were needed at all times to keep the water level down.

A variety of methods of removing the quarried slate were employed over the years as the depth of the hole increased. In the 1860s, an access tunnel was driven from below the quarry into the base of the pit. As the depth increased, it was necessary to install a water balance lift to raise slate clog from the base to the access tunnel. This operated for several years until it also became ineffective as the base was taken down further. The lift was abandoned and a Blondin Hoist installed. This was a form of travelling crane which lifted slate-bearing trucks from the quarry bed. The Hoist offered a degree of flexibility to the problem of lifting slate as the pit was constantly getting deeper.

The position of the Blondin Hoist was changed several times but ultimately it was realigned south to north to allow tubs of slate to be hoisted onto a constructed steel landing adjacent to the access

A Water Balance Incline; water was pumped into a bucket which counterbalanced the slate load below. When sufficient water was collected the slate was raised to the rim. This was superseded by the Blondin Hoist. Photo courtesy of **Coniston Institute and Ruskin Museum.**

tunnel leading into Parrock Quarry. For several years, the main route of exit for slate clog was via this tunnel. A battery-powered locomotive hauled trains of trucks through the tunnel into Parrock Quarry to the powered incline. The steam winder at the head of the incline hauled flatbed trucks of slate clog out of the quarry to be processed at High Parrock Tip.

The Blondin Hoist was used right up to the end of the working life of the quarry. Hodge Close closed in 1964. It is said that the quarry closed because the operating company could not afford a new blondin rope.

MOSS RIGG QUARRY

The enormous pit of Moss Rigg was originally a series of underground chambers. Due to their growing size, the roofs were removed in the mid 1880s. Working continued under various leaseholders until, in 1935, Moss Rigg was closed down by the Buttermere Slate Company who had been working the site for over 10 years. 13 years later, the quarry was reopened by three Coniston quarrymen who formed the Lakeland Green Slate & Stone Company.

Moss Rigg was developed over the following 40 years creating a major international supplier of decorative stone. The quarry was selected as the source of the building stone used to construct Coventry Cathedral's Chapel of Unity. Designed by Basil Spence, it was completed in 1962.

In 1990, Moss Rigg was temporarily closed but has never reopened.

During the 19th century, Lanty Slee sited one of his whisky stills in a cave in Moss Rigg quarry. This was among numerous locations used to enable Lanty to move his equipment at short notice to avoid the attentions of the excise men.

Men slate riving and dressing in **Hodge Close**. Photo courtesy of **Coniston Institute and Ruskin Museum**.

TILBERTHWAITE QUARRY

The ancient workings in Tilberthwaite Quarry were known to the quarrymen as Penny Rigg Quarries.

The quarry is one of the earliest to have been developed in the district and also one of the most productive. By 1750, lords of the manor received a considerable revenue from the workings. A stocktake in 1752 held on the quarry bank produced a figure of 600 tons valued at approximately £37, a considerable sum at the time.

The quarry worked the silver-grey slate band. The bedding plane here is almost vertical which meant that quarrying required a minimal amount of black powder. Slate clag could be peeled off the quarry walls easily by the quarrymen (and sadly, also by climbers).

Finished slates were carted to the head of Coniston Lake for shipment to the coast.

The quarry finally closed by 1930.

THRANG QUARRY

The quarry is located in Chapel Stile where in former times, most houses were occupied by quarrymen's families. Now most are holiday cottages.

The workings at Thrang are unusual in that slate was obtained from both surface quarries and underground mines. A section of the underground workings were accessed by a vertical square-sectioned shaft. A number of mining levels lead off from this shaft. Former residents can remember a stack of coal and discarded cinders adjacent to the top of the shaft strongly suggesting the use of a steam powered winder to raise slate from the depths. The mining tunnels and close heads spread out beneath the hillside and allegedly to beneath Holy Trinity church. Though unlikely, it gave rise to the local legend that quarrymen working overtime on a Sunday could hear the church bells ringing beneath ground.

The last workings at Thrang were carried out by a couple of retired former quarrymen. Fed up with domestic chores, messrs Coward and Rigg returned to 'work', repaired a riving shed and started producing slates from discarded blocks lying around the quarry floor. Their products found a ready local market. They carried on until they were unable to walk up to the quarry.

RUNESTONE QUARRY

Runestone Quarry, known locally as Betsy Crag Quarry, consists of a series of long open pit workings follow a silver-grey slate band up the fell side. The quarry, one of the earliest in the area, is likely to have been worked since the 1700s.

The quarry closed just prior to the first world war. Early transport of the slate would be by pack pony and the remains of a sledge track is evident on the eastern side of the site. Later, slate was taken from the lower quarry via an access tunnel which opened out at a small stockyard on the lower fell side. Ultimately, a cart road was constructed up to the quarry banks.

There is evidence of numerous buildings built to an exceptionally high standard by the quarrymen determined to provide good shelter in this exposed north-facing location. The **Lower Quarry** houses the remains of a riving shed. The smooth grassy floor, the **Gallery**, further up the quarry has the remains of a bait cabin and riving shed. Slate from the **Middle Quarry** was brought here through a tunnel to be processed to make roofing slates. The entrance to the **Middle Quarry** goes under an arch formed by a single slab of slate. This was used as a bridge to allow quarrymen to walk from Tunnel Hole Quarry to Betsy Crag Quarry with ease. The tunnel from the middle quarry was blocked by rockfall in the 19th century.

The obscure entrance to the tunnel became an ideal location for Lanty Slee to set up one of his illicit stills. Slee originally came from Borrowdale and lived in Little Langdale for most of his life. As well as working as a farmer, quarryman and copper miner, he had a thriving business in smuggling. Slee operated multiple illicit stills for production of moonshine whisky which he sold for 10 shillings per gallon, or smuggled with pack horses via Wrynose Pass and Hardknott to Ravenglass. He transported smuggled tobacco on the return journey. The whisky was sold to "discerning local gentry and professional classes" including a local magistrate. He was convicted at least twice although his stills and stashes of moonshine were hardly ever found by the excise men. In the early 1970s, debris from the tunnel was cleared and the remains of Lanty's still equipment were found.

Compiled with permission by AL DAVIS
from **Slate Mining in the Lake District**
by ALASTAIR CAMERON

PETER STERLING

The footbridge arch constructed from a single slab of slate. There were likely no handrails! How it was lifted in to position is a puzzle.

Slate Quarrying Historical | 97

Big Dipper E1 5b (page 127) Pete Whillance, first ascent — 📷 Pete Botterill

Saddlestone Quarry

A great place for poseurs, as tourists have a grandstand view of the action. The largest of the quarry holes on the east side of The Old Man of Coniston, below and left of Low Water. The main feature of this large hole is the impressive arête of *The Shining* on the left as one enters the quarry. This wall faces north west and only receives the sun on mid-summer afternoons, but it dries extremely quickly.

Warning: The fixed equipment in this quarry is as old as the routes and much is in a poor state; proceed with caution or a sense of adventure.

Approach: Park in Coniston or at the Walna Scar car park. Follow the main tourist track up Coniston Old Man. Enter 200m past the point where thick steel cables cross the path. These cables span the upper section of the quarry.

See map on page 100.

① **Rainey Park** 23m F6c+ ⚠
A fine route which follows the striking crack in the wall left of the awesome arête. The first bolt is very rusty with its hanger snapped off. The crack is filthy.
K Phizacklea, S Whittall 10.10.1992

② **Homeward Bound** 26m F7a ⚠
Excellent crimpy climbing up the centre of the wall. Start just right of *Rainey Park*. The first bolt is very rusty.
K Phizacklea, S Wood, K Grindrod 11.10.1992

③ **The Shining** 29m F7a
A stunning route up the left-hand side of the central prow. A difficult and sustained proposition. Start off the large boulder, directly below the arête. The first bolt is very high. There is a crevasse between the starting block and the crag. Clipstick highly recommended.
S Wood 11.10.1992

On the opposite side of the quarry is a steep wall which catches the morning sun, with an obvious ramp in its centre.

④ **Bad Moon Rising** 16m F6b ★
A worthwhile and interesting route; cruxy at the start. Follow the ramp.
S Whittall 10.10.1992

GPS 54.363923 -3.095913

HIGH BLUE QUARRY

OS Grid Ref: SD 294 985
Altitude: 380m

All the routes in the quarry are slabby, worthwhile and ideal for afternoon and evening climbing. The impoverished pioneers were unable to afford bolts and the imaginative trad-sport fusion of manufactured nut placements makes a mini-rack essential on some of the lines.

Caution: The quarry floor has many sharp-edged flakes that have caused injuries; look after yourself and your rope.

The Low Quarry was once a good venue too, but **Rascal Wall** fell down, it is unstable and the bolts have been removed.

Approach: Take the road between the Black Bull and Co-op and park. Walk up the track steeply north towards the Coppermines and take the right-hand fork up the fellside avoiding turnings to the left. The track becomes grassy and after an S-bend leave the track to walk up a spoil heap to arrive at the Low Quarry marked by a prominent cube of rock. **High Blue Quarry** is further up and is entered along an old sled track. The climbs are situated on the back and right walls.

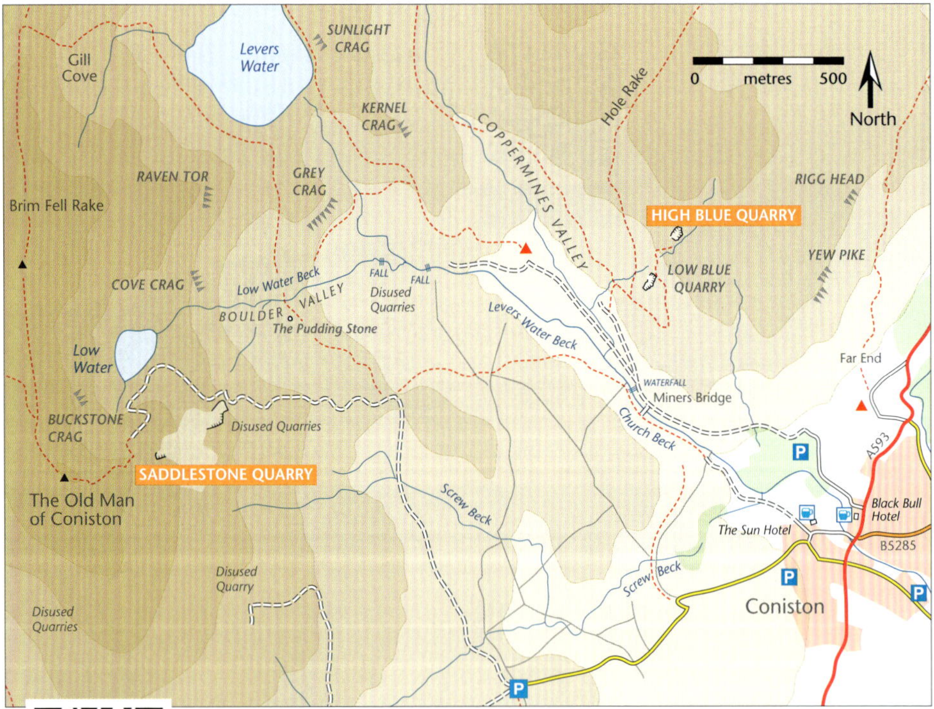

P GPS 54.373018
      -3.087751

High Blue Quarry | 101

Blue Bayou F5 (page 103) Joe Holden — 📷 Ron Kenyon

1. **Blue Riband** — E1 5b
2. **Blue Steel** — E2 5c ★
3. **Impoverished Pioneers** — E2 5c
4. **Blue Remembered Hills** — F6c ★
5. **Blue Moon** — F6b ★★
6. **The 300 Spartans** — F6b
7. **Blue Movie** — E2 5c
8. **Palmer's Performance** — F5+ ★
9. **Scallywag Slab** — F6b ★
10. **A Slight Slate Escapade** — F4+
11. **Blue Bayou** — F5

Scallywag Slab F6b (opposite) Joe Holden,
A Slight Slate Escapade F4+ (opposite) Ron Kenyon — John Holden

High Blue Quarry | 103

1 Blue Riband 10m E1 5b
Start behind an enormous leaning flake in the left-hand corner of the back wall. Climb the slanting slab to where it narrows. Make a difficult entry into the base of the higher gangway (drilled nut placement), and follow it to the top.
A Phizacklea, M Lynch, JL Holden 29.09.1991

2 Blue Steel 22m E2 5c ★
A good route. Start below a groove running diagonally up rightwards, 6m right of the enormous flake. Climb into the scoop between the slab and the groove. Follow the slab leftwards past a chipped hold and then up. Move rightwards onto steeper rock for 3m. Climb the wall passing the left side of the overhang to reach a clean-cut diagonal crack; climb this for 2m then move right onto a good ledge (peg) and continue to the lower-off.
A Phizacklea, JL Holden 21.09.1991

3 Impoverished Pioneers 23m E2 5c
A worthwhile route following the groove just right of *Blue Steel*. Follow the groove to the sharp prow of rock (small wires). Use this prow to force an entry onto the right-hand slab. Move up the rib and across left, below a roof, to re-enter the groove. Climb this for 4m until it is possible to move left on sloping holds to the lower-off of *Blue Steel*.
A Phizacklea, JL Holden 21.09.1991

4 Blue Remembered Hills 25m F6c ★
A fine route which packs a lot in to its length (and while on the subject of length, it may be impossible for the short). Start by a rectangular mottled block leaning against the wall 5m right of *Impoverished Pioneers*. Climb the slanting slab to its top. Move right with difficulty (gripper clip) and make a desperate move over the overlap onto the slab above, then continue directly up the steep groove to the small tree. Move up left and then right to enter the deep V-groove and climb it, finishing to the right. Bolt belay 6m back from the top.
A Phizacklea, M Lynch, JL Holden 29.09.1991

5 Blue Moon 25m F6b ★★
An excellent route crossing the hanging slab in the centre of the wall below the levitating block. Start in a slight corner at the left end of the impressive overhanging slab 3m right of *Blue Remembered Hills*. Make some strenuous pulls to reach the obvious traverse line on the right. Traverse the sloping gangway to a slab below the hanging block. Cross the slab to a shothole and climb up to ledges. Climb directly up the wall to reach some cracked blocks. Over these leftwards to reach a lower-off below the large overhang.
A Phizacklea, A Rowell, JL Holden 27.10.1991

6 The 300 Spartans 25m F6b
A left-diagonal line below the overhangs. Start below the corner bounding the right-hand side of the back wall. Climb the open corner for 4m then move up and left to a small tree. Cross the rib on the left with difficulty to an open horizontal shot-hole. Move up for another 4m before traversing left below the large overhangs. Climb up to just below the roof and make a long traverse to the lower-off on *Blue Moon*.
A Phizacklea, AH Greenbank 28.09.1991

7 Blue Movie 24m E2 5c
Quite thin climbing with a naughty bit at the end. Start as for *The 300 Spartans*. Climb the corner for 9m then and then make an intimidating rising traverse right across the slab, above the diagonal overhang, to the top bolt on *Palmer's Performance*. Continue rightwards delicately until below the tree. Move up to this to lower-off.
A Phizacklea, JL Holden 26.08.1991

8 Palmer's Performance 22m F5+ ★
Continuously interesting climbing starting by the triangular cracked block in the base of the slab 6m right of *The 300 Spartans*. Step off the top of the block and move up and left into a vague scoop. Go up and slightly left to reach a ragged crack. Follow this back right until below a step in the roof. Move up to the overhang and pull over on good holds to the slab above. Up and slightly left is a lower-off, or finish rightwards as for *Blue Movie*.
M Bagness, L Harrison 8.05.1991

9 Scallywag Slab 30m F6b ★
A good route. Start as for *Palmer's Performance*. Climb the thin slab directly, just left of the groove, to the overhang. Go over this with difficulty onto the slab above, and up to the tree.
Photo opposite.
M Bagness. L Harrison 8.05.1991

10 A Slight Slate Escapade 20m F4+
A nice route, with its crux just below the lower-off, taking the shallow groove just right of *Scallywag Slab* and using the same protection.
Photo opposite.
M Bagness, AH Greenbank 05.1991

11 Blue Bayou 20m F5
Pleasant enough. Start on the left of the narrow greenish slab on the far right of the quarry, easily identified by a protruding iron spike. Climb the slab gradually moving rightwards to a lower-off.
Photo page 101.
M Lynch, A Phizacklea, JL Holden 29.09.1991

HODGE CLOSE QUARRY

OS Grid Ref: NY 316 017
Altitude: 170m

Rebel Alliance F7b S0 (page 113) Neil Gresham — ALASTAIR LEE

HODGE CLOSE QUARRY

The focal point of Lakeland slate climbing, **Hodge Close** is an impressive quarry hole. The quarry offers a wide variety of climbing. However, the quality of the rock varies - generally it is solid with reasonable friction (for slate), but several areas are very unstable.

This striking location can be popular with tourists and divers (the waters are up to 32m deep); be mindful of this and take care.

Once the sun strikes **Main Wall** the intimidating nature of the quarry is somewhat diminished, but it never stops being a top class and exciting venue.

Approach: The quarry is reached from a junction on the A593 Coniston-Ambleside road, 3km north of Coniston, signposted Hodge Close.

0
metres
500
North
Hodge Close
Disused Quarries
PARROCK QUARRY
to Tilberthwaite
THE WORKS
Car Park P
HODGE CLOSE QUARRY
BAKESTONE QUARRY
to A593 and Coniston

18
54
108
35

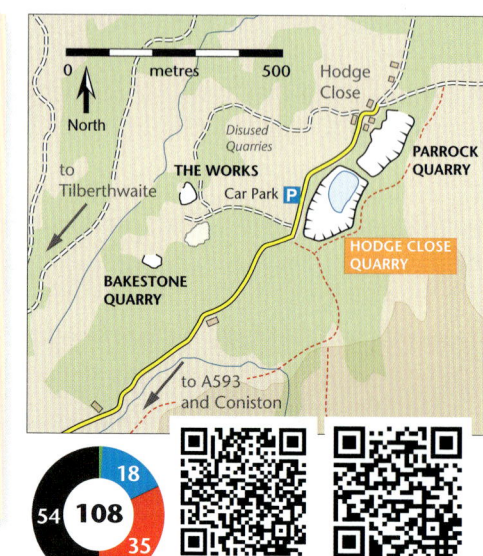

RAD Hodge Close Quarry

P GPS 54.406003 -3.055533

From
PARROCK QUARRY
Page 136
Main Wall
Page 116
Access from
All Weather Gym
(Page 114)
Pool Wall
Page 112
diving board
G-Spot
Page 113
West Wall
Page 108
PS

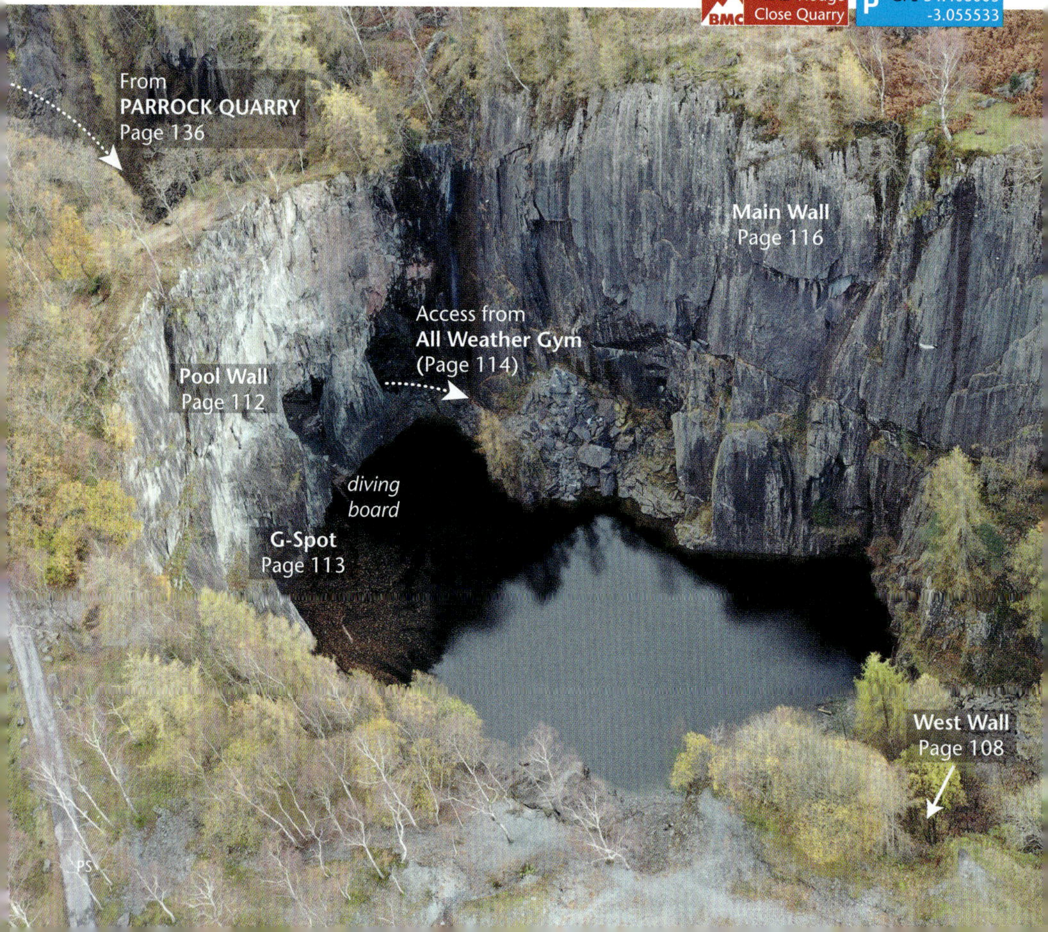

Hodge Close Quarry 107

Lower Traverse — 📷 Ron Kenyon

Main Wall - Right Sector
Page 131

From Car Park

Limestone

Slate

Micro-Granite

Sandstone

The West Wall

The quality of the rock is poor in comparison with the **Main Wall**, but it does receive the morning sun.

Approach: With care down the spoil heap at the southern end of the quarry, or alternatively abseil. The first route starts on the left two-thirds of the way down the spoil access path that one descends into the quarry.

① **Midgebite** 10m F6c+
A well bolted little problem that gets steadily harder, with the crux at the top.
A Towse 6.08.1998

The next route starts below a slabby arête which has a large dirty corner to its right, 10m right of *Midgebite*.

② **Calling the Shots** 27m F7a ★★
An excellent technical pitch which follows the shallow groove 2m left of the arête. Climb the short wall on good holds to a prickly ledge. The shallow groove is followed with increasing interest to reach a horizontal break. Continue up leftwards and gain the short finishing groove with difficulty. This is climbed using its right arête.
E Cleasby, J Eastham, M Lynch 27.06.1992

③ **Skyline** F6b+
The arête immediately right of *Calling the Shots*.
W Hannah, J Adams, W Young 16.10.1994

④ **Skyline Direct Start** F7a
K Murphy, J Adams 16.10.1994

Three steep sustained routes can be found on the friable mossy wall, right of the dirty corner. When clean they provide well protected challenges.

⑤ **Face the Times** 20m F6c
Start just right of a small sapling growing above a large wire cable lying at the foot of the left-hand cleaned streak. Climb the initial wall to a ledge, then climb the wall behind to reach a diagonal faultline which leads to a lower-off.
J Adams, TW Birkett 7.06.1992

⑥ **Face the Music** 24m F6c+
More sustained than *Face the Times*. Start in a red cave (2 bolts) in the right-hand wall, below the right-hand cleaned streak. Climb onto the large ledge. Step right and follow the cleaned streak up a slight fault-line directly to a lower-off.
TW Birkett, J Adams 4.06.1992

⑦ **Face Life** 25m F7b
Start to the right of *Face the Music*. Climb up the crack towards the right-hand end of the lower tier (2 bolts) onto a ledge. Traverse left and up the wall to a lower-off.
TW Birkett, J Adams 6.08.1995

Further along this wall of the quarry is a tunnel with a large ladder running up to it. This tunnel provides a safe, if wet, escape from the quarry. The easy but dangerous diagonal ramp running up right from here to the top of the quarry is known as The Greaser's Exit, a popular challenge for groups of inebriated Hell's Angels who party around the quarry. The first clean wall to the right of the ladder contains a chipped route with 4 bolts.

⑧ **Dogfight at Virgin Massacre Creek** 20m F7c+ ★★
A very fast drying route which is claimed to be better and harder than **Manic Strain**, the Llanberis test-piece. The holds are minute and do wonders for tendinitis. Climb the enhanced thin crease up the wall to a lower-off bolt.
P Cornforth, M Greenbank 26.11.1987

⑨ **Leicester Tit Lab** 20m E3 5b
The arête to the right of *Dogfight at Virgin Massacre Creek*.

At the end of the walkway alongside the pool is a conspicuous cave.

⑩ **Café Boys do their Thong** 10m F5+ ★
Left of the cave gain a thin rampline which leads rightwards into the short corner. Up this to a lower-off. Take a sling for the anchor.
A Hyslop, J Topping, J Goodenough 12.12.1989

⑪ **Enoc** 10m F6b ★
Direct start to *Café Boys Do Their Thong* up the leftwards trending crack.
R Widnall, N Hogg 10.08.1994

⑫ **??????** E3 (F7a) ★
Start underneath a large shothole, 2m right of *Café Boys Do Their Thong*. Pull up to the shothole (sky-hook) and then climb directly to a side-pull on a flake. Continue to a junction with the top of *Café Boys Do Their Thong*.
A Wilde, A Swainbank 9.07.1998

⑬ **!!!!!!!!!!!** 10m E3 (F7a) ★
Start 2m right at an obvious flake/crack. Climb the crack which is very strenuous. At the top pull out right and traverse rightwards using poor footholds on the right wall. Pull up onto a ledge.
A Wilde, A Swainbank 9.07.1998

⑭ **The Fang** 10m E3 (F6c) ⚠
The fang of rock has fallen down and the route is unstable. Not recommended.
K Phizacklea, S Whittall 03.05.1992

⑮ **Mowing the Lawn** 25m F6c+ ★
Start just right of the cave. Fingery wall climbing with a pleasant slab to finish.
A Towse, J Hool, J Martindale, S Harvey 29.07.2009

⑯ **Oiling the Lawnmower** 30m F6a ★★
A pleasant excursion up the slabs above the pool. Start a few metres right of the cave on a block at the edge of the pool. Step down and right beyond the diagonal crack, before climbing directly to a scoop; climb this to a large ledge. A steep wall gives way to the clean slab above.
Photo this page.

Chance Encounter VS 4b A very poor route following the rightward-slanting fault starting from halfway up *Oiling the Lawnmower*.
1980

Oiling the Lawnmower F6a Al Phizackalea — 📷 John Holden

The Pool Wall - South Face

A contorted shattered wall overhanging the pool above the mangled metal *diving board* at the north end of the main quarry. The twisted and bent metal is the result of 4,000 tonnes of rock that fell from the face above. Rocks and whole trees regularly fall off!

Two adventurous routes cross this face. The descriptions are reproduced for any would-be pioneers as there are no known repeats; a third route is known to have been completely destroyed. The condition of the rock, its features, references to fixed gear or spikes should be considered fiction.

Approach: Walk north along the road past the cottages and take the track on the right. To your right, almost immediately, a path descends a ramp and leads down through trees to **Parrock Quarry** to the huge cave of **The All Weather Gym**. The *diving board* is unmistakeable dead ahead.

⓱ Bay of Pigs   40m   E4 6a

From the point where the road passes the end of the quarry, walk rightward for 25m up the path to a large oak tree growing from the edge of the quarry. Abseil from this tree to the ledge with a quarry spike belay. Start from a ledge 5m above the pool in the back of the bay mid-way between the *diving board* and the walkway by *Oiling the Lawnmower*.

1 23m 5b From the ledge, move right into a slabby scoop and continue to an overlap (bolt). Pull over this then climb rightwards, around the edge, onto a delicate slab. Follow the left edge of the slab to a diagonal break. A stride across a short steep wall on the left gains another slab; follow this diagonally left, keeping below the steep rocks above, to a ledge at the foot of an easy corner which slants up right. Steel spike, rock spike and Rock 8 belay.

2 17m 6a Climb the broken steps directly above the belay (peg) to below the steep striated headwall (bolt). Climb up and left to a (bolt), then go right to some little incuts where a long reach enables the huge finishing jugs to be embraced.
P1 A Phizacklea, E Cleasby, JL Holden, A Rowell - P2 Cleasby, Holden, Rowell 29.08.1990

⓲ Pigs in Space   33m   F6c

A swine of a route on steep and occasionally loose rock. It follows the quartz band in the headwall left of the left-hand archway, starting from a large ledge in the centre of the face. This is reached by abseiling a couple of metres right (looking out) of the well-scratched popular abseil at the top of the wall. Bolt belay. Start in the corner right of the belay and climb up to a short ledge on the left. Ascend the steep corner above to a ledge on the right, then traverse precariously right across the leaning wall to reach the quartz band. Follow this with difficulty to a prominent gangway. Climb this at first rightwards, then back left to the top.
S Wood 15.09.1992

The obvious diagonal line leading leftwards out of the left-hand archway, following a line of ledges below the headwall, has been climbed at **VS**.

DWS Grades

S0   No particularly high crux moves. This grade is essentially safe; climb until you fall!

S1   Care required. Depth needs checking, or maybe there is a high crux.

The G-Spot | Hodge Close Quarry

The G-Spot

A slate Deep Water Soloing (DWS) venue - climb with dry boots!

Warm weather is needed so the recommended season is June to October. Beware, the water is very deep and cold!

Approach: Take a dinghy down the spoil and boulders at the south end then along the gangway to a gravel put-in near the cave. Or, use *Leo's Traverse*.

19 Kyber Crystal   F6b+ S0   ★★
Short, snappy, straightforward - a great first DWS.
N Gresham 06.2018

20 Crystal Maze   F7b S0   ★★★
A great party piece to impress your pals if you're feeling strong, or to skid off sideways and take a body-slap if you're not! A potent combination of powerful slapping and tenuous heel-hooking.
N Gresham 06.2018

21 Shock Treatment   F6c S1   ★★
A short, steep burly corner.
N Gresham 06.2018

22 Sinking Feeling   F6a+ S0
A surprisingly awkward slim groove.
N Gresham 06.2018

23 Second Order   F6c
Downclimb; the top of *The First Order* moving on to the slab right of *Sinking Feeling* at the bottom.
L Houlding 06.2018

24 The First Order   F6c+ S0   ★
Not quite the warm-up it looks. A testing bridging sequence leads to the easier upper groove.
N Gresham 06.2018

TOP 25 Rebel Alliance   F7b S0   ★★★
Technical slopers, undercuts and buckets lead to a key sequence in the final hanging groove.
Photo page 104.
N Gresham 06.2018

26 Clone Wars   F7b S1   ★★★
Big holds, burly moves and a sustained 'out-there' finish.
N Gresham 06.2018

27 Leo's Traverse   F6c+ S1
Boulder off the *diving board* to access *The First Order*, *Rebel Alliance*, and *Clone Wars*.
L Houlding 06.2018

28 Leo's Hard Traverse   F7b S1
From the beach - takes the crux of *Crystal Maze* to access all routes.
L Houlding 06.2018

The All Weather Gym

The **All Weather Gym** is the name given to the huge pillar which supports the roof of the archway between **Hodge Close** and **Parrock Quarry**. The umbrella-like headwall shelters the rock from rain, except during windy conditions, allowing climbing to take place at any time. These short bolt-protected problems are described from right to left, starting from the *diving board*.

Warning: Unstable and not recommended. Tons of rock have fallen from the wall above in to the pool in a number of separate events over the past few years. In addition, hangers have been removed from some of the routes. It's probably best to climb elsewhere.

Approach: Walk north along the road past the cottages and take the track on the right. To your right, almost immediately, a path descends a ramp and leads down through trees to **Parrock Quarry**, to the huge cave and pillar of The All Weather Gym.

㉙ **Sport for All**   12m   F4
Scramble onto the ledge on the right 3m above the pool. Climb the shallow grey groove in the centre to a bulge and pull left into a scoop.
A Hyslop, M Bagness, RO Graham 15.02.1990

㉚ **Big Gym**   10m   F5+
A good problem starting off the *diving board*. Step up to the foot of a slabby rib which is followed on its left side, then move left onto a slab.
A Hyslop, D Birkett, TW Birkett 11.02.1990

㉛ **Broken Pelvis**   10m   F6a
Start where the support girder for the *diving board* is cemented into the pillar. Climb up hollow flakes below a shallow corner, then pull right into a short left-facing corner, finishing up a slab.
A Jack, R Curly 8.08.1984

㉜ **A Spate of Slate**   10m   F6a
Step off the hollow flakes of *Broken Pelvis* and climb the groove/arête on the right.
D Douglas 17.08.1993

㉝ **Pioneer Meets His Match**   10m   F6b
Climbs the slab left of *Broken Pelvis*. Climb onto the hollow flakes on *Broken Pelvis*, then pull out leftwards onto the hanging slab.
D Douglas 17.08.1993

㉞ **Quarry Slaves**   9m   F7b+
Very few people succeed in completing this route. Start below the arête nearest **Parrock Quarry**. Climb the initial shallow groove with difficulty to a rest up right; continue steeply on desperate undercuts.
G Sutcliffe 5.06.1990

㉟ **Cellar Dwellers**   10m   F6b+
The steep arête. Step off the block and follow the overhanging arête.
A Hyslop, E Blylock 02.1990

㊱ **Northumbrian VS**   10m   F7a+
Some say it's over-graded, and more like a Cumbrian HS! Start on a ledge opposite a crack and climb the wall just right of the arête nearest the pool to enter a shallow square-cut corner. Up this (crux) to the top (sling lower-off).
G Sutcliffe, A Hyslop 18.02.1990

㊲ **OAP's Sport Climb Too**   11m   F5+
Start up the arête overlooking the pool. Trend left, under steeper rock, to finish up an awkward hanging groove to a chain.
A Hyslop, I Williamson 02.90

Second Coming F6c+ (page 116) Tom Priestley — 📷 Rory Tunnah

The Main Wall - Left Sector

This impressive 60m wall showcasing the best of Lakeland slate climbing extends the full length of the east side of the quarry.

The rock on the far left is suspect; the most unstable routes **Sideshow** (E2 5b 1980) and the very loose crack of **Stiff Little Fingers** (XS 1980) are not described.

Approach: Walk in through **Parrock Quarry** or abseil.

① Carpe Diem   18m   F7a+

The conspicuous bolted groove as you approach under the archway in the north east corner of the quarry. Climb the demanding groove until a small ledge/good hold can be reached. Mantelshelf onto this with great difficulty. Step up and move slightly rightwards onto the steep slab. Continue up the slab with continuing difficulty before finally escaping rightwards to better holds and the anchor. First two hangers damaged by rockfall.
A Towse, S Harvey 6.09.2009

② Joie de Vivre   57m   F6b+   ★★★

Start at a deceptively easy-looking ramp about 3m right of the groove taken by *Carpe Diem*. Follow the ramp rightwards to a crackline and climb up passing four bolts before moving back left to a double bolt belay. Follow the obvious grooveline past three distinct hard sections until eventually forced to make awkward moves right, up and then back left on improving holds.
A Towse, J Hool, S Harvey 6.09.2009

To the right is a large clean rock scar capped by an overhang. The shallow crease at the right-hand side is taken by the following route.

③ Second Coming   55m   F6c+   ★★★

A superb ingenious climb requiring a cool and competent approach. About 10m right of the highest point of the scree is a little alcove sporting an iron spike at shoulder height. Stand on the spike then climb up the two sloping niches on the left to gain a traverse line below the steeper rock. Move left into a hanging groove then step left onto a speckly slab using doubtful holds to reach a tiny shattered ledge below the blankness. Climb up and right to reach the shallow crease which is followed until a long stride right can be made onto a flake ledge. Boldly climb onto a good hold where an acrobatic sequence leads out right into the large bottomless groove. Follow this steadily to reach a large sloping ledge and a bolt belay is 8m from the top. Traverse left from the belay and climb the wall direct via two slim stepped grooves.
Photo page 115.
E Cleasby, P Short, JL Holden, A Towse 19.07.1992

④ First Night Nerves   55m   E5 6b   ★★★

An excellent route which provides sustained well-protected climbing up the steep black wall right of the rockfall scar, before taking a bold direct line up the left side of the **Main Wall**. Pulling ropes at the twin bolt reduces drag. Original start was *The Main Event*, or start as for *Second Coming*.
1 48m 6b Follow *Second Coming* to the hanging groove then step up and right. Climb up and right precariously across a quartzy band to reach a good hold below an undercut flake. Climb the flake then further delicate climbing leads directly to a junction with *Stage Fright* at a blunt spike. Continue directly then traverse left to reach a large sloping ledge and bolt belay in the groove of *Second Coming*.
2 7m 5a Continue up the corner to the top.
Photo opposite.
RO Graham, A Phizacklea 13.09.1987

⑤ The Big Link   50m   E6 6b

A huge, very bold and tenuous traverse of the **Main Wall**. The second pitch is protected by a single peg. Start as for *Second Coming*.
1 25m 6b As for *First Night Nerves* to the good hold below the undercut flake. Traverse right into the groove of *Stage Fright* (double pegs). Cut up and right to belay on the ledge of *The Main Event*.
2 25m 6b Traverse right for 7m (peg) then right again and straight up on scary smears for a runout top section.
S Wood, B Scroggs 2011

⑥ The Main Event   70m   E5 6a   ★★

An impressive route. Its wandering nature, poor protection and difficulty add spice. Start below the overhanging wall, a few metres right of *Second Coming*, at the foot of a steep thin crack.
1 28m 6a Climb the crack using a sloping ledge out left to reach a traverse line below the overhanging wall. Traverse right, following the flake, to reach a large ledge.
2 45m 6a Traverse back leftwards along a ramp below the steep wall for 4m, pull up right, then back left to gain the upper wall (peg). Follow the thin flake up and left then rightwards to good ledges, then climb the shallow groove on the left to a ledge (bolts). Climb up for a couple of metres before stepping right to finish more or less directly.

Alternative start to p2: The short open corner above the belay can be followed (peg). Thin moves lead to a junction with the main pitch at the good ledges reducing the grade to E4 6a.
P1 P Whillance, R Parker / P2 P Whillance, R Parker, P Botterill, D Armstrong, A Murray Spring 1980

First Night Nerves E5 (opposite) Caroline Ciavaldini — 📷 David Simmonite

Sky F6b+ (page 125) Ed Luke — 📷 JOHN HOLDEN

The Main Wall | **Hodge Close Quarry** | 119

⑦ **The Idaho** 9m F7b+ ★
Connection Wave
A short impeccable test piece. Start by two shot-holes below 2 bolts 4m right of *The Main Event*.. Gain the shallow hanging corner and continue straight up into a little runnel.
K Phizacklea 08.1992

The next three routes start in the final little bay, just above the water's edge at the foot of a large corner adorned with two bent spikes.

⑧ **Chestnut Mare** 15m F7b ★
This elegant route climbs the clean pillar to the left of the corner. Start up a short rib below the lower arching overhang to enter the scooped depression on the left (bolt). Exit right (bolt) to a shothole, then back left to the arête using a ridiculously minuscule hold. Continue easily.
S Wood, K Phizacklea 04.1992

⑨ **First Footing** 13m VS 4b
The large corner passing two bent quarry spikes to the ledges. A good way of approaching any of the routes between *Stage Fright* and *Life in the Fast Lane*.
M Lynch, P Rogerson E Cleasby 1973

⑩ **The Plunger** 15m F6b+ ★★ ✏
A good technical problem up the right arête of *First Footing*. Climb the thin diagonal crack rightwards (wires) to the arête (bolt). Follow the arête above to a good flake runner and continue to the ledge.
Photo this page.
P Cornforth, A Phizacklea 4.05.1987

The following four routes climb the steep clean wall which rises straight out of the right-hand end of the pool, reached using metal rungs just above the waterline.

⑪ **Creative Contortions** 15m F7b+ ★★
A desperately difficult problem up the right-hand side of the wall. Start from the fifth rung; bolt belay. A hard move leads to the diagonal crack. Climb the intricate quartz speckled wall directly then climb slightly leftwards to a ledge.
S Wood 30.09.1992

⑫ **Contorted Creations** 14m E5 6b ★
An easier but bolder companion right of *Creative Contortions* which starts from the sixth rung. At great risk of intimate personal injury, step up to reach the diagonal crack. Climb up (bolt) to a flake then left and boldly up (bolt). Follow a very slim groove to a tiny pocket then grab the arête on the right and romp to the top.
S Wood 6.10.1990

⑬ **Titbits** 12m F6b+
The short groove on the right of the smooth wall. A bolt belay at its foot can be reached either by climbing *First Footing* and abseiling down or, more adventurously, by following the iron rungs above the water. Climb the groove to where a secondary groove merges on the left. Climb either groove to the ledge - the left-hand one is easier.
M Lynch 21.05.1992

⑭ **Movement** 22m E3 6a
A link from the belay of *Titbits* to *The Plunger*. Climb the diagonal crack running across the steep wall above the iron rungs (peg) to reach the arête (bolt); finish up this.
M MIller 1990

The Main Wall | Hodge Close Quarry

21	Sky	F6b+ ★★★		34	Arm & Hammer Slab	F6c
22	Great Expectations	F7b ★★★		35	Limited Edition	E4 6a ★★★
23	Hodgetastic	F6c		36	Haggis	E6 6a
24	Way of the Wyrd	E6 6b		37	Nocturnal Emissions	F7c
25	Life in the Fast Lane	E5 6b ★★		38	Stinky Dinks	E2 6a ★
26	Amphibian	F7a ★★		39	Mirrormere	E2 5b ★
27	The Entertainer	F6a+ ★		40	Randolph Scott	E1 5b ★
28	Entertainment Value	F6c		41	Viennese Oyster	E4 6b ★★
29	Return to Year Zero	E4 6b		42	Blank Expression	E5 6a ★
30	Power Transmission	E5 6c ★★		43	Behind the Lines	HVS 5a ★★★
31	Beef Jerky	F7a ★★		44	Curtain Call	F7a+ ★
32	Big Dipper	E1 5b ★★		45	Malice in Wonderland	E4 6a ★★★

Malice in Wonderland E4 6a (page 129)

The Main Wall - Upper Sector

Arguably some of the best and boldest slate climbs in the country are found here. By today's standards they seem wild with absurd protection. Let's keep it that way.

The routes start from the ledge system which runs across the foot of the **Main Wall**, about 20m above the pool. *First Footing* makes an easy approach from the edge of the pool. The first pitch of *The Main Event* also reaches the ledge system; or more conveniently, abseil.

15 Stage Fright 50m E6 6b ★★★
A superb, sparsely-protected and intimidating route demanding fearless determination. Its focus is the stark isolated groove. An extra rope is required to reach a belay. Start from a large flake on the left-hand side of the ledge. Traverse leftwards across a short ramp below the steep wall for 4m. Up right, then back left to gain the upper wall (peg). Traverse delicately left across the slab to a rib (peg). Step left, using a hidden foothold, into the slim leftwards leaning groove; climb to a poor resting place (peg). Move left and up to a good ledge then climb the wall trending rightwards for 10m, until a thin flake leads directly to the top.
P Whillance, D Armstrong 21.05.1983

16 Command Performance 47m E6 6b ★
A rather unbalanced route which demands a cool confident approach. Follow *Stage Fright* until half-way across the traverse (peg) then move up to a good finger jug. Stand on this (bolt). A difficult move gains the base of the shallow flakeline which is followed to the ledge (twin bolts). Step right and climb up to another ledge, then continue diagonally leftwards, boldly at first, to reach the top section of *Stage Fright*.
D Pegg, J Gaskins 29.04.1990

17 The Final Act 44m E6 6b ★
Possibly the most frightening lead on this wall, very direct and a bold lead. Follow *Stage Fright* to the peg then mantelshelf onto the small finger jugs above with difficulty (poor RP 2). A hard move leads up to a good hold on the front face of the flake; climb directly up this to reach a ledge and (twin bolts). Move up to another ledge then continue in a straight line up the headwall.
S Wood, J Hughes, K Hughes 27.03.1993

18 Ten Years After 45m E5 6a ★★★
Sustained elegant climbing above well-spaced gear; too spicy to be an E4. Start off the left-hand ledge, at the foot of a tapering groove. Climb the groove then move leftwards onto the undercut wall. Step delicately left and climb up to better holds (micro cam; wire) then rock over leftwards to reach some ledges (wires). Step right from here and climb the wall to reach a shallow stepped groove. Climb this (peg) then continue directly up the wall to a small groove; follow this (wire) to an awkward finish.
R Matheson, E Cleasby Easter 1980

19 Wicked Willie 45m E5 6b ★★★
A superb and audacious assault of the wall with widely-spaced gear. Climb *Ten Years After* to the sanctuary of the 'better holds'. A hard move up and right (peg) leads to easier ground (bolt). A thin flake (small cam) with a final wild move rightwards gains a friendly ledge. The wall above, climbed first on the right (wire) then left leads to a good hold below the fir tree.
A Phizacklea, G Cornforth, P Cornforth 3.05.1987

20 Wings 42m E4 5c
A worrying route with some doubtful rock. Start below the tapering groove at the wall's centre. Climb the groove then make a poorly-protected traverse right to gain an open corner above and left of the large roof. Climb the corner to the top.
P Botterill, D Armstrong, P Whillance, R Parker, A Murray 30.03.1980

21 Sky 47m F6b+ ★★★
Excellent climbing. Abseil to the left-hand end of a large ledge below an arête; above the corner of *First Footing*. Climb the arête to a ledge below a thin flake/crack; follow this strenuously to where it peters out level with the big roof. Make a hard move left into a short corner and out again to join a grooveline. Step back right onto the headwall and traverse rightwards across the ledge system above the big roof to reach a shallow groove. Climb this to the top.
Photo page 16 & 118.
E Cleasby, R Matheson Easter 1980

22 Great Expectations 42m F7b ★★★
A very technical exercise up the vague rib and roof right of *Sky*. Start as for *Sky* and climb up and rightwards to a prominent overlap then traverse out right to the rib. Hard climbing up the rib leads directly to a good side hold, where a move left enables a flake to be reached; this is followed to the roof (wires). Hand traverse the lip of the roof rightwards to a little flake and pull over the roof to reach the upper traverse of *Sky*. Climb directly up the wall to finish with a long reach.
A Phizacklea, J L Holden, B McKinley 3.07.1990

The next three routes start from the right-hand end of the cleaned ledge above *The Plunger*, at the foot of the large slabby groove which slants down from the big roof.

㉓ Hodgetastic 18m F6c
An awkward fingery line which climbs to the foot of the prominent fang below the big roof. Climb up the lower part of the groove for 6m (wires) then pull out left onto a steep speckly wall. A vague line leads left then back right to the lower-off below the roof.
K Phizacklea, S Whittall 3.07.1992

㉔ Way of the Wyrd 42m E6 6b
A route of contrasts climbing the easy open groove below the large roof before venturing boldly above it in a most committing manner. Start at the foot of the groove. Climb the groove (wires) to a point about 3m below the roof where it is possible to traverse delicately rightwards to the top of an arête. Arrange vital protection in the groove on the right, then step left onto the crucial traverse, just above the main overhang. From the peg pull directly over the bulge to gain the upper wall which is climbed with great commitment, (pathetic hand-inserted RURP) to reach a horizontal crack (peg). Finish more easily directly to the top.
M Miller, P Hadfield 1990

㉕ Life in the Fast Lane 45m E5 6b ★★
Some holds have broken off low down and it is likely that this route hasn't been climbed for many years.
The culmination of the 1980 Carlisle siege. A classic audaciously climbing the prominent rib leading to the right-hand side of the big roof. A courageous and controlled approach is required to deal with the sparse protection. From the foot of the groove, a shattered flake runs up right to the rib (cam). A very difficult smear leads to easier climbing directly up the rib to the right-hand side of the overhang. Step right into a dirty corner (runners), then traverse back left directly above the roof (peg) to reach and climb a shallow grooveline (peg).
Photo page 5.
P Whillance, A Murray, R Parker 04.1980

The Main Wall - Central Sector
Most routes start from a large tree-covered terrace reached by abseil - please use a sling around the tree.

㉖ Amphibian 60m F7a ★★
Good sustained climbing, but slow to dry. The line of grooves between the **Central** and **Main Walls**. Abseil from a bolt to a small ledge just above the right-hand end of the pool.
1 18m F7a Step left below the groove (steel rung, bolt); follow this and the crackline above to the ledge on the extreme left side of the main ledge.
2 42m F6c From the flake on the left, step into the groove and pull round the overhang and continue with difficulty to a ledge. Climb the easier groove above and to the right to gain a ledge (bolt belay). Move right and climb the stepped rib directly to the top.
E Cleasby, R Matheson 6.04.1980

㉗ The Entertainer F6a+ ★
A good entertaining route which starts as for *Amphibian*, just above the pool. Climb the shallow clean groove above the right-hand end of the ledge with dexterity to the ledge below **Central Sector**.
S Whittall, K Phizacklea 30.09.1992

㉘ Entertainment Value F6c
From the third bolt, traverse left for 2m then climb the steep committing wall to the ledge.
S Whittall 7.10.1992

㉙ Return to Year Zero 29m E4 6b
An interesting but awkward pitch. Start at the extreme left-hand end of the tree-covered ledge, at the top of pitch 1 of *Amphibian*. A logical lower extension would be to climb *Entertainment Value* to reach the ledge. From the flake on the left, step into the groove and pull round the overhang. Traverse right with difficulty, just above the overhang, to reach a good foothold. Follow the thin crack directly to ledges (bolt belay).
S Wood, S Whittall 11.05.1993

㉚ Power Transmission 40m E5 6c ★★
A route for geckos which claws out leftwards from *Big Dipper*. Climb *Big Dipper* to the top of its initial flake (wire), then step down and traverse left (bolt) to reach the vaguest of ramplines running up left. Follow this (bolt) to a good hold up left, then swing right into a sentry box in the overlap above (wire). Climb out of this directly to reach the belay ledge on *Amphibian*. Step up the arête then go right to join *Limited Edition* which is followed to the top.

An easier escape for those unable (or unwilling) to reach the sentry box can be made up left from the second bolt to large ledges on *Amphibian*.
A Gridley 05.1988

The Main Wall | **Hodge Close Quarry**

㉛ Beef Jerky 40m F7a ★★
'cause there ain't nothin' tougher'. Traverse left out of the base of *Big Dipper* above the roof, and climb straight up. Make a traverse right to a rest in a scoop. Climb straight up then traverse right to a good egg cup. Finish up and left.
K Phizacklea, C Matheson 17.07.1998

㉜ Big Dipper 46m E1 5b ★★
A pleasant way of discovering the intricacies of **Hodge Close** climbing. This follows a diagonal ramp rightwards. Start on the large terrace below a steep flake/crack, towards the left end of the ledge. Climb the flake which leads strenuously to the ramp. Follow this rightwards (bolt) and climb the continuation groove to a bollard (bolt belay). Climb the wall on the right to finish up a groove.
Photo page 97.
P Whillance, R Parker 9.03.1980

TOP ㉝ Big Mirror E2 5b ★★★
This combination makes a great climb - scary, but never desperate. Start on the large terrace below a steep flake/crack, towards the left end of the ledge.
1 34m 5b Climb the flake which leads strenuously to the ramp system. Follow this right (bolt) and climb the continuation groove to a bollard and bolt belay.
2 30m 5b Traverse the wall on the left for 8m, then up (bolt). Continue leftwards (bolt), then step down and traverse delicately left onto the arête which is followed directly to the top.

㉞ Arm & Hammer Slab 12m F6c
Climb the wall above the bolt belay at the top of p1 of *Big Dipper*.
M France, D Duxbury 20.09.1994

TOP ㉟ Limited Edition 33m E4 6a ★★★
An excellent route which climbs the left side of the wall and feels distinctly trad. Start from the bolt belay at the top of the ramp on *Big Dipper*, reached by abseil. From the lower left point of the ramp, step across left to gain a shallow right-facing scoop and find the right sequence to reach an excellent hold. Traverse diagonally left across the wall to reach a flake then up and slightly right to better holds below the slight steepening of the headwall. A hard move on quartz holds leads to a tiny right-facing flake; finish up this.
Photo page 92.
P Carling, P Noble 24.05.1986

㊱ Haggis 42m E6 6a
A fairly pointless and protectionless variation to *Limited Edition* - climb to the excellent hold above the scoop, step left and climb the wall directly to the top bolt.
I Turnbull 06.1989

㊲ Nocturnal Emissions 38m F7c
A very direct line up the wall giving well-protected technical climbing low down and a scary finish. Climb up to reach the ramp on *Big Dipper*. Step up directly to the slab above where a very hard move leads to a traverse line (*Stinky Dinks*). Climb up and right to a rock scar then back left (ring bolt). Follow a thin crack in the steeper headwall to a bold finish slightly rightwards.
S Wood, S Whittall 26.04.1993

㊳ Stinky Dinks 45m E2 6a ★
An engaging technical traverse is the focus of this route. From a ledge below the centre of the wall, 8m right of *Big Dipper*, climb a shallow scoop to a small conifer (wire), then go diagonally left, delicately, to a ramp (bolt). Climb the flake on the right to a good spike then step left onto the thin wall and traverse (bolt) to reach a good hold. Climb a rampline back up right to the headwall (ring bolt). Step right to a flake and finish direct (peg).
A Phizacklea, P Cornforth, G Cornforth 3.05.1987

㊴ Mirrormere 52m E2 5b ★
An absorbing route with a long intricate traverse. Start on a ledge below the centre of the wall as for *Stinky Dinks*.
1 22m 5a A bold pitch. Climb directly to a small conifer. Step right and continue directly up until a step left enables the upper part of a flake to be reached. Climb this (bolt belay).
2 30m 5b Traverse the wall on the left for 8m, then climb up (ring bolt). Continue leftwards (bolt), then step down and traverse delicately left onto the arête which is followed directly to the top.
E Cleasby, A Phizacklea, R Matheson 4.04.1980

㊵ Randolph Scott 39m E1 5b ★
A direct route up the wall, starting up *Stinky Dinks*.
1 22m 5a Climb directly to a small conifer then traverse right across the wall for 5m to reach a short groove which leads to a ledge. Climb leftwards to a spike in the centre of the wall then move right to the edge of the flake and follow it to a bollard (bolt belay). Or **6a** climb the smooth-looking wall directly to the short groove.
2 17m 5b Traverse left for 3m and follow the obvious curving grooveline which leads to a dirty finish.
J Daly, K Phizacklea P1 A Phizacklea 2.05.1987

Through the Looking Glass E2 5c (page 131) James Pearson — David Simmonite

The Main Wall | **Hodge Close Quarry** | 129

❹❶ Viennese Oyster   33m   E4 6b   ★★ TOP

An artistic sort of route which requires a bold approach low down and a delicate finishing touch by the white streak high on the wall. The section above the peg provides a superb intricate sequence of climbing - take plenty of small wires. Start by a large pine tree growing at the right end of the ledge. Follow *Behind the Lines* for 5m then step left on large holds to reach a good diagonal crack. Ascend the thin slab above to a slight bulge, pull over into a shallow niche and breathe again. Climb the small groove (peg) and swing left (bolt), then carefully caress the crease above to stretch for a ledge out left. Step back right and follow a short crack to finish just left of the large tree.
P Carling 20.04.1989

❹❷ Blank Expression   33m   E5 6a   ★

Seldom led, the short shallow groove high on the wall left of *Behind the Lines* is the focal point of this route. Either follow *Viennese Oyster* and step right, or climb *Behind the Lines* to the good spike and step left to the base of the groove (tiny wires). Pull leftwards on nothing to enter it. Climb up precariously and exit right, using a good hold on the right-hand rib and continue to a sloping ledge below a corner. Climb the short stepped rib on the left to the abseil tree.
E Cleasby, R Matheson 26.04.1980

TOP **❹❸ Behind the Lines**   33m   HVS 5a   ★★★

The slabby corner which forms the angle between the **Central Sector** and the arête of *Malice in Wonderland* makes a classic line with ample protection after a bold start. Start by a large pine tree growing at the right end of the ledge. Not all the holds can be trusted. Climb delicately left from the tree to reach a short corner. Bold moves enable the main corner line to be gained, then with protection and the occasional dubious hold, climb this to the bulge just below the top. Traverse right to finish.
R Parker 30.03.1980

❹❹ Curtain Call   40m   F7a+   ★

A transgressional route up the centre of the smooth slab. Climb *Behind the Lines* for 15m; take a thin crack rightwards to the centre of the slab. Tenuous moves lead directly to the tree.
J Bird, A Tilney Spring 1988

★★ TOP **❹❺ Malice in Wonderland**   43m   E4 6a   ★★★

A beautiful route climbing the bold graceful arête. Start at the pine tree, as for *Behind the Lines*. Climb the slab on the right to a rib and follow it to the overhang. Step right (bolt) and pull directly through the overhang on good, but widely-spaced holds, to land on the slab above. Traverse left, just above the roof, to reach the arête. Climb the left side of this, passing a good diagonal crack, to a tree on its right flank. Step back onto the arête and climb it with conviction, past a thin crack on the left (micro wire), to a delicate and gripping finish.
Photo page 124.
P Whillance, R Parker, E Cleasby 20.04.1980

The Main Wall - Right Sector

The routes right of *Malice in Wonderland* all start from the quarry floor reached by scrambling down the spoil heap at the southern end of the quarry or by abseil from the trees above *Sasquatch*.

The next four routes all climb a short subsidiary wall below the foot of *Malice in Wonderland*. This wall is guarded by a small pool at its base.

46 Bright Eyes n' Blue 55m E4 6a ★
The longest single pitch in the quarry. Start by the right-hand end of the little pool. Traverse left above the pool past a large flake to gain a cleaned red corner. Climb this to a narrow ledge level with the large tree-covered ledge on the left. Continue directly up the narrow rib (bolt) to a little sapling on the arête then follow the slab above. Move right to join *Close Call* below the niche. Finish up that route.
P Short, A Towse 12.07.1992

47 Easy Rider 13m F5+
This fine little line starting from the right-hand side of the pool needs traffic to keep it clean. Traverse left above the pool to gain broken rocks below a thin shallow groove in the centre of the slab. Climb this to the ledge.
S Whittall, D Kells 04.1992

48 Timeless Flight 12m F7b ★
A very thin route with a tricky third clip.
S Wood, K Phizacklea 04.1992

49 Trivia 13m HVS 5a
Inconsequential. Climb a short corner right of *Timeless Flight*. Continue rightwards and take the shallow groove just left of the rib to the top.
M Lynch, J Eastham 27.06.1992

50 Close Call 42m E4 6a ★
An entertaining and varied route. At the left corner of the ledge, a quartz band runs up diagonally right. Follow the quartz and enter a slim hanging gangway which leads precariously to an awkward exit left at its top. From the large metal spike, traverse left across the slab (bolt) and ascend directly to the prominent niche in the overhangs above. Climb up this with difficulty onto the slab and follow a flake/crack on the left to pass to the right of the tree on *Malice in Wonderland*. Climb the steep wall above directly (bolt), avoiding both the arête and the groove on either side.
E Cleasby, JL Holden 12.06.1992

51 Through the Looking Glass 42m E2 5c ★★★
Another excellent sustained route. Protection is reasonable and the rock is sound, except for a couple of hollow flakes. Start about 6m right of *Close Call*, below a short rib which leads to the right-hand side of a low blocky overhang. Climb the rib to where it merges into the wall above. Step left, below the roof (peg), and stand up on good holds in the clean wall above. Cross the lip of the roof leftwards to gain a good ledge. Arrange gear and climb the fine flake/crack above to enter a long shallow groove which snakes upwards to a tricky finish.
Photo page 128.
E Cleasby, R Matheson 3.04.1980

52 Shattered Image 41m F7a+ E4 6b
Sustained climbing up the wall just right of *Through the Looking Glass*. Start at the base of a slabby groove, below and left of the slabby corner of *Dan Dare*. Climb up leftwards to the top of a rib. Step right (bolt) to reach easier ground (bolt). Traverse left (bolt) with difficulty for a couple of metres until a direct ascent can be made to a roof (bolt). Enter the red niche below the left end of the roof (wire), and lurch over this to a horizontal break. Stand on this (bolt), step up, (bolt) and follow a slim ramp which runs slightly right up the headwall, before finishing directly up the brittle top wall.
S Wood, D Kells, M Lynch 21.05.1992

53 Mirror Image 40m F7b+ E5 6c
The steep furrowed wall left of the dirty corner of *Dan Dare*, where poor rock, excellent protection and technical climbing blend together to provide a memorable outing. Follow *Shattered Image* to the second bolt then continue directly up a shallow groove. From here, a series of shallow channels continue with increasing delicacy to a climactic move past the fifth bolt to gain a hold in a horizontal break. Step right to a rest place on the arête, then pull back left and climb the rickety headwall (Rock 8). Climb back left to reach the top.
A Phizacklea, JL Holden (PA) 27.07.1991

54 Mirror Mirror
A dangerous proposition since a large rockfall from its middle section.

55 Dan Dare 39m VS 4c
A dirty neglected route. Climb the initial groove to a ledge. Continue up the main corner for 10m until forced right to a thin crack which leads to the top.
M Lynch, E Cleasby 27.07.1980

56 Gone Surfin'   42m   E2 5c
A wet route with loose sections. Start 3m left of *Sasquatch* below the magical flowing shotholes, which provide an endless supply of clean water. Climb the slab, slightly leftwards, to a bulge (bolt). A thin crack just to its left and a continuation layback crack lead into a mossy scoop (peg). Above is a hollow flake. Follow this rightwards into a dirty crack. Cross the slab on the right (2 bolts) to reach the top arête, just left of the finish of *Sasquatch*.
J Daly, K Phizacklea 20.05.1989

57 Oswald Moseley   37m   F6b E3 6a
This route is lacking in many things - solid rock, quality and bolt hangers. It takes a direct line up the fragile slabs left of *Sasquatch*.
A Tilney 04.1991

58 Sasquatch   38m   HVS 5a   ★★
Wait for a dry spell to climb this good route taking the white-streaked open groove/flake which runs diagonally right up the slab. Beware of some loose holds. Start a couple of metres right of the flowing shotholes. Climb the shallow white-streaked groove with difficulty to a ledge then the wall behind to a second ledge. Climb steeply above (caution) to finish up a flaky crack in the upper slab.
R Matheson, E Cleasby 04.1980

59 The Cleaver   41m   E4 6a   ★
A potential chop route up the brittle slab. Climb *Sasquatch* for a couple of metres then move right onto the slabs. Poorly protected moves lead up, then right along a faint break to reach a thin flake in the slab above. Climb this (2 bolts); fingery moves out right enable a large sloping ledge to be gained. Follow this rightwards to a small tree; from here a ragged crack leads leftwards to the top.
K Phizacklea 4.06.1986

60 Fatal Attraction   43m   F7b
Intense and exacting climbing across the glassy slabs right of *Sasquatch* - one of the thinnest problems at Hodge Close. Unfortunately the rock is rather fragile. Start below a thin quartz flake 5m right of *Sasquatch*. Stand on the quartz flake with care, then traverse diagonally right without respite to reach better holds. Move up then back left across blank slabs to reach a tiny nubbin and a welcome rest. Climb a shallow groove above to reach an expanding ledge then continue up the wall to a good hold by the small tree at the foot of the upper slabs. Finish up the ragged crack cutting through the moss to the top.
P Carling 1.06.1989

61 Hoof Hearted   40m   E4 6b
Another sustained slab climb with some suspect rock and spaced protection. Start 12m right of *Sasquatch*, on the left side of a large flake leaning against the slab. Bridge up the flake to its apex then enter a scoop. Climb carefully up left (bolt), then follow a thin crackline above with difficulty to a large ledge with a flake above (bolt). Step left and pull up to gain a sloping ledge with a small tree on the left. Finish direct up the ragged crack.
A Phizacklea, TW Birkett 14.06.1987

62 Beaver Patrol   32m   F7b   ★
The blunt rounded rib at the right-hand side of these slabs presents a very technical challenge. To the right of the flake of *Hoof Hearted*, the slabs recede to form a dirty corner and a vile flake system. Start below the corner. Step left onto the slab then climb directly up this to reach a small overhang. Step right and continue up to a loose ledge system. Step up then climb right to reach the crest of the rib. Follow this delicately, first left, then back right, to the top.
A Phizacklea, M Dale 26.09.1987

63 Lucky Ray   32m   E3 6a
The blunt rib right of *Beaver Patrol*. There are six bolts but take medium nuts and cams.
R Faragher 13.07.1994

64 Soap Opera   32m   F7a
Start about 12m up and left of *Mad Alice*. Climb directly with difficulty to the left side of a diagonal bulging overlap. Traverse right under this to meet the top section of *Daytime Blues*.
A Towse, P Bartlett 20.08.1995

65 Daytime Blues   32m   F6b   ★
The line of bolts behind a tree 8m left of *Mad Alice*. Make a couple of delicate moves to get established in a scoop then continue directly.
A Towse, JL Holden 13.08.1995

66 Mad Alice   30m   F6a+   ★★
A great route up the well-bolted groove and blunt rib.
M Danson, I Cooksie 2.05.1981

67 Moonlight Sonata   30m   F6a
A decent route until the hangers were stolen. Some 5m right of *Mad Alice*, below a prominent slab. Climb the corner to the slab. Up this more easily to the headwall and the top.
A Towse, JL Holden 9.08.1995

68 The Lobsters' Quadrille   30m   F6a
Hangers again stolen. 4m right of *Moonlight Sonata*. Move up to a short wall to get established on the slab. Climb the right-hand side until it is possible to traverse right for 5m; gain the slab above and climb the steepening slab to an interesting finish.
JL Holden, A Towse, C Towse 15.08.2005

The Main Wall - Right Sector | Hodge Close Quarry

69 The Tommy Knockers F6a
Start up the boulder slope 5m to the right of *Moonlight Sonata*.
J Adams, TW Birkett 5.08.1995

The **Main Wall** of the quarry has two girdle traverses which cross the face in opposite directions. These routes share the same belays, and in places they climb the same line, but they are surprisingly independent and both give fine outings. Care is needed to protect the second man and back-ropes are advised on some sections.

70 Close Encounters 174m E5 6a ★
A left to right girdle which takes the lower line across the **Main Wall**, utilising a line of old bolts giving an easy aid pitch below the large overhang. Start at the top of the quarry, above the main archway, a couple of metres left of the top of the corner of *Play for Today*.
1 24m 5c Descend a ramp easily into the corner and follow a thin crack out right, above a roof (peg). Continue in the same line (2 pegs) to a belay on a sloping ledge about 6m below the top of the crag (bolt, peg).
2 15m 6a Downclimb the corner to a sloping ledge then cross the wall on the right with difficulty (bolt). Descend slightly to a spike foothold. Move up and right to a belay (bolts).
3 40m 6a Climb down the groove below the right side of the belay to a ledge. Step down and make a thin move right (peg). Climb down and right into a groove. Follow this for a couple of metres then cross the wall on the right on brittle flakes to a spike. Belay on the right at the left-hand side of the big roof (bolt, nuts).
4 25m 6c A0 Traverse under the roof until a desperate move can be made into a groove. Move across onto the arête and climb this delicately to the base of a dirty corner then traverse right to a sloping ledge (bolts).
5 30m 5b Climb up slightly to the rib on the right, move right onto a flake and downclimb this to a good foothold. Climb the shallow ramp for a couple of metres, then traverse a ledge line right to a flake; belay.
6 30m 5c Descend the grassy corner to the right then traverse delicately right into a corner. Follow a diagonal crack in the right wall which leads to an arête. Climb this to a tree.
7 10m 5c Step right and finish up a groove.
P Carling, G Sutcliffe 10.05.1987

71 Standing Ovation 157m E4 6b ★★
A right to left girdle, taking a high line across the **Main Wall** and giving a superb sustained route. Start as for *Through the Looking Glass*.
1 25m 5c Climb *Through the Looking Glass* to a tree and flake belay on the left.
2 30m 5c Step left onto a rib and move down this for 2m. Descend the crack on the left which leads down to a groove. Traverse delicately left to gain a grassy groove which leads to a belay (bolts).
3 27m 6b Reverse the ramp on the left to a spike runner and traverse leftwards across the slab (bolt) to gain a good hold. Climb leftwards to a flake then step left around the rib to belay (bolts).
4 50m 6a A sustained pitch. Cross leftwards to gain a dirty corner; climb this until a horizontal crack crosses the left wall. Follow this (peg) to gain a shallow groove (peg). Traverse left across the blank wall above the big roof to (peg) and better holds, then climb up and left to gain a ramp. Reverse down this (bolt) to gain a groove. Climb down this crossing left into a larger groove. Step down and across onto the left wall (peg and bolt) then climb down and left until a long reach can be made to a hollow flake. Move down and across to a ledge, then climb the slim groove to a belay (bolts).
5 25m 5c An unprotected pitch. Step down onto the wall to the left and climb an upward-rising line of holds, delicately, to gain a sloping ledge (peg). Finish on the top, 6m above. Alternatively, climb down the flake below the left side of the belay for a couple of metres and traverse delicately left (bolt), then continue up to the sloping ledge.
A Phizacklea, S Hubbard 10.05.1987

PARROCK QUARRY

OS Grid Ref: NY 317 018
Altitude: 180m

Parrock Quarry is adjacent to and joined with **Hodge Close**.

The **Upper Slabs** are clean, open, fast drying, and sunny, while the lower quarry, **Slobs** and **Cable Wall** remain dank and are slow to dry.

Approach: The quarry is reached from a junction on the A593 Coniston-Ambleside road, 3km north of Coniston, signposted Hodge Close.

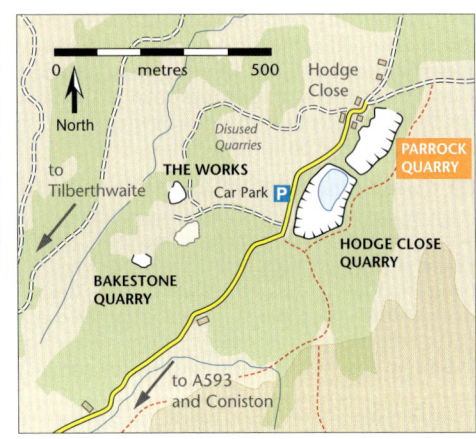

RAD Parrock Quarry

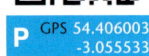
GPS 54.406003 -3.055533

The Upper Slabs

These pleasant slabs and grooves are found on the left as one enters the quarry, above a short scree slope. Most routes employ lowering off staples, but there is an easy scrambling descent to the right of the slabs.

Warning: The left-hand section of the quarry has collapsed and is unstable. There were some entertaining problems here - the enigmatic slab of **Cryptic Contortions** and the innocuous off-width **The Groove**. All of the routes on the buttress to the left of *Far Out* are considered dangerous. To the right of these walls is an area of slabby ribs and grooves, which has a prominent glacis running up rightwards below the right end of this area. The next routes start at the highest point of the scree slope, just left of a slabby groove.

❶ Far Out   12m   E5 6a

Thin flakes and hyphens to the top of *Cup and Lip*.
A Chambers 19.04.1992

❷ Cup and Lip   13m   F6b

Climb the centre of the smooth slab past a desperate mantelshelf.
P Whillance, D Armstrong 02.1983

③ Celica Groove   12m   F5+

The first open grooveline.
Photo page 139.
I Williamson, J White 30.03.1982

④ G.F.I.   13m   F6b

A very thin problem up the polished slabby arête. A couple of mantelshelves lead to the upper section - easy but loose.
I Williamson, J White 13.07.1982

⑤ Showroom Dummy   15m   F4+

From the base of the glacis, a slab runs back up left to reach the upper part of the arête of *G.F.I.*.
J White, I Williamson, P Cornforth, A Tilney 20.02.1982

⑥ The Model   13m   F5+

Pleasant climbing up the left-hand of two shallow grooves.
I Williamson, J White, P Cornforth 20.02.1982

⑦ The Gambler   12m   F6c

Climb the thin slab and arête between *The Model* and *One Arm Bandit*.
RP Cooper 07.1984

⑧ One Arm Bandit   12m   F5+

A good little route up the right-hand groove.
A Tilney, I Williamson 14.02.1982

The Slobs

The overhung walls and wet slabs on the east side before the tunnel through to **Hodge Close**. The routes see little sunshine and suffer from constant seepage. Those to the right were considered to be adequately bolted - all of the gear is old.

Approach: From the quarry entrance, continue down the ramp; **The Slobs** are on your left.

Descent: For routes 1 - 5 walk off. All of the others have lower-offs.

The left-hand end of these slabs terminates in a prominent sharp fin climbed by *An Oasis of Tranquility*. Up and left of this is a ledge formed behind a battlement of perched blocks, about 10m below the top of the quarry. This ledge is reached by scrambling up the scree on the left and across bramble strewn ledges. This ledge is the starting point for two short esoteric gems.

① Speed of Light   13m   F7a+   ★

A desperate route up the undercut left-hand arête of the slabs. Climb the bulging lower section then make a hard move onto the slab. Follow the right side of the arête (Rocks 1 and 3) then trend diagonally rightwards on thin holds to finish at a tree.
K Phizacklea, J Daly 20.02.1992

② Magenta De Vine   14m   F7a+

Another awkward route starting at the same point as *Speed of Light*. From the first bolt, climb awkwardly right below the top roof to its right-hand end, where the slab above can be gained. Climb up into a bottomless corner (peg and small wire) then pull out right at its top onto another slab and continue diagonally right to a mantelshelf finish.
K Phizacklea, J Daly 21.01.1992

The whole of this area, around the fin and the groove to its right, is very unstable and large blocks have come down or are slipping. The next two routes are not recommended.

❸ An Oasis of Tranquility   30m   E4 6b

Starts below the corner to the left of the prominent sharp fin, near an ash tree. Good sustained slab climbing in an unusual position up the fin. Climb the corner for 6m then move right using the wide crack. Clip the bolt in the slab above, pass it on its right and glide smoothly to the capping roof. Step right to a spike (The Oasis) from where a delicate move up and left across a hanging slab leads to a flake/crack. Climb this to the trees.
P Short, A Towse 10.09.1989

(4) Jim of Shadows 32m E3 5c

At the left end of the main wall is a red groove, formed by the right edge of the sharp fin. A route with a foreboding atmosphere. Climb the initial blocky corner then pull right into the main bottomless slabby corner which leads to the immense brooding overhang. Escape is via the strenuous off-width flake/crack on the left. (A car jack is rumoured to be *in-situ* here for a runner; if not, take your own!) This finishes with a risk of gelding by the sharp fin to reach The Oasis, which is followed to the top.
M France, J Evans 26.10.1991

(5) Hang 'em High 49m F7a+ ★★

A highly improbable line breaking through the overhangs at the left end of the wall. Start 7m right of *Jim of Shadows*
1 17m Climb up to a prominent layaway, swing up rightwards over the overlap and move right frantically below the roof. Climb a very steep wall to enter a bottomless corner/groove, where a delicate traverse right across the lower lip of the slab leads to a small belay ledge. Sensational!
2 13m Climb delicately up the slab on the left then move up and right passing a sapling on the left then climb directly to the top.
K Phizacklea, J Daly 4.04.1992

20m right of *Jim of Shadows* is a cave below a compact slab capped by a huge band of overhangs. The routes suffer from deposits of pine needles and leaves washed off the top after heavy rain. Bring a brush.

(6) The Underworld 16m F7a

A sustained delicate traverse below the roof - frequently wet. From a ledge at the left end of the cave, climb the thin crack to the roof then traverse rightwards to a lower-off bolt at its right-hand end.
J Daly, D Geere, K Phizacklea 22.05.1992

(7) Michael Angelo 11m F6c

A finely chiselled line starting just right of the cave. Step left onto a good hold above the lip of the cave. Climb the thin line above to a lower-off bolt on *The Underworld*.
Direct start - pull directly over the cave mouth to gain the good hold (small wire).
M Bagness 4.06.1990

(8) Banana Slide F6a

Start below the first right-facing groove 18m right of the cave. Climb a short slab past a bolt to enter the grooveline. This leads up left, from where a pull up is made to a lower-off bolt in a niche below the overhangs.
J Daly, K Phizacklea 29.05.1991

(9) Going Ballistic 14m F7b ★

A very technical problem which climbs the large corner at the left-hand end of slabs.
K Phizacklea, J Daly 28.05.1992

(10) Permitted Development 13m F7a+

A good sustained slab climb starting below a shothole 2m off the ground. A very direct line up the rounded rock.
A Hyslop, V McClelland 17.06.1990

(11) The Slobs 16m F6a ★

A very pleasant line. Gain the first bolt on *Permitted Development*, then step delicately right across a minute ledge to stand on a quartz band. Continue up a small short groove to reach a ledge. Step right and ascend the largest of the hanging grooves.
M Bagness, A Hyslop 4.06.1990

(12) Slobodan Zhivovinovics 12m F6a

Another thin problem starting from a little step at the foot of the slabs, 5m left of *Gorilla Groove*.
A Hyslop, AH Greenbank 10.08.1990

(13) Autan 28m F6c

Takes the bottomless V-groove at the right-hand side of the slabs.
J Daly, S Merry, K Phizacklea 30.05.1992

(14) Gorilla Groove 30m F6a+ ★

An unusually exciting outing up the arched groove sandwiched between two sets of overhangs at the right-hand side of the slabs. Start below the red-coloured groove on a tree-covered ledge just left of the waterfall. Climb the groove to a rounded ledge out right. Continue up the groove (wires) until the overhangs force a delicate traverse leftwards across the slab to a ledge. Finish up the easy rib, taking care with loose rocks in the retaining wall at the top.
J Daly, K Phizacklea 25.04.1992

(15) Desperate Dan the Dyno Man 22m F6c+ ★

A pleasant route up the stepped arête right of *Gorilla Groove*. Climb *Gorilla Groove* to the rounded ledge. Continue up rightwards to a good flat ledge and pass a bulge to grab a wobbly jug. Pull up carefully and step right onto the slabby arête. Climb this delicately.
J Daly, S Wood 4.04.1992

The final 2 routes start from a ledge behind a small tree 8m above and right of *Gorilla Groove*, which is reached by a steep scramble by the waterfall. This final hanging slab dries more quickly than those in the quarry bottom.

⑯ Pleasantly Slobbish   10m   F6c
From the tree, go up to the first bolt then reach a short flake out left. Climb this then continue directly to the top.
A Hyslop, M Bagness 12.06.1990

⑰ House of Correction   10m   F7a+   ★
From the first bolt on *Pleasantly Slobbish*, step right and climb the slab!
A Hyslop, V McClelland 19.06.1990

The Cable Wall

This is the large vertical wall of brittle slate to the right of the entrance to **The All-Weather Gym** and opposite **The Slobs Area**. It derives its name from the thick wire cable hanging from it. The face is impressive, but with old gear, moss and dirt, it is singularly unattractive.

Approach: From the quarry entrance continue down the ramp southwards.

① Gratuitous Violence   52m   F7a   ★ ⚠
The white streak is wash-out from above which makes the holds dusty. Start in the mouth of a cave. The first gear (peg & bolt) needs a clipstick.
1 30m Ape up the rope to the crackline in the overhanging wall. This is followed strenuously to gain a band of poor rock. Follow this up left on large holds to a tree-covered ledge and bolt belay.
2 22m Climb out rightwards on fragile holds (bolt) to a small ledge below the white headwall (bolt). Gain the ledge, step up left, and using tiny layaways gain a shothole (bolt). Stretch up right to a diagonal flake (possible runner over a sawn-off metal stake on the left). Follow the break leftwards to gain a shattered ledge and hanging trees above.
K Phizacklea, R Matheson 21.04.1993

② A Sorry Affair   24m   F6c+   ★ ⚠
A surprisingly entertaining route with well-spaced protection. Better than appearances first suggest. Start just left of the cable. Climb steeply to a sloping hold then continue on large holds. A sloping diagonal finger traverse runs up leftwards with increasing delicacy to below an arched flake. Power up this to a lower-off.
S Wood 16.09.1992

Celica Groove F5+ (page 137) Joe Holden
📷 Ron Kenyon

THE WORKS

OS Grid Ref: NY 314 017
Altitude: 180m

Transfusion M8 (page 131) Simon Frost — Andy Rutherford

THE WORKS

This impressive hole offers a range of routes from a slightly overhanging wall to the "upside-down world" of the cave's roof. The quarry is close to areas where material is still excavated; please do not enter other areas or antagonise relations with the quarry owners.

Approach: On entering **Hodge Close** car park there is a track behind a locked gate on the left. A track leads from the gate down to a large working quarry. The track bends rightwards and descends. On the left there is a quarried hole. The quarry is accessed making use of fixed equipment from a tree near the lip.

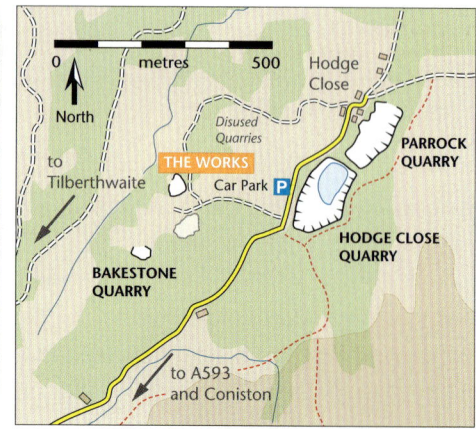

 RAD The Works   P GPS 54.406003 -3.055533

Industrial Sector

The slightly overhanging wall on the left as you descend into the quarry. Popular - many of the placements are severely worn and some have pulled through. Preclipping the first bolts is recommended.

There is a warm-up traverse below the long roof, M5+ until the last move which may be M8.

1. Time and a Half   9m   M5
2. Double Time   9m   M6
3. Overtime   9m   M6   ★
4. Stein Pull   M6   ★
5. Grand Design   9m   M7   ★

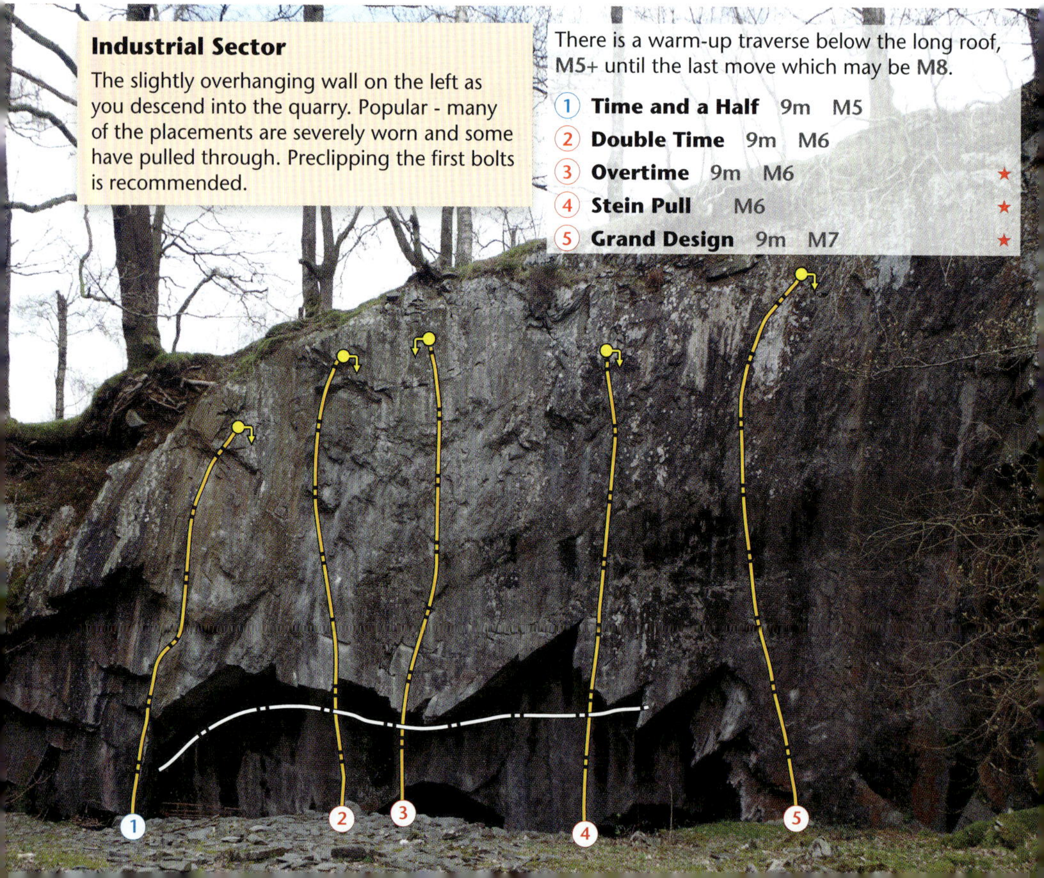

Left Hand Cave

⑥ Newbie M7

⑦ Going for a Swing 15m M9+
A combo, start with *Newbie* and swing right to join *Polish Direct* and the hanging bosun's chair.

⑨ Swingers Extension 25m M11
If you've not had enough try the extension, the UK's first multi-pitch dry tooling route. First climb either *Polish Direct* or *Going for a Swing* to the bosun's chair. Next, from the chair, break through the roof and traverse right to the corner. Finally tackle the right wall to a lower-off.
2016

⑧ Polish Direct 35m M12
Start on the pillar at the back of the cave between the two tunnels. Climb the pillar and out across the roof past 12 bolts to reach the bosun's chair on the right of the cave.
2015

⑩ Lakes Ethics 25m M9+
The first route added to this cave. Climb the right side of the arch in the lower cave then break through the first roof and cross to the arch and the lower-off left of the arch.
2013

The People's Slab
The slab between the two main caves.

⑪ Left Route M4
The left side of the slab. Traverse right near the upper vegetation to the *Middle Route* lower-off.

⑫ Middle Route M4

⑬ Right Route M4

Quick Release M11 (page 146) Steve Johnstone — 📷 Andy Rutherford

Right Hand Cave

This cave has been the focus of much strong arm action since the beginning of development in the quarry. It offers climbing in the dry when the rest of the Lakes is wet.

⑭ **Bloodline** 20m M10
The crackline running parallel to the roof starting from the left side of the cave. A long powerful reach near the end.
2012

⑮ **Let there be Light** 30m M10+
From the upper groove of *Bloodline* break out right across the steep wall. Cross *Blood Donor* and continue with some downward moves to link with the final section of *First Blood*.
Photo page 31.
S Chevis 2012

⑯ **Blood Donor** 15m M9+
Cross the steep roof to a fierce final move into the groove and lower-off of *Bloodline*.
2012

⑰ **First Blood** M9+
Start up *Blood Donor* and link a series of roofs rightwards to a lower-off on the lip out to the right.
2012

⑱ **Quick Release** 15m M11
Start at the slab to the left of *Guardian of the Underworld* and follow a crack through the roof to join *First Blood* two bolts from the lower-off.
Photo page 145.
2012

⑲ **Guardian of the Underworld** 30m M12
Start deep in the cave just before a section where the cave floor drops away at an awkward step. Climb the prow to the roof then use figure of 4, 8 and whatever other numbers are required to reach the lower-off of *First Blood*.
A Turner 2012

⑳ **Project**
Project. An incomplete line of 13 bolts starting at a dangling rope in the middle of the back of the cave and crossing the cave roof to join *Guardian of the Underworld* at its 12th bolt.

Right Hand Cave | **The Works** | 147

㉑ **Transfusion** 15m M8
Offers a different style using many natural placements. Deceptively steep. There is a bolt in place for the belayer on the ledge at the foot of the route. Climb the arête that forms the right-hand side of the cave entrance. After a blind move to gain the arête and crackline climb the arête on torques and enhanced edges. At about 2/3 height move leftwards out of the crack onto a series of natural edges with a thin move giving access to the good upper crack/flake and lower-off.
Photo page 140.
2012

Just right of the **Right Hand Cave**.

㉒ **Steve's Corner** 15m M6
Climb the slab to gain the corner and climb this to exit out left at the top. Some open torques can be used in the upper corner or a long move made to bypass them.
Photo page 280.
2012

㉓ **Fallen Roof**   M6+
A line of bolts right of *Steve's Corner* starting right of a hole in the floor, that was the roof of a tunnel. Some ledges in the lower half lead to a left-to-right diagonal crack using natural features.
2013

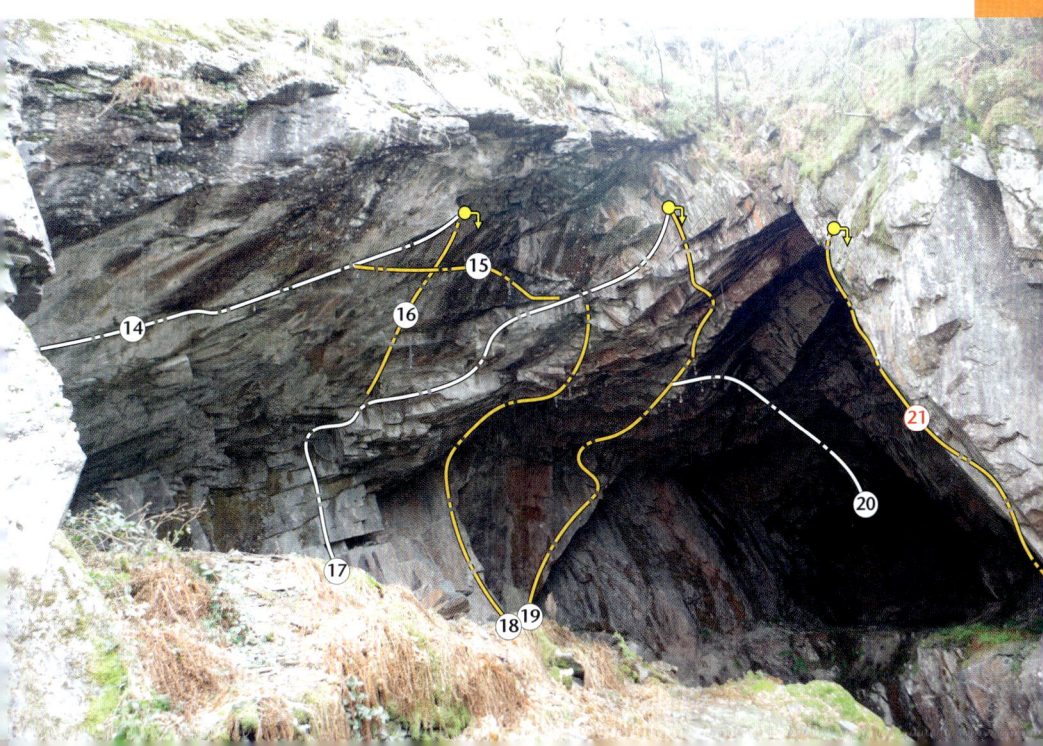

24 Winter is Coming 10m M7
The lowest point of the quarry towards the east has a partly filled tunnel. This is down and right from the usual quarry access. Climb the wall right of and above the tunnel entrance.
P Holder 2013

BAKESTONE QUARRY

OS Grid Ref: NY 313 017
Altitude: 180m

15mn

This cave boasts one of the hardest routes in the country - *Powerdab*.

The Wicket

The manicured grassy quarry path leads to the cave with *The Fang* in its centre. There is a slabby corner to the right and a wall above the cave on its left.

Approach: Park as for **Hodge Close** and take the track through the gate heading west. Take a path to the right of the active quarry (stay clear of the crumbling quarry edge) to reach a flat mossy area. Pass this to a higher terrace and an old tunnel entrance then traverse scree to two old quarry buildings. Go up the steps and the quarry is on the left.

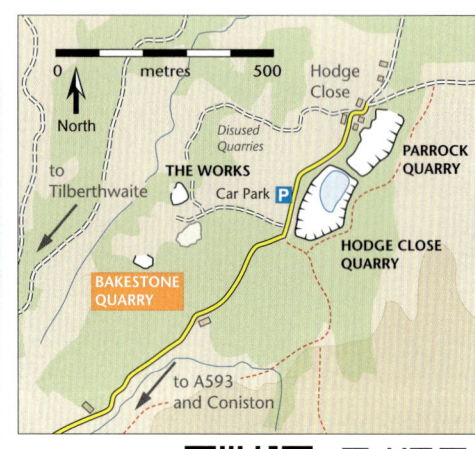

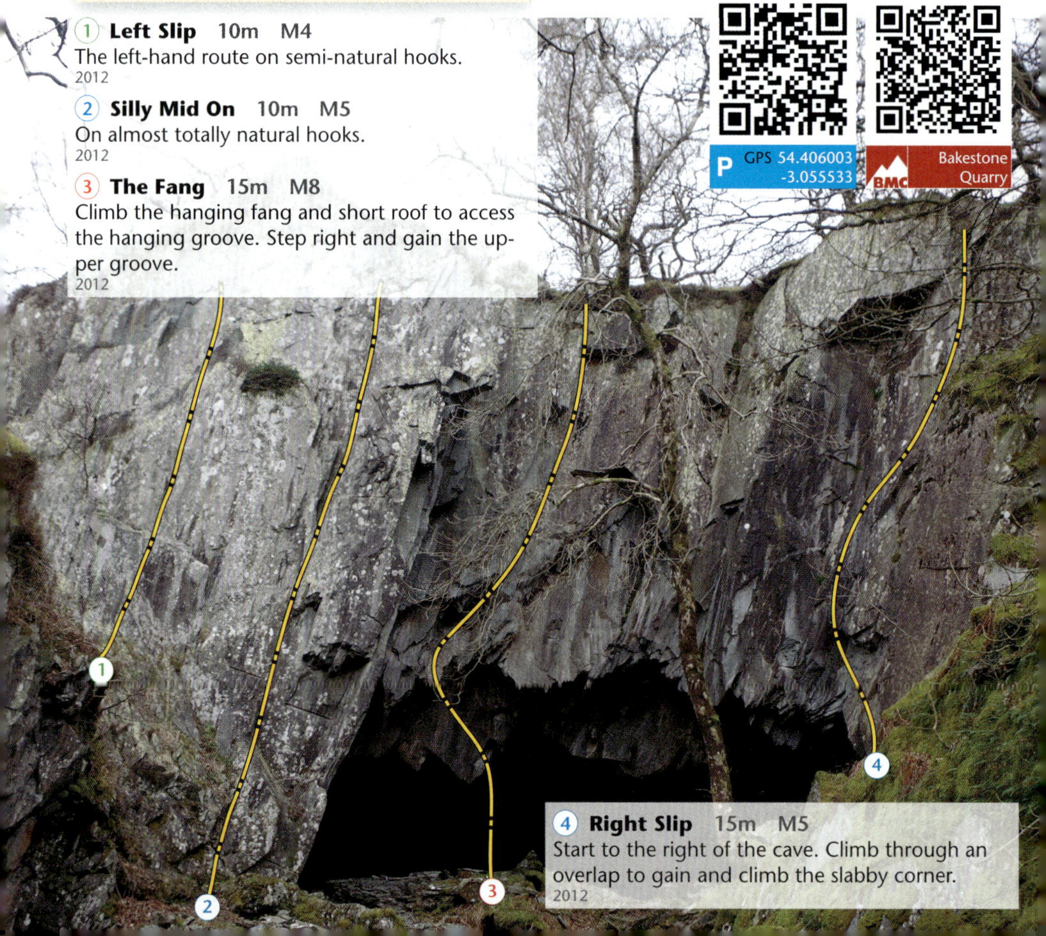

P GPS 54.406003 -3.055533

BMC Bakestone Quarry

1 **Left Slip** 10m M4
The left-hand route on semi-natural hooks.
2012

2 **Silly Mid On** 10m M5
On almost totally natural hooks.
2012

3 **The Fang** 15m M8
Climb the hanging fang and short roof to access the hanging groove. Step right and gain the upper groove.
2012

4 **Right Slip** 15m M5
Start to the right of the cave. Climb through an overlap to gain and climb the slabby corner.
2012

The Wicket Bakestone Quarry

5 Outside Leg 12m M5
Climbs the arête to the left of the cave via the large flake; then make a move onto the sloping ledge. Finish as for *Outfield* to a shared lower-off.
2012

6 Dibdab M7
Climb the wall to join *Powerdab*.

7 Nisbet Memorial Link M6+
A harder start to *Outfield*.

8 Outfield 20m M6+
Climb the shallow groove to the roof. Traverse leftwards, below the roof, to mantel onto a sloping ledge. Step right to final steep moves and a lower-off.
2012

9 Powerdab 20m M13
One of the hardest dry-tooling routes in the UK. The line of bolts across the roof to the right of *Outfield* has big powerful moves throughout.
G Boswell 2013

10 Low level Traverse M4
To the left of **The Wicket** is a rubble-filled hole with a long flat roof and a smooth left wall. A low level traverse can be followed along the base of the smooth left wall from the back of the hole. A good warm up.

MOSS RIGG QUARRY

OS Grid Ref: NY 312 025
Altitude: 180m

Moss Rigg offers adventure in a setting of brutal beauty. The climbing is protected by bolts, yet to classify this as sport climbing is a little misleading due to the approach and the universal instability of the rock.

Approach: Park at **Hodge Close**. See map page 106 for **Hodge Close**. From the parking, head north on the road and take the wide gated track on the left between houses. Follow this, always downhill, to cross a slate bridge over the beck to meet the High Tilberthwaite to Little Langdale track. Turn left towards Tilberthwaite and take the track right passing a locked gate. Ascend through disused slate workings to the rim. Descend the south slope or abseil from trees down *Train Crazy Boys*.

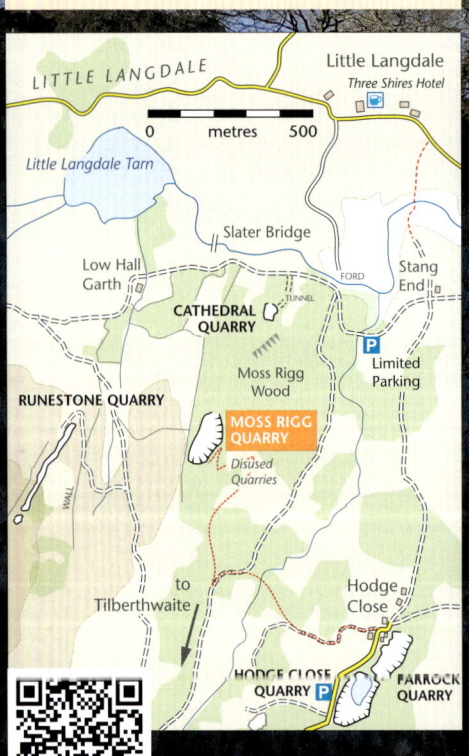

GPS 54.406003
     -3.055533

Titanic Arête F6c+ (page 154) Dan Robinson — Bob Curry

Slate

❶ Borrowdale Lad's Day Out   40m   XS 5c

A bold and dangerous undertaking. Although the line is still there, a recent huge area of rock immediately to the left has fallen away lending an uneasy feel to the free-standing pillar taken by the first pitch, with sky visible through the crack. Potentially unstable, dangerous, dirty, overgrown and not recommended. Scramble up unstable boulders to reach the base of the groove.
1 22m 5b Climb the short flake on the right then move left and up into the groove. Follow the crack strenuously to the haven of a belay (bolts).
2 18m 5c Climb the groove on the left of the belay then balance up to a good foothold on the exposed edge. Difficult moves on undercuts are made to enter the groove on the right; follow this, finishing out on the left crest. Take extreme care with the rubble and root cornice.
P Ross, D Byne-Peare, AH Greenbank 10.07.1990

❷ Titanic Arête   50m   F6c+   ★

A compelling line soaring skywards into the trees. Start up a short steep wall just right of the arête. Helmets and life-boats should be taken.
1 26m F6a The innocuous initial wall is awkward. Tackle the loose rib above with vigilance to reach the safety of a comfortable ledge.
2 24m F6c+ Climb the right-hand side of the arête. An enigmatic sequence, or a French-free move, above the peg may enable you to grab a large hold. From here reaching the top is inevitable.
Photo page 153.
P Ross, D Byne-Peare 8.07.1990

❸ Train Crazy Boys   45m   F6b+

Constantly morphing, this fluid adventure demands competence and awareness. Superficially clean and sound, the enticing pillar is remarkably loose and any large hold must be treated with suspicion. Seconds should definitely not stand directly below the leader. With a couple of stainless exceptions the bolts are rusty mild steel expansion bolts with stainless hangers. Climb into a shallow corner stepping right to avoid steepening rock. Continue through the bulging rock above trending left to enter a very smooth groove at 35m. The bulge provides an interesting entry to the steep final wall.
Photo this page.

Train Crazy Boys F6b+ (this page) Steve Scott
Keith Sanders

TILBERTHWAITE QUARRY
OS Grid Ref: NY 305 009
Altitude: 220m

Kick Off HVS (page 160) Caroline Ciavaldini — David Simmonite

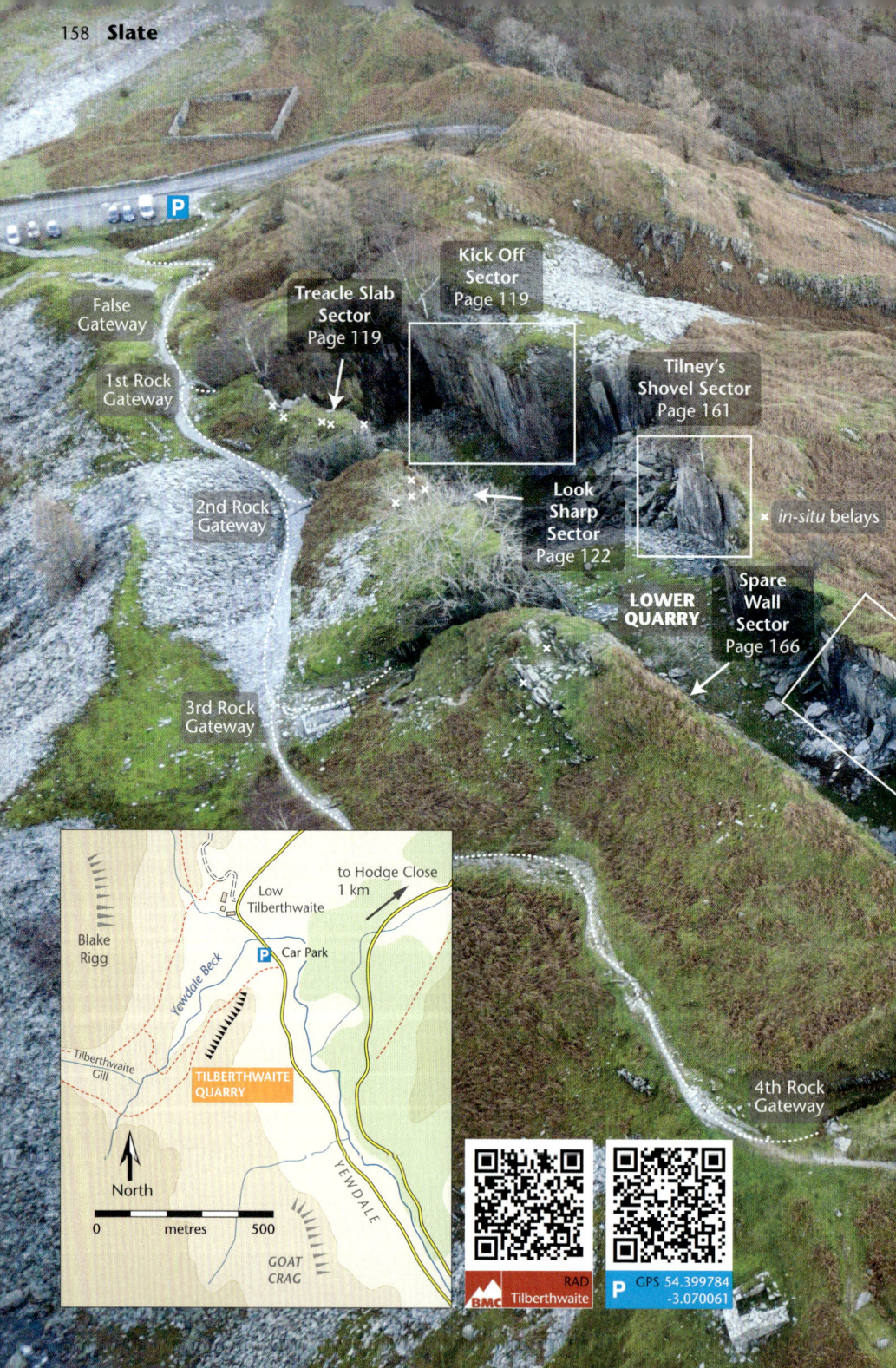

TILBERTHWAITE QUARRY

A sheltered location with a sunny outlook. The **Upper Quarry** in particular with its flat grassy base is an excellent picnic site. The quarry offers a range of styles from sporty slate to traditional climbing and even has a beginners' top-roping area. It is very suitable for a short day or evening's climbing.

⚠ Despite the quarry's popularity many loose flakes retain the notoriety of adventure; be careful!

Approach: Quickly reached from the main A593 Coniston to Ambleside road, about 3km north of Coniston signed to Tilberthwaite.

From Coniston and A593

Big Tree Corner Sector
Page 113

Rhode Island Red Sector
Page 127

UPPER QUARRY

Limestone

Slate

Micro-Granite

Sandstone

BB

Kick Off Sector

The first route is on the wall opposite the first rock gateway.

① Rusty Wall 18m E3 6a
An interesting crimpy route. Start at the blunt arête to the right of the cave, directly below a large tree. Climb to a ledge and sapling then use a hollow flake on the left. Climb the wall rightwards to a diagonal crack; climb this to a loose finish.
J Daly, K Phizacklea 11.04.1987

To the right of *Rusty Wall* lies a weirdly beautiful wall of horrible red rock resembling dried manure in texture and quality. The right-hand side of this wall has two prominent flakes; the next route starts just left of the impressive left-hand flake.

② Pressure Drop 11m F7a+
Thin friable climbing up the blunt arête.
M Millar 5.12.1990

③ Kick Off 10m HVS 5a ★★
The left-leaning Yosemite-style flake.
Photo page 156
C Brown 1976

④ Christmas Cracker 10m HS ★
The right-hand flake; *Kick Off* with footholds.
J Daly, K Phizacklea 14.12.1986

The canyon behind a slipped megalith a little higher up the slope was once **Big Crack**.

Tilney's Shovel Sector

5 Peapod 15m HVS 5a ★
Thrutch the short chimney to finish up the cracked slab above.
J Daly, K Phizacklea 24.01.1987

6 Solitaire 15m 5b ★
Unprotected.
J Daly, K Phizacklea 31.01.1987

7 Life in the Bus Lane 5b
A direct start to *Tuxedo Junction*.
E Blaycock 10.07.1991

8 Tuxedo Junction 16m VS 4b
Thuggy then thin; follow the leftwards sloping shelf to a flake finish.
J Daly, K Phizacklea 31.01.1987

9 More Come and Rise 11m E4 6b ★
The fierce crack has a reachy finish.
T Walkington 05.1988

A few metres right of *More Come and Rise* is a green wall below a silver birch tree, just left of a large flake.

10 Slow and Easy 10m 5b
An unprotected highball. Climb the shallow green depression.
N Franklin, N Reid 8.04.1990

11 Slip of the Tongue 10m VS 5a ★
The large flake is awkward to protect.
D Taylor 8.04.1990

12 Morecambe and Wise 9m E3 5c ★★
The thin crack.
T Walkington 05.1988

13 Tilney's Shovel 9m E2 5c ★★
Type 2 fun. 5.9+ The enigmatic left-facing V-cleft with a crack in its right wall gives a full-body pump.
C Brown 1976

Big Tree Corner Sector

Tilberthwaite at its best and worst. This sector has some of the most interesting and challenging climbs, yet has recently suffered a huge rockfall and there may be more to come down. The short wall opposite the gateway gives some boulder problems. A massive rockfall occurred left of *Juggler's Crack* in 2018; this area is still unstable.

Approach: This is the pleasant flat-bottomed quarry above the scree slope. It can also be entered by following the path up to the third rock gateway.

14 Pedestal Corner E2 5b

Not recommended due to instability and loose rock. Climb either groove to the finishing corner.
K Phizacklea, J Daly 31.01.1987

A huge flake, effectively the top wall between *Pedestal Corner* and *Juggler's Crack*, fell in 2018. Take great care here as the area is unstable.

15 Juggler's Crack 12m HVS 5a ★★

A fine problem starting behind an embedded split flake. Climb the thin flake up the steep slab.
J Daly, K Phizacklea 22.03.1987

16 Punchy Patterson 12m E4 6a ★

The first moves have become more difficult due to movement of the split flake. A bold mantelshelf to reach the bolt marks the crux of this sketchy slab. Skyhook recommended!
K Phizacklea, J Daly 23.10.1988

17 Anvil Arête 12m E3 6a ★★

The fine delicate central arête is climbed on its left side; a single bolt and sky hook are the only protection.
K Phizacklea, J Daly 30.03.1987

18 Spycatcher 13m E5 6b ★

Hard climbing on snappy flakes up the shallow scoop between *Anvil Arête* and *Big Tree Corner*.
A Greig, R Parker 15.08.1987

19 Big Tree Corner 13m E1 5b ★

The prominent right-facing corner. Marred by polish and its proximity to The Death Flake.
C Brown 1976

Big Tree Corner Sector | Tilberthwaite Quarry

The Death Flake Routes - home to some extraordinary climbing this massive flake is unstable and considered to be dangerous literally and physically - these are chop routes.

20 Flake and Corner 13m HVS 5a
Traverse the flake and climb the corner.

21 The Curver 12m E2 5b
Gear has been known to rip from the massive flimsy flake. Traverse right across its top to a sequency finish up the stiff crack.
K Phizacklea, J Daly, M Wright, N Russell 07.1988

22 Slate Dancer 12m F7b
A direct on *The Curver*, fairly sustained and harder than *Histocompatable Hanger*.
J Burrell

23 Histocompatable Hanger 15m F7b ★
A snappy wall climb.
J Burrell 18.09.1993

24 Latex Generation 15m F7a+ ★
With old rotting gear and unstable rock this is considered dangerous. Climb the red-arched groove into a short triple corner. Continue up the prominent flake, which is now missing, finally escaping left.
D Green, M Radtke Summer 1988

25 Megabyte 15m E5 6a ★★
The shallow corner gives poorly-protected sustained climbing of considerable character.
J Daly, K Phizacklea, K Garstang 15.02.1987

26 Ingham's Route 16m F7c ★★
A solid problem up the front of the clean pillar which forms the narrows of the **Upper Quarry**. Start up the left side of the pillar, then follow the thin seam to a good hold in the centre. A desperate sequence leads directly to an easing - but only slightly.
P Ingham, P Cornforth 22.05.1988

27 Violation 16m F6c ★
Forceful but elegant climbing up the steep grooved face right of *Ingham's Route*. Climb the V-groove to a metal spike, move left over a bulge and up to a block beneath the overhang. Pull up onto the slab to a good foothold. Climb awkwardly back left to a thin crack.
K Phizacklea, J Daly 4.04.1987

164 Slate

- 24 **Latex Generation** F7a+ ★★
- 26 **Ingham's Route** F7c ★★
- 27 **Violation** F6c ★
- 29 **Foghorn Leghorn** VS 4c

28 Violation Variation 17m F6c
Climb over the bulge above the top slab and follow a jamming crack rightwards to the tree.
J Daly, K Phizacklea 11.04.1987

29 Foghorn Leghorn 16m VS 4c
The ferny V-groove 5m right of *Violation* to a ledge overhung by a tree. Bushwhack up the slab on the left.
K Phizacklea, J Daly 4.04.1987

Rhode Island Red Sector

A clean wall on the left of the upper scree slope has a rightwards-slanting diagonal corner up its centre, the line of *Rhode Island Red*.

30 Captain Pugwash 16m HVS 5a ★
The ragged right-facing crack leads steeply to finish left of the tree.
J Daly, K Phizacklea 23.10.1988

31 The Vexed Question 10m F6c+
Hard climbing. Climb the thin slab to an awkward mantelshelf; span left to a large hold and the finishing crack.
M Miller, T Peak 7.07.1991

32 Jitterbug 12m E3 6a ★★
A challenging route up the leftward-curving finger crack. Often worked. Watch out for hollow flakes as you finish!
J Daly, K Garstang, K Phizacklea 22.02.1987

33 Rhode Island Red 14m E3 5c ★★
A sequency strength sapper.
K Phizacklea, J Daly 22.02.1987

34 Top Shot 15m VS 4b
The wide crack.
J Daly, K Phizacklea 2.03.1987

Spare Wall Sector

At first fractured, the south face descends towards the third rock gateway where the remains of a Tilberthwaite original, **The Rib**, now lie amongst the short grass on the quarry floor.

Due to the dangerous condition of the rock and gear, routes to the left are not described. The first route of merit takes the slabby arête left of a right-facing corner and opposite *Anvil Arête*.

35 **Barnes Big Day Out**   15m   F6a
Climb the arête. Take care with the anchor.
I Barnes, C Rabone 20.05.1998

4m left of a prominent low ash tree growing from a flake is a light-coloured wall with a narrow ledge at head-height.

36 **A Meeting with Don Juan**   12m   F6c   ★
Start just right of a corner at the left end of the wall. Layback to a sloping hold in the centre of the wall. A hard mantelshelf leads to skittery climbing and a span to the top.
T Peak, P Hadfield 1.06.1991

37 **Lorna's Orifices**   12m   E3 6a
Considered dangerous. Left of the low ash tree sprouting from a flake is a thin flake/crack. There are two shotholes and two old bolts just to its left. The chossy crack has filled with dirt washed out from above. Climb up to the diagonal line on sharp holds and follow the flake to a loose finish.
J Metcalfe, PW Cox 06.1989

38 **Acrachnophobia**   15m   VS 4c
Climb the crack then pull over a large flake.
M Hartley, A Clark 22.07.2006

39 **Spare Wall**   15m   F6a+   ★
An interesting slabby problem.

The clean polished slab to the right is a major attraction for beginners. The next routes are on the steep wall to the right of the third rock gateway.

40 **Making Peace With God**   10m   HVS 4b
A heart-stopping series of very delicate moves with sparse protection. Start on the wall of the gateway. Some 2m left of a tree stump climb to the shallow vertical crack. Follow this the top.
M Hartley, A Clark 22.07.2006

41 **Stump Flake Wall**   10m   HS 4b   ★
Start just below the tree stump and climb the crack over the flake.
A Clark, M Hartley 22.07.2006

Tilberthwaite Quarry 167

Treacle Slab E3 5c (page 169) James Pearson — 📷 David Simmonite

Slate

Beginner's Top-roping Area

Look Sharp Sector

To the right of the scree slope is a light-coloured wall to the left of a hanging rock gateway.

42 Split Wet Beaver 18m F6b ★★
A fingery route with disposable holds. Start behind the large flake below the left end of the wall. Step onto a good hold and follow the thin crack up a shallow groove.
J Metcalfe, PW Cox 06.1989

43 Elicit Scenes of 18m F8a ★
Sex and Violence
A finger-searing problem on slopey crimps with only one obvious hold at mid-height. Start at an old rail line on the ground.
P Cornforth 27.01.1991

44 Fat Guy goes Nutzoid 18m E6 6b ⚠
Another fine route. Climb the shallow crease to better holds then step right to gain a good hold. Pull back left to reach a thin crack then finish direct.
M Radtke, J Metcalf 07.1989

45 Look Sharp 19m E2 5c ★★
A good strenuous route with a fine crack. Start at the foot of the scree slope. Gain the ledge then follow a thin crack to a good rest out right. Traverse left using a shothole to reach the jamming crack which leads elegantly past a short wall to the top.
K Phizacklea, J Daly 25.01.1987

Treacle Slab Sector

An impressively steep pillar rises to the right of the hanging gateway.

Belay stakes have been placed along the top of this sector.

46 Act of Contrition 21m E5 5c
A high-ball. Climb the arête.
J Burrell 20.02.1998

47 Major Misdemeanor 20m F7c+ ★
Dry-tooling has damaged the line of manufactured holds up the front of the pillar to the right of the hanging rock gateway.
P Cornforth 9.04.1992

48 Treacle Slab 20m E3 5c ★★
A great climb; some say it's **E2**. Set off with intent on flat holds to reach a left-trending gangway; follow this to a ledge. Hollow flakes lead to the top.
Photo page 167.
J Daly, K Phizacklea 31.01.1987

49 Death Warrant 20m E5 6b ★★
The crack and wall to the right of *Treacle Slab* with one stopper move above the bolt. Climb *Treacle Slab* to a small layaway and make a big rock up to latch a good hold on the right. Climb up on crimps, then more easily up the crack to a lower-off.
M Johnson, G Atkinson 20.10.1993

50 I Sold my Soul for Whisky and Mushrooms 20m E3 6a
Climb the corner to the right of *Treacle Slab*.
P Smallwood, B Rudd 12.11.1996

Round to the right is a right-facing flake-filled dank corner which the next route is believed to take. Be careful here.

51 Rabbithole Redemption 20m HVS 4b
Climb the flake to reach a narrow ledge. Exciting unprotected moves lead to a grassy scramble for the top. Belay on trees 6m left in the second archway entrance.
M Fletcher, A Fletcher 19.09.1995

52 Belay Bunny 20m F6b ★★
The eye-catching left-slanting flake 5m left of *Nebbie*.
B Davison, P Clay 25.10.1993

53 Nebbie 20m E3 6a ★
A strenuous battle up an impending crack.
K Phizacklea, J Daly 11.04.1987

RUNESTONE QUARRY

OS Grid Ref: NY 306 024
Altitude: 250m

Runestone Quarry

Ska Train F6b (page 172) Rob Illingworth — 📷 Ron Kenyon

RUNESTONE QUARRY

Ignored for a generation, this easily-reached sheltered quarry has been transformed into a great venue with extensive views across Langdale and Tilberthwaite. Almost 30 years after first being explored, volunteers supported by the **Cumbria Bolt Fund** inspected, cleaned and replaced many of the bolts in 2019 and 2020. Lower-offs were added and some new lines climbed. The **Middle Quarry** offers the best selection of routes.

The wet February weather and lockdown during the Covid-19 pandemic delayed and then interrupted the bolting. The projects are expected to be completed at some point in 2020. Work is ongoing so expect to find some changes.

Approach: From the A593 take the Tilberthwaite turn and park as for **Tilberthwaite Quarry** (see map on page 158). Walk north along the road through the farm. Follow the bridleway branching up left for about 1km, until it levels out with a view of the Langdale Pikes. Up on the fell to the left is a spoil-heap with a conspicuous left to right inclined path; this path leads into the quarry. Continue along the bridleway and take the second track on the left. Cross a stone stile next to a gate and then take that inclined path into the **Lower Quarry**.

Alternatively, the quarry may be reached from the **Cathedral Quarry** parking (page 182). Follow a track west alongside the river to some cottages (no parking). Continue up the track away from the river; the quarry spoil heaps can be seen above. Take the track to the left, go through a gate, and continue to where the track branches right to the quarry and the stone stile and inclined path as above.

A mountain bike can make the return trip speedy and fun.

Lower Quarry

① **Finger-tips of Civilisation** Project　　F6b+
Climb the wall, move round the arête and scuttle up the slab.

② **Ska Train**　12m　F6b　　★
Climb the awkward corner to gain the slab then continue leftwards, with a decidedly difficult move, to an easier finish.
Photo page 171.
M Miller 27.08.1990

③ **The Narrow Land** Project　　F5c
Climb the hanging corner and slab.

④ **Monster Dog**　10m　F7a　　★
A technical exercise maintaining the *Monster Dog* experience. The lower slab leads to a tough pull over the overhang.
M Miller 25.08.1990

⑤ **Power of Sila**　　F5b
Lovely climbing with one awkward move.
E Parker, H Mawson 29.05.2020

⑥ **Caspian**　15m　F5b
Immediately left of the entrance to the quarry. Climb a small undercut nose and wall then trend left to the final shallow groove. Rather dirty but should improve with use. Belay bolts over the top.
B Pilgrim, M Edwards 8.03.1992

⑦ **Gandalf**　13m　F6b+　　★
The square-cut pillar just left of the chimney – Gollum's Gully. Move up left to gain and climb the arête. The route originally went up to a peg then left to the arête. Belay bolts over the top.
M Miller, P Hadfield 25.08.1990

⑧ **Gollum's Gully**　12m　VD
The conspicuous chimney.
M Bagness 18.04.1991

⑨ **New Booties**　10m　F6b
Fingery climbing below a huge detached block. Climb up to a loose flake (bolt); cross to the block. A diagonal crack leads back right to finish direct.
S Halton, L Harrison 04.1991

⑩ **Arthur Dolphin isn't**　10m　HVS 4c
　　Dead, I've Seen Him in News World
The name is in poor taste, the climbing and the protection is no better! A leftward-slanting line up a protruding buttress about 10m left of *Lynn-er Motion*.
T Peak, E Blylock 7.04.1991

13　40　23

P GPS 54.399784 -3.070061

RAD Runestone

174 | Slate

11 Lynn-er Motion 10m E1 5b
The clean slab with a prominent horizontal crack at 4m (old bolt) - 10m right of *Arthur Dolphin isn't Dead, I've Seen Him in News World*.
P Hadfield, J Walmsley 18.06.1991

12 Yo! Pick Poe! 10m HVS 5b
A large corner in the level below the extensive scree slope.
E Blylock, T Peak 7.04.1991

13 Fancy a Jump 10m F6b
Follow the hanging slab, with an undercut start, half-way up the scree slope, on the left. In 2020 the bolt hangers are missing; earmarked for re-bolting.
B Pilgrim, M Edwards 21.04.1992

Above the scree slope at the head of the **Lower Quarry** is a flat area, **The Gallery**. The left wall provides a dozen boulder problems between **V1** and **V3** which can be identified by the scars. The prominent arête is **Phantom Arête** V3, best approached by the path coming in from the right.

1	Finger-tips of Civilisation	F6b+	4	Monster Dog	F7a ★
2	Ska Train	F6b ★	5	Power of Sila	F5b
3	The Narrow Land Project	F5c			

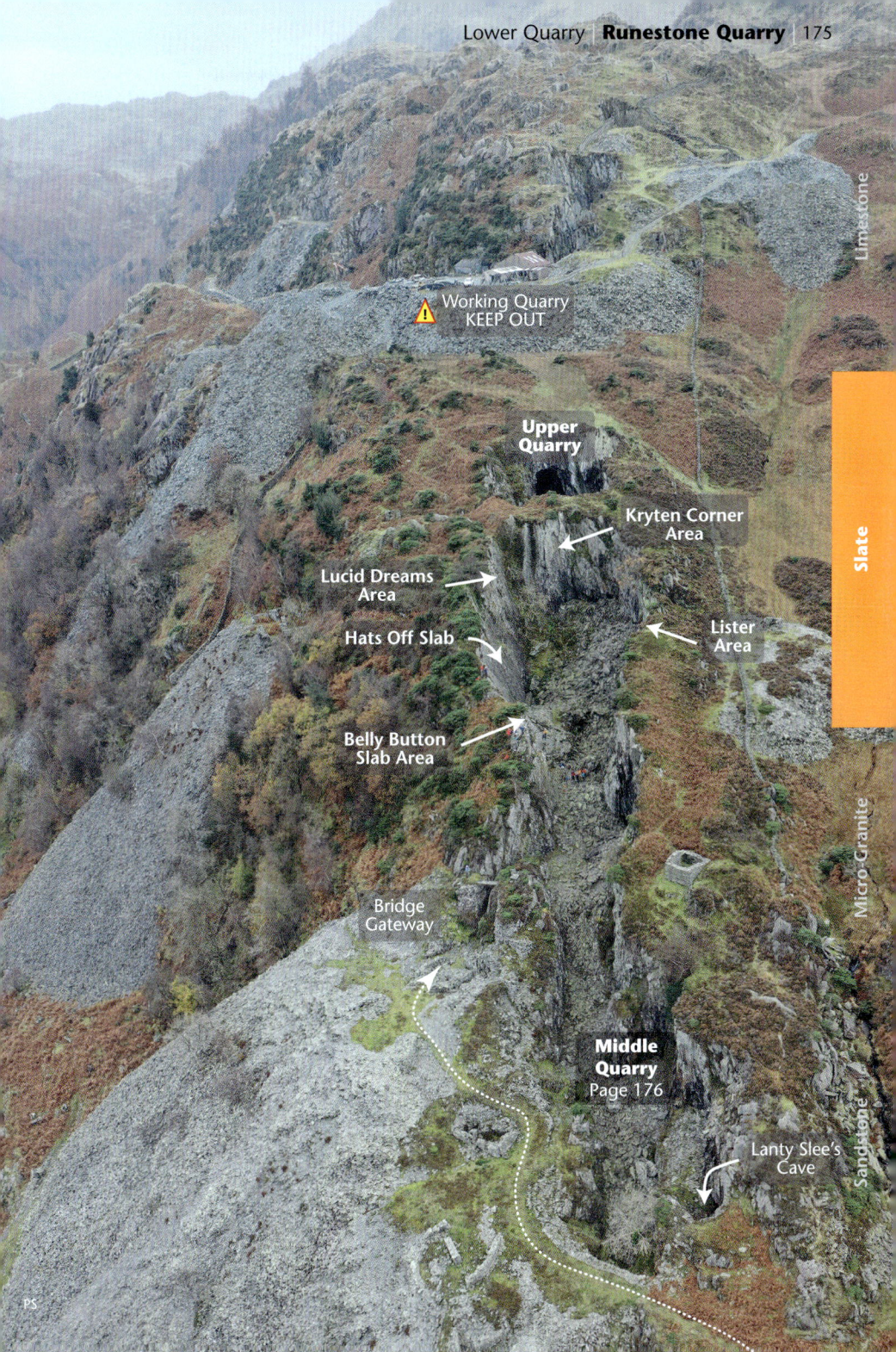

Middle Quarry

A fine spread of routes at a mixture of grades.

In the lower (northern) end of the quarry is the cave once used as an illicit whisky still by the notorious Lanty Slee. It was said that the resultant product was the best thing that ever came out of the quarry.

Approach: From the entrance to the **Lower Quarry** follow the path up the right (west) side of the quarry to eventually reach a flat area between the quarries, from which the **Middle Quarry** can be seen. One may also easily access **The Gallery** from this flat area. On the left (east) side of the quarry there is a pathway which leads under a huge impressive slab bridged across the entrance gangway. *Belly Button Slab* area is about 30m up to the left.

① **Hang Like a Hound** 10m F7a+ ★
A hard pull over the overhang leads to sustained climbing on the arête.
A Hyslop, M Bagness 15.04.1991

② **Coye Dog** 10m F6a
A rib eases the step into the corner; climb this then swing left to share the anchor on *Hang Like a Hound*. The direct start goes at **F6b**.
V McClelland, E Blylock 9.04.1991

③ **Nice View, Petunia** 13m F6a
Pull onto the narrow ledge on the right at 3m. Climb the shallow groove above joining the top slab of *Clutching at Straws*.
T Peak, V McClelland 13.04.1991

④ **Clutching at Straws** 13m F6a+ ★
A rectangular slab guarded by an overhanging wall gives a fingery problem!
P Hadfield, T Peak 24.04.1991

⑤ **It's Moi Land** 12m F6a
Climb the slabby corner, then rightwards through tiers of overhangs to a curving overlap. Step left, up to a ledge, then finish more easily. Or, step right with more difficulty to finish up the rib on the right.
T Peak, S Halton 27.04.1991

Just left of *Hang Like a Hound* a fine, steep slab has potential.

Middle Quarry **Runestone Quarry** 177

6 There's Nae Fat on me Taties 12m F6a+ ★
Good sustained climbing. From a thin rib climb into a dark scoop flecked by rusty streaks. Following a vague groove-line aim for a protruding nose of rock at the upper bulge.
E Blylock, L Harrison 3.04.1991

7 Belly Button Slab 13m HVS 5a ★
From a small walled enclosure a diagonal flake/crack leads into a broken niche, step left onto the large hanging slab and climb this directly over a small overlap to reach a lower-off over to the left. To be retro-bolted, **F5c**.
M Bagness, L Harrison 18.04.1991

8 Self Isolation 11m F6a ★
From a pointed block move left and climb the slab. Making use of the groove on the left is much easier.
R.Kenyon, R Illingworth 19.03.2020

9 The Burning 10m F6a+ ★
From a pointed block pull onto the slab with difficulty. Climb a vague flake continuing past a small overlap.
V McClelland 9.04.1991

10 Smile at the End of the Rainbow 10m F6a+ ★
Pull over the right side of the overhang then follow the shallow groove.
R Kenyon, R Illingworth 26.05.2020

11 Hats Off to Linten Miller 10m F6a ★
The left-facing groove.
V McClelland 13.04.1991

12 Hats Off Direct 10m F6b
Follow the bolts directly up the slab to join *Hats Off to Linten Miller*.
R Illingworth 26.05.2020

13 Runestone Cowboy 10m F5b ★
A direct line up the fine slab.
Photo opposite.
R.Illingworth, RJ Kenyon 19.01.2020

14 Rust Bucket 10m F5a
Climb the rust-coloured groove reaching left to clip the bolts on *Runestone Cowboy*.
A Davis 26.05.2020

15 Greasing My Teapot 10m F6a ★
Climb the slab with interest.
E Blylock, V McClelland 9.04.1991

16 Wide Open 11m F5a ★
The faint grooveline just left of the bolts.
V McClelland 9.04.1991

17 Yodelling in the Canyon 11m F4
The left-slanting groove; shared protection from bolts to the left.
E Blylock 9.04.1991

18 Runestone Cross F5b
The easier groove of *Self Isolation* to the 5th bolt and then follow an ascending traverse to finish at the top of *Greasing My Teapot*.
Consider double ropes.
P Sterling, L Sterling 30.05.2020

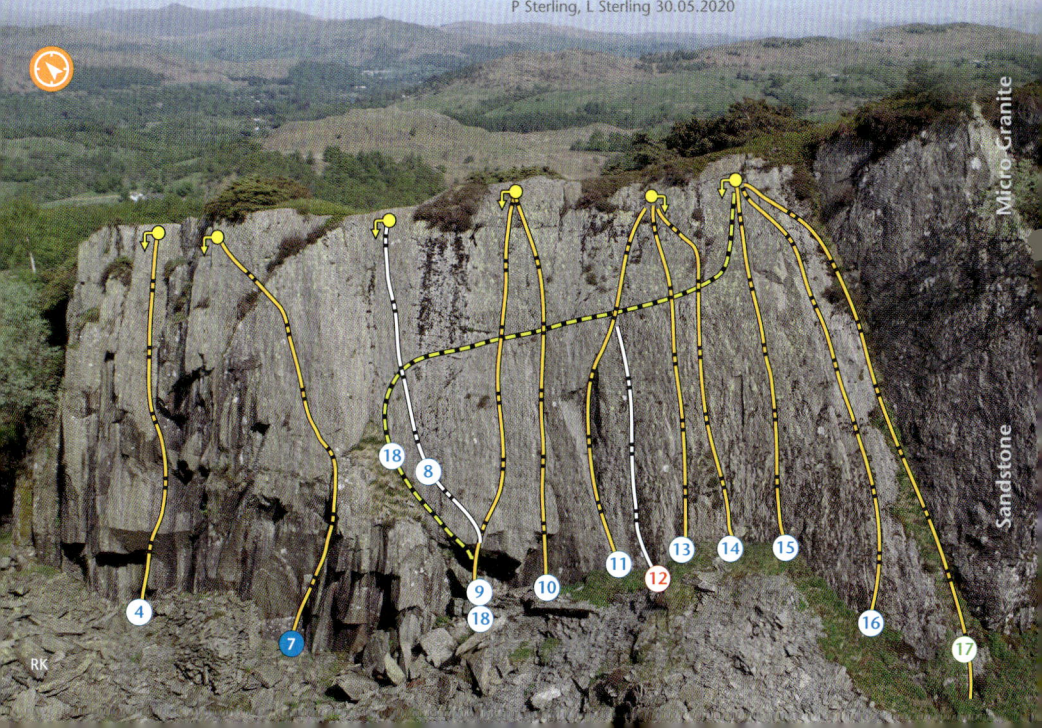

19 Viral Visions 15m F6a+ ★
An interesting line up the left side of the slab taking a faint groove and rib.
R Illingworth, E McKenna Parker 20.05.2020

20 Corona Nightmare 15m F6a+ ★
A hard start leads to a faint crackline.
R Illingworth, E McKenna Parker 20.05.2020

21 Lucid Dreams 16m F6b ★★
A great route following discontinuous grooves.
G Campion, A Campion 29.07.2018

There is scope to the right. A route could be made starting at the grass ledge, well to the right of the overhung base, making an ascending traverse leftwards.

22 Kryten Corner 17m F6b ★
At the top (south) end of the quarry there is a prominent pillar containing a steep clean-cut corner. Climb the corner with increasing difficulty. The route suffers from wash-out from the soil above - so may need a clean.
P King, S King 28.03.1991

23 Arnold Rimmer 17m E3 6a ⚠
Climb *Kryten Corner* for 8m then head up rightwards and up the rib.
P King, S King 14.04.1991

24 Lister 16m E3 5b ⚠
Poor protection. The broken wall opposite the slab of *Greasing My Teapot* has a series of hanging slabs. Start below and left of a large tree growing on a ledge at 10m. Climb diagonally left up a gangway and step left below a cracked nose to reach the slab.
P King, S King 16.04.1991

25 Lockdown Project 10m F6a+
The arête on the left of the open corner of *Contagion*.

26 Contagion Project 10m F6b
Opposite *Belly Button Slab* is a fine, clean open corner reached by scrambling up from the left.

27 Nirbhaya Project 18m F6b+
Opposite *Hang Like a Hound* a curving corner rises the full height of the quarry. Just right is a fine steep wall. Hard moves gain the wall.

As one goes underneath the bridged block, a fine narrow wall opposite, just right of *Nirbhaya*, would seem to merit attention.

Middle Quarry | **Runestone Quarry** | 179

CATHEDRAL QUARRY
OS Grid Ref: NY 313 028
Altitude: 150m

I Got Horribly Drunk F6c+ (page 182) Caroline Ciavaldini — David Simmonite

CATHEDRAL QUARRY

An impressive hole in the ground! Home to some spectacular climbing in a surprisingly sunny location that also benefits from being sheltered from the wind (a feature local midges can often use to great effect).

The quarry can be heavily used by groups.

Approach: The quarry is near to the ford that crosses the River Brathay between Little Langdale and Tilberthwaite. The ford can be reached from the A593 along a minor road signed High Park 1/2km south of the Little Langdale turn. Take the right fork on the minor road and go through two farmyards, the tack is unmetalled beyond here. Dropping near to the river there is limited parking, no mini-buses. Alternatively, thinking ahead to great post-climbing refreshment, find parking in Little Langdale and walk down the lane 100m west of the Three Shires Hotel to the ford. There is no parking down this lane and the ford is more suitable for hovercraft than cars. From the ford, 100m west is a steep path up a spoil heap. A tunnel leads from here in to the 'Cathedral' cavern. The climbs are located in the open part of the quarry visible through the 'window'; most easily gained by a scramble out of the cavern, beyond the column.

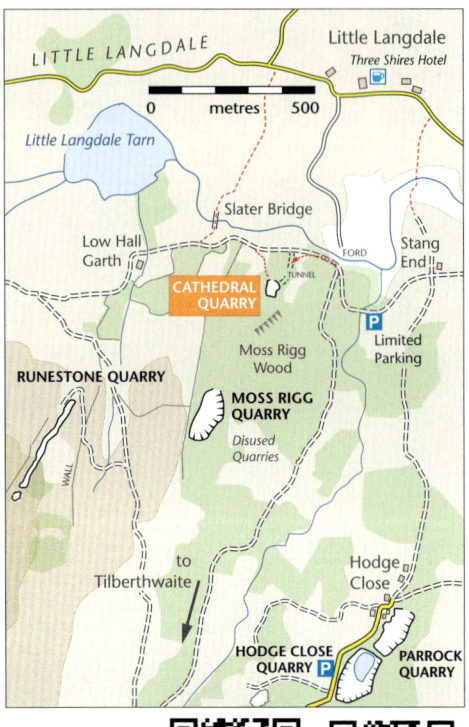

GPS 54.416726 -3.055767

RAD Cathedral

① **Caveman** 22m F8b+

The overhanging wall left of *Orifice Fish*. This wall is currently very unstable and the route should be avoided. For the record, the route climbs up the overlaps to crimps on the headwall. The final move reputedly uses a drilled pocket that is: (i) unreachable for the short (ii) the same diameter as Dave's middle finger and (iii) almost impossible to use.
D Birkett 30.05.1994

② **I Got Horribly Drunk** 10m F6c+

A rum little problem starting 4m left of the cave mouth at a small protruding toe of rock. Climb into an open groove (cam in shothole) to reach the first bolt in the bulge. Follow the rising rampline rightwards.
Photo page 181.
A Hyslop 7.08.1989

It is possible to link *I Got Horribly Drunk* and the top groove of *Orifice Fish*.

③ **Orifice Fish** 40m E4 5c ★★

Not to be missed - the unique V-chimney above and left of the cave! Start at a protruding arête just right of the cave.

1 23m 5b Climb the arête to the steeper rock at 9m (bolt). Move left and swing round a bulge to enter a smooth grooveline (bolt). Climb the prominent crack on the left until a standing position can be attained on the short arête to its left. A descending traverse left, across the polished slab above the lip of the cave, leads to a bolt belay in the groove.

2 17m 5c Climb left around the bulges to enter the holdless bottomless and merciless V-chimney. Sustained back and foot floundering leads precariously to an awkward exit up the right-hand groove.
Photo page 190.
K Stephens, P Morris 12.06.1988

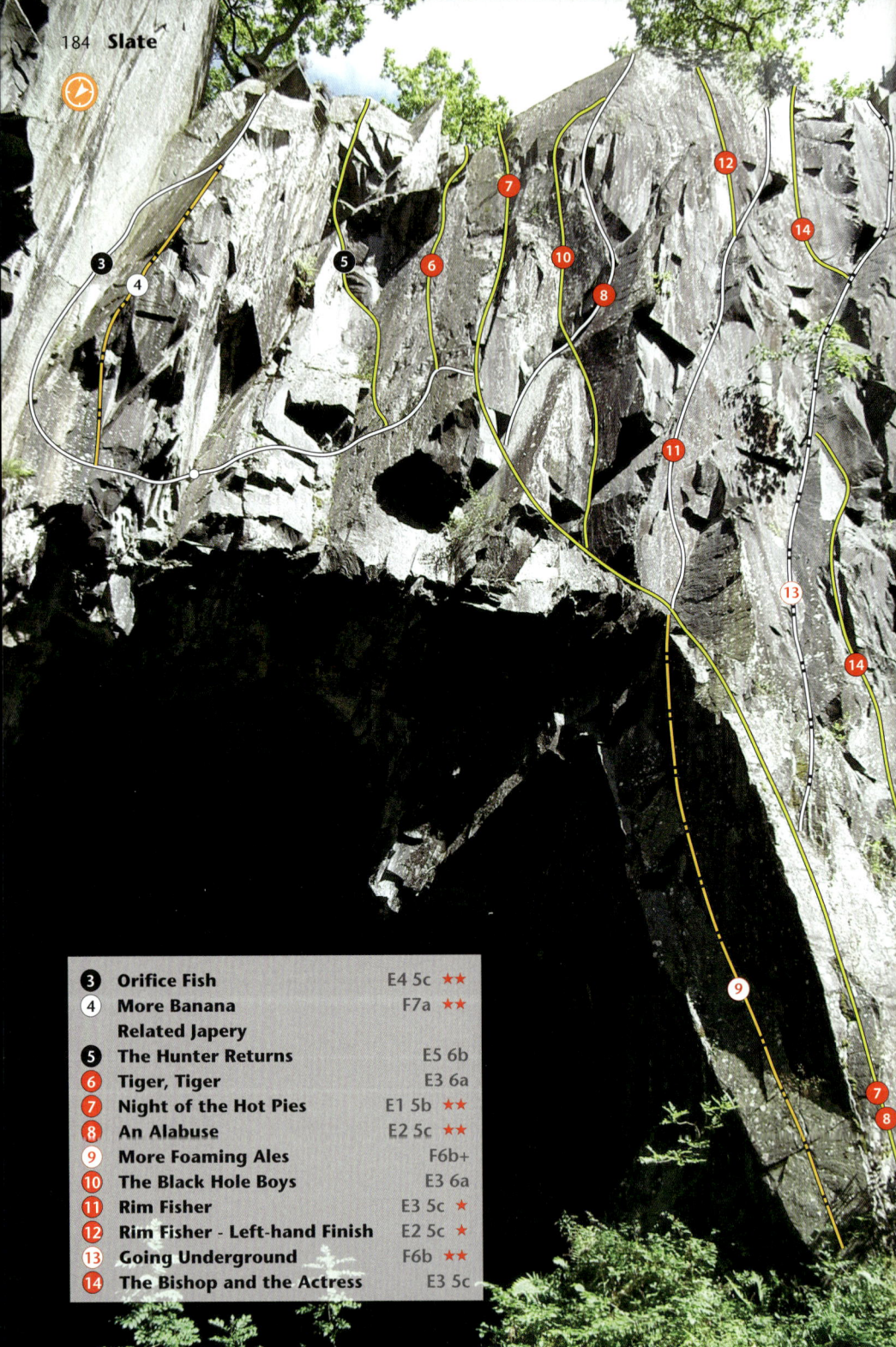

③	Orifice Fish	E4 5c ★★
④	More Banana Related Japery	F7a ★★
⑤	The Hunter Returns	E5 6b
⑥	Tiger, Tiger	E3 6a
⑦	Night of the Hot Pies	E1 5b ★★
⑧	An Alabuse	E2 5c ★★
⑨	More Foaming Ales	F6b+
⑩	The Black Hole Boys	E3 6a
⑪	Rim Fisher	E3 5c ★
⑫	Rim Fisher - Left-hand Finish	E2 5c ★
⑬	Going Underground	F6b ★★
⑭	The Bishop and the Actress	E3 5c

Going Underground F6b (page 187) Justin Shiels — 📷 David Simmonite

Cathedral Quarry | 187

④ **More Banana** 32m F7a ★★
Related Japery
The soaring arête provides an incredibly exposed technical challenge above the yawning chasm! Step left from the *Orifice Fish* belay and climb the arête to a good finger slot. Continue over the bulge with difficulty where thin climbing leads to a finale in the final groove of *Orifice Fish*.
A Hyslop, I Williamson 15.06.1989

⑤ **The Hunter Returns** 35m E5 6b
Tackles the overhangs just left of the upper section of the hanging slab. Follow *Orifice Fish* to the straight crack of *Night of the Hot Pies* then traverse across the slab to reach the scooped corner on its left-hand side. Follow this (2 bolts and peg on left) then pull directly through the overhangs with difficulty to finish.
D Bates 29.01.1989

⑥ **Tiger, Tiger** 34m E3 6a
An eliminate line up the centre of the hanging slab. Follow *The Hunter Returns* to the slab then climb this directly up its centre. Finish up the short hanging groove on the left.
D Bates, J Cooper 29.01.1989

TOP ⑦ **Night of the Hot Pies** 30m E1 5b ★★★
An excellent route with wild exposure to reach the crackline on the right of the hanging slab. Climb the arête to steeper rock (bolt). Move left and swing airily round a bulge to enter a smooth grooveline (bolt). Climb the prominent crack on the left directly slab to the top (wires).
R Brookes, M Dale 3.07.1987

⑧ **An Alabuse** 32m E2 5c ★★
A superb route. Follow *Night of the Hot Pies* to the smooth groove then continue rightwards to a prominent hanging flake (bolt). Layback around this to stand on a good hold on the rib. Continue directly, passing a spike, to finish delicately up the top slab (bolt).
R Brookes, S Alden, N Toledo, A Warrington 28.07.1987

⑨ **More Foaming Ales** 10m F6b+
A variation start for any of the previous six routes. Climb a shallow groove on the left side of the arête then go left to reach some undercuts on the very lip of the cave (bolt). A sharp pull directly over the lip leads into the foot of the smooth grooveline of *Night of the Hot Pies*.
J Topping, J Goodenough, A Hyslop 12.12.1989

⑩ **The Black Hole Boys** 30m E3 6a
A direct and fairly bold eliminate. Climb the lower arête to the steeper rock, step left and climb a short square groove above (bolt) to the hanging flake on *An Alabuse*. Pull up leftwards and enter an awkward shallow groove and climb this (RP 3) until the rib out right can be reached; finish up this.
R Brookes, N Collier 23.09.1989

⑪ **Rim Fisher** 33m E3 5c ★
Good climbing up the narrow hanging ramp between *An Alabuse* and *Going Underground*. Climb the initial rib to the steeper rock then trend right and pull up over the bulge to good holds (bolt). A hard move right over a long thin overhang leads to a ledge below the ramp. Climb this past a spike (bolt), then move right below an overhang to enter an open groove. Follow this to the top (wires).
M Dale, T Atkinson, R Brookes 15.05.1988

⑫ **Rim Fisher - Left-hand Finish** E2 5c ★
Up the clean headwall.
A Phizacklea, A Towse, JL Holden 29.03.1997

⑬ **Going Underground** 40m F6b ★★
The original route of the quarry which follows the diagonal fault across the wall and is well worth doing. Start up *Night of the Hot Pies*. Step right and follow the rampline rightwards through some awkward bulges to enter the final groove. Climb this with difficulty.
Photo page 185.
P Clarke, R Brookes 23.08.1981

⑭ **The Bishop and the Actress** 30m E3 5c
A direct line up the wall crossing *Going Underground* with some interesting climbing past the two features which give the route its name. Start about 4m right of *Night of the Hot Pies*. Climb a short slab up easy broken rock to the foot of a sharp protruding fin - The Bishop (wires). Climb the left side of this to its top (wires), where a short groove leads leftwards to a sapling on *Going Underground*. Climb awkwardly into the niche above, then out right to a good spike, below and right of a clean open corner - The Actress (bolt). Stretch left and swing around on two good jugs to join *Rim Fisher*; follow this to a sapling. Finish directly, slightly right of the tree - but don't stand on the loose flake on the right!
A Phizacklea, A Rowell 22.05.1993

⑮ **Ringpiece Activist** 35m F6c+ ★
Good climbing with reasonable protection starting from a slight indentation in the wall 6m right of *Night of the Hot Pies*. Climb a slight groove to a roof at 6m (bolt), pull over this on the left and continue directly up a blocky wall (wires) to a small overhang (bolt). Pass this on the left (spike) then above, move back rightwards to a sloping ledge (bolt). From this a precarious move right leads into the final shallow groove.
R Brookes, M Dale 15.05.1988

Darklands F6b (opposite) James Pearson — 📷 David Simmonite

Cathedral Quarry

⑯ Darklands 38m F6b ★★★
A spectacular route which forces an improbable line straight through the overhangs. Start at the same point as *Ringpiece Activist*. Climb the slab to the overhang at 6m and move up a V-notch (bolt) into a scoop (Friend 1.5 in shothole). Cross the red wall on the right to reach a large bollard on a ledge at 10m. Take the slab on the left to below the large roof then pull up right into a bottomless V-groove (bolt). Step right airily (bolt) to below a second large jagged overhang; hidden pocket (bolt). Make a wild pull over the roof onto a hanging slab then follow the groove up right to a narrow slot. Climb past this and continue up a shallow groove.
Photo opposite.
M Dale, R Kirby 6.08.1988

⑰ Murder in the Cathedral 40m E4 6a
A poor route superseded by later developments. Start by a large flake perched against the rock face. Climb into a scoop then follow a line of weakness left through the small overlaps to join *Ringpiece Activist* below the roof (bolt). Continue left to join and follow *Going Underground*.
J Cooper, J Kelly 11.06.1987

⑱ The Turbulent Beast 33m E5 6b ★★
An excellent blend of strenuous, awkward and atmospheric climbing through the overhangs. Start just left of a small holly tree, directly below the steepest section of the quarry wall.
1 12m 6b Climb up (bolt) and pull over the bulge into a groove. Continue to the overhang (bolt) where strenuous moves up and left enable the groove on the left to be entered. Follow this to a bollard and belay on *Darklands*.
2 21m 6b Step right onto a ledge below a set of triple slanting grooves (Rock 7 in shothole). Climb the grooves (bolt) to blind moves rightwards onto a sloping ledge (bolt). Pull leftwards over the capping roof to a hanging niche; a bold exit rightwards leads to the finishing slabs.
D Bates, T Walkington Summer 1988

⑲ China Crisis Direct 20m F7a+ ★★
Supersedes an earlier version which moved right to join *Burly Dudes*.
6m right of *The Turbulent Beast* is a red alcove with several blocks at its foot. Start off the left-hand block. Climb steeply on good holds to the third bolt where a tricky traverse left gains a ledge. Pull into a recess above then head right up the hanging flake. Lower-off on ledge above.
23.06.1989 D Bates / Direct - K Phizacklea 1996

⑳ Burly Dudes 22m F7b ★★
Another strenuous offering taking an impressive line through the bulges left of the cave below the huge smooth wall. Start below the large overhanging grooveline 5m left of the tunnel. Climb just right of a small grey niche to reach undercuts (bolt). Swing right and up (2 bolts) to a crucial shothole below the curving groove. Traverse left using a high foothold to reach a rest ledge below a roof and a hanging flake (bolt). Swing up right and back left above the overhang to enter a shallow groove. Climb this (Rock 8) then step right past a tree (bolt belay).
A Hyslop, I Williamson 7.06.1989

㉑ Diet of Worms E6 6b
A desperate direct on *Burly Dudes*. From the first bolt, powerful moves up and left lead to a red hanging groove. Climb this directly (bolt) to reach the resting ledge on *Burly Dudes*.
D Bates 24.06.1989

㉒ I Got Horribly Sober 40m F8b ★★★
The undercut wall leads to the blank groove right of *Burly Dudes* joining *Basilica* high up.
D Birkett 1.01.2001

㉓ Cold Turkey 10m E4 6b ★
The excellent thin hanging slab left of the large smooth wall. Start on a small ledge half-way down the left edge of the slab, belay on bolts and the abseil rope. Very Exposed! Reach right and clip a bolt then step down and traverse delicately right across the slab to its centre (bolt). Climb the centre of the tapering slab directly to the top (2 pegs).
D Bates, T Walkington 3.12.1988

㉔ Hot Tuna 13m E2 6a
Start from hanging belays, reached by abseiling from the top of the quarry. A deceptively awkward route up the shallow leaning groove forming the intersection of the *Cold Turkey* slab and *Basilica* wall.
R Brookes, P Morris 07.1988

㊁ 25 Basilica 45m F7a ★★★
A brilliant route which traverses above the cave mouth to finish up the notorious line of chipped holds in the centre of the smooth wall. The climbing is fingery and sustained; the positions are excellent. Start below a smooth clean wall at the right-hand arête of the huge cave mouth. Climb the steep arête until a line of shotholes on the right wall lead to a ledge and an old abseil point. Pull up to a bulge where fingery climbing (often damp) leads to a good handrail. From here, traverse left into the centre of the wall and make a very hard move to gain the first chipped hold. Follow the shallow groove above to good ledges where sustained climbing on widely-spaced pockets leads directly to the top.
R Matheson, D Donnini, K Phizacklea 15.04.1993

26 Barbi Junior 10m F6c
Arête to the right of the cave mouth 4 bolts to pigs-tail lower-off. This is the first section of *Basilica*.

To the right, a path winds its way to the top of the quarry.

27 No Face for Dwarfs 13m F7a+ ★
Start in a grey recess on the left, 10m below the top. A worthwhile diversion taking the diagonal line up a very thin ramp.
T W Birkett, J Adams 28.05.1992

28 The Black Beast Returns, 70m E4 6b ★
  Bottom Line Creeping with the
  Crypt Trip Boys
A left to right girdle of the steep section of the quarry. Abseil down the polished slab above the Cathedral window to the belay on *More Banana Related Japery*.
1 32m 5c Traverse right above the lip of the cave and up to the rib by the crack of *Night of the Hot Pies*. Climb down this, reversing the smooth groove and traverse right into *Going Underground*. Step right then climb upwards 5m to gain a smooth slab; cross this to the large bollard belay on *The Turbulent Beast*.
2 20m 6a Follow pitch 2 of *The Turbulent Beast* to the first bolt. Make hard moves round right (bolt) to gain a ramp which leads down to the crack on *China Crisis*. Climb up and rightwards, past a tree, (bolt belay).
3 18m 6b Step down and right onto the hanging slab (bolt) and climb the slab to a horizontal break. Traverse right to the groove of *Hot Tuna* which is followed to the top.
D Bates, J Cooper, J Kelly 09.1988

Orifice Fish E4 5c (page 182) Rory Tunnah
TUNNAH COL.

Cathedral Quarry | 191

19	China Crisis Direct	F7a+ ★★	24	Hot Tuna	E2 6a
20	Burly Dudes	F7b ★★	25	Basilica	F7a ★★★
21	Diet of Worms	E6 6b	26	Barbi Junior	F6c
22	I Got Horribly Sober	F8b ★★★	27	No Face for Dwarfs	F7a+ ★
23	Cold Turkey	E4 6b ★			

COMMON WOOD QUARRY

OS Grid Ref: NY 203 947
Altitude: 150m

The main south-facing wall offers steep climbs up to 20m in height. Down to the right is a shorter west-facing slab offering grooves and cracks.

Approach: Park at a layby on the west side of the road, just north of Low Wood House. Walk south to a rough cobbled track that zig-zags up to the right through woodland. Pass through two gates; the quarry lies to the north, just above the final spoil heap.

Access: The quarry is on CROW access land with no restrictions on climbing. The situation regarding the bolts is unclear.

Caution: The quarry was formed by the collapse of a huge underground chamber which has left deep hidden clefts and tottering blocks. Special care should be taken with a gaping hole beneath the right side of the main wall which drops about 15m into a watery black abyss. Many of the bolts are mild steel and are rusting; these date from 1998. However, the newer staples are stainless steel. Many landings are dangerous so a clipstick is essential to protect the starts of some of the routes. There are no fixed anchors for lowering off. Re-bolting is in the **Cumbria Bolt Fund** pipeline.

Descent: On foot is possible through shrubs and brambles but do take care; and secateurs.

There is an abseil/belay stake belay above the main wall by a grass mound and a large block. Many of the finishes require fighting through heather to top out.

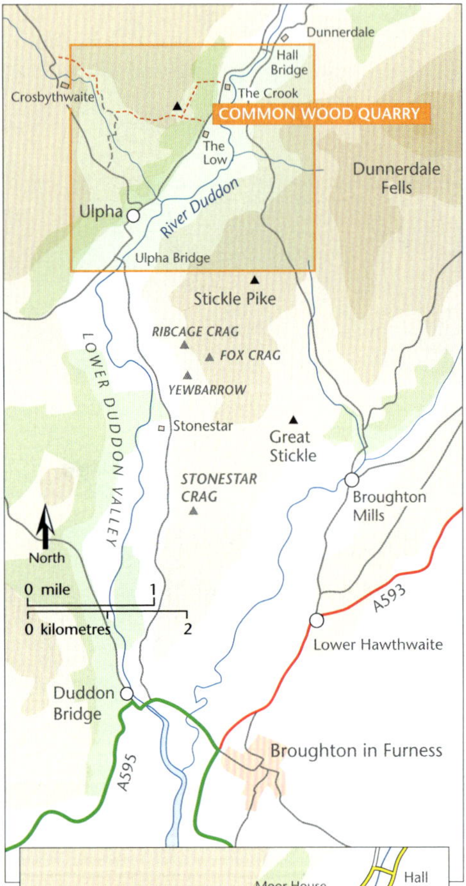

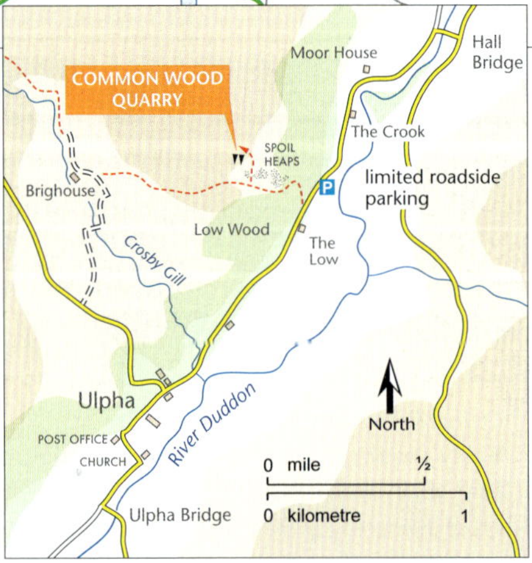

GPS 54.341054 -3.221439

Common Wood Quarry

1 Publish And Be Damned 12m F6a+
Step onto a ledge and make a couple of long reaches up to gain a short black sandwiched slab. Up this breaking out right on dubious flakes to finish as for The Provocateur.
J Daly, D Geere 23.05.1998

2 The Provocateur 12m F6c+
Make a hard step off the ground. Sustained climbing then leads diagonally up right to beneath a flaky overhang. Surmount this to gain a flake and short easy rib to finish.
J Daly, D Geere 9.05.1998

3
An unknown line of staples.

4 Hound Dog 9m F5+ ★★
A fine left-facing slab.
Photo page 195.
J Daly, D Geere 15.02.1998

Round the corner to the right is an impressive overhanging wall with a black corner/groove to its right. The next route starts beneath the bottom left corner of the overhanging wall. It has also been climbed via a direct start.

5 Meltdown 18m F6c
Pull onto the overhanging wall and climb to a thin diagonal crack on the left to gain the central ledge. Above the ledge, a continuation crack and small overlap provide sustained climbing to the top.
J Daly, D Geere 16.05.1998

6 Cold Fusion 18m F6c
A diagonal route across the wall. Clip the first bolt to the right then climb the curving weakness up left. Gain a standing position on the ledge above then traverse left onto the slab and finish up its right edge.
J Daly 31.05.1998

7 Boob Tube 17m F6c+ ★
An excellent climb up the black corner/groove. Delicate, strenuous and always precarious. Pull onto a sloping ledge in the base of the groove then climb the corner/groove in its entirety.
J Daly, D Geere 16.05.1998

8 Fall From Grace 17m F6b ★
Step across the void and climb rightwards following a line of razor sharp fins to a steep finish onto a ledge 2m below the top.
J Daly, D Geere, JJ Geere 10.04.1998

9 The Tormentor 16m F6c
Pull rightwards onto a small sloping ledge where an awkward sequence gains a ledge beneath a V-groove. Up the V-groove passing an overlap to finish.
J Daly, D Geere 16.05.1998

10 Gravity Blade 17m F7a+ ★★
K Phizaclea, I Cooksey 05.2020

11 Black Mamba 19m F6a ⚠
A huge block that formed an overhang and the finishing crack has fallen from the top of this route. In the centre of the wall is an open right-facing blackish corner. Start just right of the corner and climb leftwards to a block then follow the corner and wall to the right.
J Daly, D Geere 9.03.1998

12 18m
The line of staples in the left-hand side of the impressive arête.

The next route starts at the base of the pod to the right of the arête. Bolt belay well back.

13 Wild Garlic 17m F6a
Climb the pod and continue up a flaky rampline above. Near the top pull steeply out left to finish up the left side of a hanging flake.
J Daly, D Geere 23.05.1998

194 | **Slate**

(14) **Fly By Wire**   17m   F6a+
Pull onto a wobbly block at chest height and continue to where the angle eases. Move up and step right to a ledge, then delicately climb the rolling slabs above to a teasing stretch to the finishing V-nick.
J Daly, D Geere 28.03.1998

(15) **Hell's Mouth**   17m   F6b+
Start beneath a short finger-jamming/cam crack just right of *Fly by Wire*. Step onto a tall rock spike and climb awkwardly up right to gain a short hanging groove. A dynamic move up the groove leads to a ledge on the right; continue to a roof which is climbed via a short wide crack.
J Daly, D Geere 13.04.1998

Situated 50m down and right of the main wall is **The Slab**. The central feature of this sector is the deep V-groove taken by *Brilliant Disguise*. Some 5m left of this is the V-groove of *Dead Head*.

(16) **Dead Head**   14m   HS
Make a tricky move to gain the V-groove then climb to a roof formed by a hanging flake. Step right and surmount the flake via a crack to finish.
Geere, J Daly, JJ Geere 10.04.1998

(17) **Licking The Wounds**   15m   VS 4b
Start 3m left of *Brilliant Disguise* and climb the shattered crackline to the top.
D Geere, J Daly 9.03.1998

(18) **Dead Calm**   16m   E1 5c
Takes the slabby pillar. Pull up to gain a V-groove in the rib and climb it to a small overhang (bolt). Surmount the overhang and use its right edge to smear delicately up to better finishing holds.
D Geere, J Daly, JJ Geere 10.04.1998

(19) **Brilliant Disguise**   16m   E2 5c
A good route starting at the base of the prominent V-groove. Climb the groove to a roof at 11m then swing out left to gain a good foothold at the base of a hanging V-groove above. Teeter precariously up this to the top.
D Geere, J Daly 8.03.1998

(20) **Dick Tatoes**   14m   F5+
Just right is a slab with 2 prominent cracklines and a flake leaning against its base. Up the front of the flake then climb the left-hand crack up the slab in its entirety.
J Daly, D Geere 8.03.1998

(21) **The Toulouse Sausage**   14m   F5
Pull onto the flake and layback up the wider right hand crack to a finish over blocks at the top.
J Daly, D Geere 9.03.1998

Hound Dog F5+ (page 193) Peter Sterling 📷 Keith Sanders

THRANG QUARRY

OS Grid Ref: NY 318 055
Altitude: 160m

An unmistakeable overhanging amphitheatre at the left end of the quarry workings. It provides sport routes on overhanging slate.

Approach: From Chapel Stile walk up the short road leftwards beneath the church and follow the track beyond.

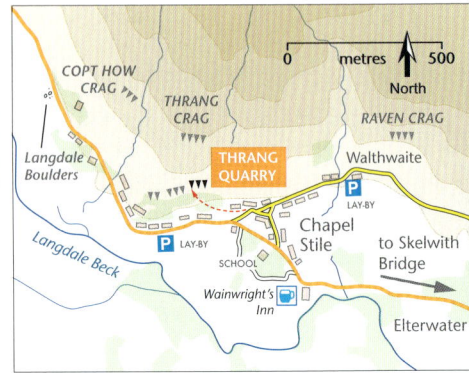

① **Left-Hand Line**   9m   F6c   ★
Warm up on this with a high crux.

② **Hello Helen**   10m   F7b+   ★★
A good looking line up the main corner via an initial hanging slab. From a spike of doubtful character a hard sequence right gains the slab. Cross to the corner with the crux at the final bolt.
D Birkett V McLelland 07.1990

③ **Keep On Keeping On**   9m   F8a+   ★★
Straightens out *Scared Rabbit* to take the back wall direct. Climb two moves up *Scared Rabbit* then levitate up the middle of the wall to a jug. Titanium fingers a definite advantage.
D Birkett 06.1991

④ **Scared Rabbit**   12m   F7a+   ★★
Relatively straightforward up the groove to a line of holds leading left to the jug and lower-off. Easier said than done.
D Birkett 06.1989

⑤ **Kept Woman**   F7c+
Links *Keep on Keeping On*, moving left at the second bolt, to finish up *Hello Helen* with a gnarly match in the chipped pocket.
R Davies 08.2012

GPS 54.439165 -3.048007

Thrang Quarry | 197

DALT QUARRY
OS Grid Ref: NY 248 165
Altitude: 120m

The Seam F6a (page 202) Justin Shiels — 📷 David Simmonite

Dalt Quarry | 199

Limestone

Slate

Micro-Granite

Sandstone

Slate

DALT QUARRY

Short enjoyable lines hidden away in the trees below Castle Crag. Take a clipstick to this sheltered quarry developed in the 1990s. Apparently sound yet recent rockfall demonstrates the instability of slate!

Approach: The track south from Grange leads past Hollows Farm campsite and along the river; leaving the campsite the track deteriorates, cross the stream then branch right for 125m into the quarry.

GPS 54.547163 -3.155408

RAD Dalt Quarry

South (Dark) Side | **Dalt Quarry** | 201

South (Dark) Side

① **Dark Angel** F7b+
Gymnastic pocketed wall.
M Johnson, A Hocking 13.08.1995

② **Shadow Warrior** F7c
The pink wall; the distinct colour does not help with climbing! Technical wall to crackline.
M Johnson 7.07.1994

③ **Bat out of Hell** HVS 5a
(a.k.a Mac's Crack)
There will be no queues for this!
R McHaffie, J Bosher 21.11.1993

④ **Skegness is so Bracing** F6a+
Amazing layaway on flakes.
A Nichol, D Nichol 1990s

⑤ **Hothouse** F6b+
Left side of arête.
A Nichol, D Nichol 1990s

⑥ **Backfire** F6b
Right side of arête.
A Nichol, D Nichol 1990s

⑦ **Nameless** F5
Wall past poised block.
A Nichol, D Nichol 1990s

⑧ **Zima Junction** F6a+
Shothole may help start up corner.
A Nichol, D Nichol 1990s

⑨ **Valdez is Coming** F6b+
Arête with layaways to left.
A Nichol, D Nichol 1990s

North (Sunny) Side

⑩ Al's Slab F5+
Sustained grooveline.
A Nichol, D Nichol 1990s

⑪ Panzerfaust F6c+
Rib and slab gives a fine challenge.
A Nichol, D Nichol 1990s

⑫ Heart of Glass F6b
Awkward crackline.
A Nichol, D Nichol 1990s

⑬ Better Red than Dead F5+
The reachy wall.
A Nichol, D Nichol 1990s

⑭ Laguna Verde F5+ ★
Fine ledgey groove.
A Nichol, D Nichol 1990s

⑮ Blue Oyster Cult F6a ★
Fine cracked arête - F6b when taken direct.
Photo opposite.
A Nichol, D Nichol 1990s

⑯ Zipcode F5+
Athletic start - easier above.
A Nichol, D Nichol 1990s

⑰ Chickenhawk F5+ ★ ⚠
Interesting corner.
A Nichol, D Nichol 1990s

⑱ The Seam F6a ⚠
The corner has suffered rock fall and has been cleared of loose rock - but beware! Climb the wall left of the corner with a long reach to finish.
A Nichol, D Nichol 1990s
Photo page 198.

⑲ Dalt Loch Monster F6a ⚠
Start up the broken corner and crack on the left.
A Nichol, D Nichol 1990s

⑳ Dalt Loch Chimney F5
Broken corner and wall above.
A Nichol, D Nichol 1990s

㉑ Wounded Knee F5
V-groove and wall.
A Nichol, D Nichol 1990s

㉒ Ian's Day Off HVS 5a
V-Groove
M Johnson, A Hocking 13.08.1995

㉓ Bury my Heart F3
Pleasant corner.
A Nichol, D Nichol 1990s

㉔ Legless in Gaza F6c ★
Long way to the first bolt - then rattle up the arête
A Nichol, D Nichol 1990s

㉕ Baywatch F6b
Desperate corner.
A Nichol, D Nichol 1990s

㉖ Little Sydney F5
Pleasant wall.
A Nichol, D Nichol 1990s

North (Sunny) Side | **Dalt Quarry** | 203

Blue Oyster Cult **F6a** (opposite) Michael Kenyon — 📷 Ron Kenyon

MICRO-GRANITE

Arc-de-Triomphe F6a+ (page 230) Caroline Steel — David Simmonite

HISTORICAL

Threlkeld quarry was opened in 1862 by George Boulton as a convenient source of stone to provide ballast for the Cockermouth-Keswick-Penrith railway line. Granite from the quarry was also used to provide masonry for the 135 bridges erected during the construction of the railway.

The quarry at this time was a private concern made viable by its proximity to the railway which allowed the stone to be transported easily. The stone was used by Manchester Corporation Waterworks for their Thirlmere scheme including the dam; for ballast for the Crewe - Carlisle railway; for roadstone, kerbing; and for facing buildings with dressed stone. Vast numbers of "setts" - small cube-shaped cut blocks for paving city roads - were also made by highly skilled workers who served a long apprenticeship. These skills were very different to those of the local slate quarrymen. In 1900, the Threlkeld Granite Company was formed and this company built the high quality terraced houses on the approach to the main Threlkeld Quarry to attract skilled quarrymen from the Midlands.

As demand for granite grew, the narrow gauge railway operating in the main quarry was extended south, first to Middle "Spion Kop" Quarry and then further to Bramcrag Quarry. Rock from these quarries was taken to the main quarry for processing in the crushing plant. From the main quarry, the rock was transported to the mainline in Threlkeld down a self-acting incline using gravity to allow the laden wagons to pull empty wagons back up into the quarry.

All of the quarries closed in 1937 as the company took over Embleton Quarry. New plant had been installed here in 1932 which made the rock much easier to work. Much of the plant at Threlkeld was antiquated and inefficient. As the sill at Embleton was worked out, the Main Quarry at Threlkeld was reopened in 1949. During the subsequent modernisation the narrow gauge railway line was removed.

Bramcrag was reopened in 1955 with a heading blast. A tunnel was driven into the face and branched off into a T-shape. This was then packed with explosives. A new explosive mixture was being used - ammonium nitrate and red diesel.

Photo from the 1920s showing the narrow gauge railway which was used to transport stone from the quarry to the crushing plant at the main quarry in Threlkeld. The line was removed in the 1940s. The area behind the train is now the **Bramcrag Wall** sector.

The crushing plant in the main quarry at Threlkeld. Rock from Bramcrag Quarry was brought here by rail.

The gases released had a slow expansion rate but the effect was ultimately dramatic. Rock landed on the St John's road and in the fields beyond. The rock was now used for road and railway ballast (Kingmoor marshalling yard in Carlisle). The micro-granite in Bramcrag Quarry is slightly more brittle than that in the other quarries and was particularly useful in the production of "setts". The rock from Bramcrag Quarry, unlike other local granites, would not take a polish and retained its rough texture after heavy use. This bodes well for the future of climbing in the quarry.

Around 70 men were employed in Bramcrag Quarry at this time using road wagons with a cut down body. The company invested in Euclid dumper trucks bought second hand having been previously used for open cast mining in the Second World War. Euclids were from America and named after the town where they were built.

Bramcrag Quarry was worked until 1967 though by then, cleaner rock was available in the main quarry. The final nail was supplied by a quarry inspector who shut down the quarry as access to quality rock was becoming too dangerous. The quarry stood neglected, though still owned by the mining company.

In 1982, the Main Quarry finally closed. In 1986, Ian Hartland, whose land backed onto Middle Quarry, approached the company and purchased it. Subsequently he bought Bramcrag Quarry to install a sawmill. This is the building in Top Sink below **Charcoal Burner's Buttress**. Later still, he bought Main Quarry and began ongoing restoration work which includes the development of the museum now popular as a tourist attraction.

Ian Hartland
Owner of **Bramcrag Quarry**

This photo is looking north across the main quarry at Threlkeld. Rock from Bramcrag Quarry was brought here for processing.

This photo dating from the 1950s shows rock being loaded by two Ruston Bucyrus excavators into Euclid dumper trucks which transported 14 ton load of granite to the crushing plant at Threlkeld Quarry. The lower excavator is in Top Sink - where the current buildings (formerly used by charcoal burners) are located. The upper excavator is sitting below what is now referred to as **The Dark Side**.

BRAMCRAG QUARRY

OS Grid Ref: NY 320 220
Altitude: 200m

Blank on the Map F6c (page 212) Cam Fowler — 📷 David Simmonite

Micro-Granite

BRAMCRAG QUARRY

A high-quality sport venue with fun climbing, clean sticky rock and a superb outlook; the quarry attracts many climbers. However, like all old quarries, there are areas of unstable rock and the quarry needs to be treated with respect.

In particular, the quarry is not suitable for groups, instruction and, particularly, children.

Danger: Despite the removal of huge amounts of loose rock, rockfall frequently occurs almost anywhere, even below seemingly safer sectors. Do not stand under climbers and consider wearing a helmet. In addition, some areas are susceptible to more substantial rockfall. There have been three such rockfalls recently and these are indicated on the relevant photodiagrams. Areas believed to be particularly affected are mentioned in the text.

Approach: The quarry is privately owned. Climbers are on good terms with both the landowner and the user of the quarry. In the past selfish parking has created issues. Park sensibly where shown and follow the approach indicated. Please do not park on the road or block the access track into the quarry. If you do not observe these simple courtesies you risk losing access to this venue.

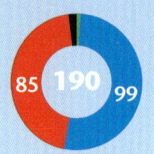

85 190 99

 60m rope

 12 quick draws

- Bramcrag Wall — Page 212
- The Dark Side — Page 216
- The Charcoal Burner's Buttress — Page 218
- Grand Wall — Page 222
- Sunburst Slab — Page 224
- Promontory Buttress — Page 228
- Main Wall — Page 229

Bramcrag Quarry 211

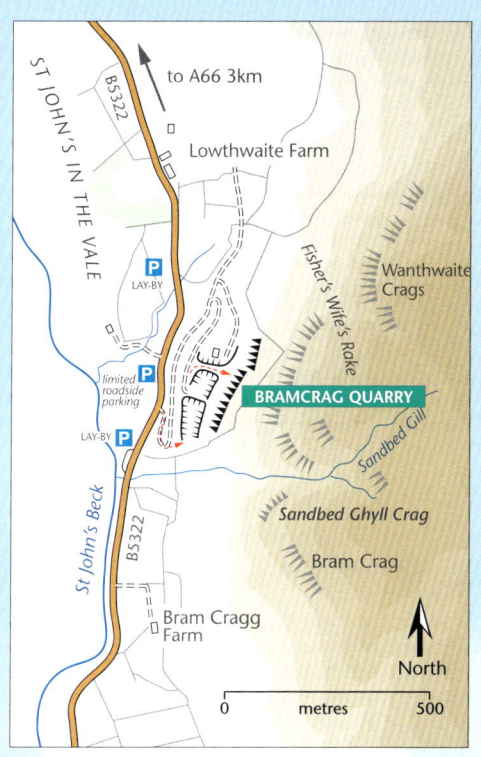
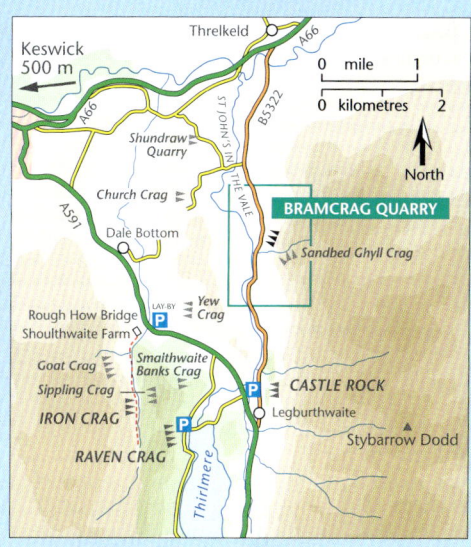

GPS 54.586310 -3.057183

RAD Bramcrag Quarry

Micro-Granite

Bramcrag Wall

Facing south, this wall gets all the sun going and dries quickly. On the left the rock is slick, lacking the excellent friction found elsewhere. To the right are some excellent wall climbs in the mid grades. However, on the routes *Shot in the Dark* to *Roughneck* the brown juggy rock is subject to water absorption and the rock becomes brittle and snappy. Take care after rain.

Approach: Cross the access ridge then head left along a path, above the buildings, to the base of the wall. Following the track to the top bend then continuing rightwards along a faint path leads to the base of the wall.

① **Michelangelo** 16m F6c ★
The rock on the traverse is slick with poor friction especially on warm days - save it for a cool evening. Start beneath the obvious rising crack on the left. Climb the short wall to gain a huge flake. Climb the flake on its right to gain the crack above. Difficult, but never desperate, moves rightwards across the crack lead to a niche.
M Norbury 12.06.2010

② **Middle Earth** 16m F7b
A direct route up the shield. From the first bolt, step right and attack the shield to a stopper move - continue to a niche.
M Norbury 12.06.2010

③ **Bramcrag Wall** 19m F6c+ ★★
Technical, sustained and quick-drying. Start at the large flake leaning against the centre of the wall. Great moves up the steep slab lead to a rest at a large block. Climb over this and the steeper wall above to the niche of *Michelangelo*. Step back right and make thin moves (crux) to the lower-off.
M De Vaal 14.06.2010

④ **Wai Lord** 19m F7b+
Start at the ramp right of *Bramcrag Wall* and follow the obvious curving line with desperate moves to reach the lower-off.
M Greenbank 08.2010

⑤ **Combi** 12m F5b
No new climbing but pleasant enough. Climb *Wai Lord* to the 4th bolt then move right and climb a short groove to the lower-off below the corner.
W Young, C Downer 20.09.2016

⑥ **Yazidi** 10m F6a+
Climb the black slab and short groove.
W Young, C Downer 20.09.2016

⑦ **The Hurt Locker** 20m F6c ★★★
A brilliant strenuous climb up the prominent arching corner. Climb the flake/crack; where it peters out make an awkward move left then climb to the corner. Continue to the jammed block, step left and climb the wall for a few metres before rejoining the corner to finish.

The first part to the lower-off below the corner gives a short pitch **10m F6a+**.
C Downer, W Young 4.10.2016

⑧ **Northern Soul** 20m F6b+ ★★★
Climb the crack and its continuation to slabby rock leading to an overlap left of the edge. Move round the edge then immediately right into a groove then finish up the line of flakes.
The bottom section traversing left to the lower-off in the corner gives a short pitch **8m F6a+**.
C Downer, W Young 30.04.2019

The next three routes start above a rock step; the ground-level belay bolts should be used.

⑨ **Blank on the Map** 20m F6c ★★
Another brilliant pitch - strenuous initial moves lead to more delicate steep slab climbing. Start immediately above a rock step which is below the large protruding flake. Belay bolt just to the right. Climb up to the flake then layback furiously to reach the finishing moves up and right.
Photo page 209.
D Ward, C Downer 13.06.2018

⑩ **Looper** 15m F6b+ ★
From the leftmost of the two belay bolts, climb up for 2m then make delicate moves right to gain the flake on the right. Junction with *Bolt From The Blue*. Climb up the flake for 3m then move right onto the wall. Up this to better holds at the bulge. Over this then move rightwards to the lower-off.
C Downer, W Young 15.03.2017

⑪ **Bolt from the Blue** 20m F6b ★★
The line of left-leaning flakes. Belay bolt at the foot of the route. Climb the flakes to their top and step left to finish up the groove.
W Young, C Downer, J Adams 27.08.2016

⑫ **Shot in the Dark** 20m F6b ★★
Steep enjoyable climbing. Start at a small overlap split by a crack. Climb the crack then the wall above by the discontinuous cracks.
Photo page 214.
C Downer, D Sperry, W Young, J Fotheringham 16.07.2016

Micro-Granite

13 Marginal Gains 20m F6b ★★
Delightful climbing taking an elegant line. Bridge the chimney for 2m then step onto the wall. Clip the first bolt then move left up the wall into a slabby scoop. Move right under the overhang then up to a flake/crack. From its top step left and continue to the lower-off.
C Downer, W Young 24.08.2016

14 Roughnecks 20m F6a+ ★
A juggy wall followed by a delicate slab. Named after the hammer used for cleaning routes. Bridge the chimney for 2m then step onto the wall. Climb the wall to a tricky move right to gain an easy-angled slab. Step immediately left then up to the lower-off.
W Young, C Downer, A Davis 20.07.2016

Shot in the Dark F6b (page 212) Peter Sterling — 📷 Bill Young

Bramcrag Wall | **Bramcrag Quarry** | 215

Bramcrag Wall - Right
- (7) The Hurt Locker — F6c ★★★
- (8) Northern Soul — F6b+ ★★★
- (9) Blank on the Map — F6c ★★
- (10) Looper — F6b+ ★
- (11) Bolt from the Blue — F6b ★★
- (12) Shot in the Dark — F6b ★★
- (13) Marginal Gains — F6b ★★
- (14) Roughnecks — F6a+ ★

216 | Micro-Granite

The Dark Side
With excellent rock this sector offers a selection of outstanding routes taking powerful lines. Originally called 'The Danger Zone' as it appeared particularly prone to rockfall though time has shown this to be no more of an issue than other sectors.

Approach: This sector is 20m right of **Bramcrag Wall** across a large triangular scree fan.

(1) The Visionary 20m F6a+ ★
Start near the top of the scree fan below a short groove at 4m. Climb the short groove and easy rocks to below a black slab. Climb this then over an overlap.
C Downer, D Sperry, W Young 27.03.2017

(2) The Flying Dutchman 25m F6b+ ★★
A fine route with intricate climbing weaving through the upper section. Start below a prominent quartz vein high on the route. Climb the slabby rib then up the wall to a diagonal crack beneath an overlap. On the right are three bolts close together. Step onto the ramp below the bolts and move up to its end. Above is a flake which is used to gain the groove on the left. Up this for a few metres then pull into the easy-angled groove on the left. From its right-hand edge climb the wall then reach left to the lower-off.
C Downer, W Young 5.04.2017

(3) This Charming Man 15m F6a+
This eponymous route starts at an easy-angled left-leaning slab. Climb the slab to its top at a diagonal crack. Move right and climb the awkward black wall to a finish up delicate slabs.
C Downer, W Young, RO Graham 11.10.2015

④ **The Darkness Beckons** 25m F6b ★★
Steady climbing leads to a difficult finish. Beware of rope drag. Start at the right side of the slabs. Climb the easy-angled groove followed by a steeper groove to its top. At the third bolt (ignore the 4th bolt up and right) pull left onto the slab then trend up and left to a break in the overhang. Climb into the groove above to exit left below the bush stumps. Pull awkwardly into a leaning corner which is followed through another overlap then right a few metres to the lower-off.
C Downer, W Young 03.07.2018

⑤ **Charm Offensive** 15m F6b+ ★★
An excellent sustained pitch. Start at a short slab below a rib. Climb the left side of the rib to gain the slab then up to the short wall. Pull left into a sloping groove then continue up the steeper groove and short wall to reach an easy slab.
C Downer, W Young, RO Graham 11.10.2015

⑥ **Vanished Times** 15m F6b ★
Climb the obvious steep corner then delicate moves rightwards lead to the lower-off.
C Fowler, C Downer, L Jones 27.05.2012

⑦ **Antiques Roadshow** 25m F6a ★
Steep juggy climbing. Start at a steep slab below a cracked wall. Climb the slab leftwards to a ledge. Follow the cracked juggy wall for 5m, move left onto an easy-angled ramp and finish steeply up the black wall.
Photo this page.
W Young, C Downer, G Lee 8.10.2015

⑧ **Cool Hand Luke** 25m F6b+ ★★
The conspicuous diagonal crack gives an excellent route. Two bolts close together mark the crux.
L Jones, C Downer, D Sperry 19.05.2012

⑨ **Helter Skelter** 25m F6b+ ★★
Great technical climbing - a stunning pitch. Climb the short groove then move right under the overhang onto the left wall of a large open groove. Make difficult moves up and right into the back of the groove and climb it to its top. Using a diagonal crack, pull over the small overlap then left into a niche. Exit this with difficulty up right then move left and up.
C Downer, W Young 21.07.2018

⑩ **Dancing in the Danger Zone!** 35m F6b+ ★★★
Simply brilliant. A very sustained pitch which sweeps elegantly across the buttress. Pull onto the slab and traverse left and then up to a good handhold. Pull out left onto the wall and then, with difficulty, gain the groove. Traverse left to the arête. Difficult moves round the arête lead into a groove. Follow the fine slab diagonally left, then back right into a fine groove.
C Downer, L Jones, D Sperry 16.05.2012

Antiques Roadshow F6a (opposite) Al Davis — Ron Kenyon

Micro-Granite

The Charcoal Burner's Buttress

The routes weave intricate lines through capped grooves. To keep grades consistent lines often cross and careful study of the photo-diagrams will aid route finding.

Approach: Cross the access ridge then head slightly leftwards across boulders to a scree slope that runs up rightwards under the buttress.

The Charcoal Burners worked in the sheds below this sector.

① **Best Western**   25m   F6a+   ★
Satisfying juggy climbing. Starts at the left side of the buttress at a large embedded block. It is probably better for the second to retrieve the gear. Climb the overhanging crack to a good hold then pull left into the corner. Step right and follow the steep arête to a slab. Climb the slab direct and the leftward-slanting ramp above.
C Downer 5.08.2014

② **Ring of Fire**   52   F6c+
A girdle of **Charcoal Burner's Buttress**. Start as for *Best Western*.

1 27m F6c+ Climb the steep rib up to the slab. Move right to stand on the top of a block; *Arcade Fire*. Pull onto the slab then traverse delicately right (*The Deviant*). Step right into a crack (*Silicone Crack*) and up to belay on the lower-off.
2 25m F6b Move rightwards past a lower-off (*The Culling*) to the edge of a slab. Cross the slab to the right-hand bolt line (*Sunbeam Talbot*).
C Downer, W Young 27.06.2015

③ **Jack the Dripper**   25m   F6b+   ★
Well named. Often wet but can be climbed in less than perfect conditions as the holds are generally good and stay dry. Climb rightwards up the wall to the apex of the overhang. Pull strenuously over this and up to a block (*Arcade Fire*). Climb the slab and shallow groove.
C Downer, W Young 29.06.2015

④ **The Deviant** 25m F6c+ ★
From the edge of the crevasse, step down and move left under the overhang. Using a block, pull over then step right to the rib and make a difficult move to reach a traverse (*Arcade Fire*). Traverse leftwards past a block and onto a slab. A thin and crimpy traverse leads horizontally right, then move up to the lower-off. Rope drag can be an issue.
C Downer, W Young, C Wornham 8.09.2014

⑤ **The Deviant Direct** 25m F7a+ ★
From the traverse climb the steep wall and continue straight up to enter a slabby groove.
C Downer, W Young, C Wornham 21.07.2016

⑥ **Arcade Fire** 25m F6a+ ★★★
Delightful delicate climbing. Climb the right-hand side of a large flake then traverse left until tricky moves lead to a large block on a ledge. Use this to gain the slab and head up and right.
C Downer, P Ross 24.07.2013

⑦ **Keep the Car Running** 27m F6a+ ★
Follow *Arcade Fire* to the block then continue traversing horizontally left for another 8m. Climb straight up the excellent slab. Best for the second to retrieve the gear.
C Downer, T Daly, S Murphy 9.08.2014

⑧ **Silicone Crack** 15m F6c
Silicone sealant was used to divert seepage away from a crucial foothold. Short and sharp. From the first bolt move up and right to a steep finger crack. Climb this to an easing in angle.
C Fowler, C Downer, C Wornham 2.09.2014

⑨ **The Culling** 20m F6c ★★
An excellent route which starts at a fine groove with 2 bolts. Climb the groove to the overhang. Move left to reach a flake and pull steeply over to a good foothold. Continue up the groove (crux), moving right avoiding the large block.
C Downer, C Fowler 28.09.2013

⑩ **The Twisted Wheel** 15m F6b ★
Climb the two short offset grooves direct to the overhang. Step right and climb the overhang then easily to the lower-off.
C Downer, W Young 13.07.2019

The Sperry Finish 10m F6b+ ★ From the lower-off climb the wall slightly left to a crack in the bulge. Awkwardly over the bulge, up the short crack then rightwards to the lower-off.
D Sperry, W Young, C Downer 13.07.2019

⑪ **Slaying the Badger** 25m F6a+ ★★
Great climbing. Starts at a short slabby corner on the right side of the slabs. Climb the short corner then pull onto a ramp until a traverse left leads to a corner. Make a long reach left to a good hold and swing round onto a ledge. Clip the bolt above; step down whence interesting moves left gain easier ground. Pull onto the flake and finish up the crack above.
Photo cover, page 225.
C Downer, C Fowler 25.08.2013

⑫ **Ripping Yarns** 25m F6a+
Starts below a short chimney/groove. Climb the groove and continue, using holds on the right, to the third bolt. Step left and finish steeply (easier than it looks).
C Downer, D Sperry 6.05.2014

TOP ⑬ **The Charcoal Burner** 25m F6b ★★★
Delightful balancy climbing - a gem of a pitch. Climb a short chimney/groove to an awkward move right onto a ledge. Follow the groove above stepping right at the bulge and continue up the arête to a tricky move left to gain a crack; follow this to the lower-off.
Photo page 221.
C Downer, D Sperry 9.06.2013

⑭ **Sunbeam Talbot** 20m F6b
An unbalanced route which is slow to dry. An easy approach rightwards up a slanting crack leads to a difficult finish.
D Sperry, C Downer 9.06.2013

⑮ **Bramcrag Corner** 20m F6a ★
Slow to dry. Climb the corner direct to the overhang. The lower-off is across to the left.
W Young, C Downer 1.09.2017

The Charcoal Burner F6b (page 219) Colin Downer — David Simmonite

Grand Wall

Brilliant steep climbing with atmospheric positions. This impressive wall gives a number of satisfying routes.

Approach: From the access ridge head up leftwards between boulders and the base of the quarry.

(16) Grand Designs 25m F6c ★

Steady climbing with a short sharp crux. Climb the corner to the second bolt then take the right wall to a ledge. Up the groove, formed by blocks, to the overhang. Make difficult moves over the overhang into a groove and up this to a short overhanging wall. Step left and pull over the bulge (2 bolts close together) then trend up right.
C Downer, W Young 27.08.2017

TOP (17) The Mission 25m F6b ★★★

A brilliant route with varied climbing. The name derives from the 8 days spent cleaning!! Climb easily via a short corner to ledges. From blocks, pull over the overhang then step left into a large hanging groove. Climb the groove to its top then step right to a good flat handhold. Stand on this then climb the wall leftwards under an arching overlap to an exit up to the lower-off.
C Downer, W Young 27.07.2017

(18) Spook 30m F6a+ ★★

Climb easily via a short corner to ledges. Follow the broken crack/groove right of the blocks for 4m then traverse left across a very large groove. From its left edge move up to below a short overhanging wall. Pull over this and up to the lower-off. It's best for the second to retrieve the gear.
C Downer, W Young 25.07.2017

(19) Spectre 22m F6b ★

Follow *Spook* to the left traverse. Climb the groove and wall above to reach a ledge and lower-off to the left.
C Downer, W Young 27.09.2017

On the next three routes it's probably easier for the second to strip the gear.

(20) The Wrecking Crew 28m F6a+ ★★

Steep juggy climbing with fine positions - an excellent route. Climb the slabby wall to ledges. From the right-hand side climb the corner to its end under an overhanging wall. Traverse left along a fault on large holds in a very exposed position. Pull onto the ledge with interest then move left and up.
C Downer, W Young 12.07.2017

(21) Heaven Can Wait 25m F5c ★★

Climb the slabby wall to ledges. From the right side of the ledge, climb the corner under the overhanging wall and continue across the slab heading rightwards to the lower-off.
W Young, C Downer 8.07.2017

(22) Heaven Sent 25m F6a

Start just right of a bush stump 2m right of *Heaven Can Wait*. Climb into the short corner and immediately traverse left along a curving ledge and up to easy ground which leads to a big slabby corner. Pull into the corner then traverse right with feet on the very edge of the slab. Moves right lead to the lower-off.
C Downer, W Young, A Inglis, M Houlding, M Lowther 25.08.2019

(23) Rebel Yell 20m F6a+

Worthwhile. The first corner is usually wet but can be can be climbed in those conditions. Climb the short corner then easily up left to the second bolt. Move up and traverse the slab rightwards to the edge of the permanently wet rock. Above is a groove; climb this to reach a slab then moves right lead to the lower-off.
W Young, C Downer, M Houlding, M Lowther 25.08.2019

Grand Wall | **Bramcrag Quarry** | 223

Micro-Granite

Micro-Granite

Sunburst Slab

This slab, with intricate short grooves on the left and long pitches to the right, is the last area of the quarry to receive the sun; perfect for those scorching Lakes summer days and balmy evenings.

⚠ **Care should be exercised when lowering off if you are using a 60m rope - tie a knot in the end!**

Approach: Head left up grass and scree when you arrive at the crag. A prominent right-to-left diagonal crack marks the start of *The Sunshine Gang*.

① **Tin Can Alley** 20m F6a
Starts at a wet corner at the top of the scree slope. Usually wet, it is well worth waiting for a dry spell. A prominent icefall forms here in winter. Climb the wet crack in the slab to gain a ledge. Pull out left onto a slab (bolt on left over a bulge). Tricky moves back right lead to easier ground. Finish by the fine groove above.
C Downer, M Armitage 13.07.2014

② **Coup-de-Grace** 20m F6b+ ★★★
Steep juggy and excellent. Follow a slabby rib to gain a large flake. Up and right is a block; use this to pull steeply up. Move left onto a slab then climb the overhanging wall/groove above.
C Downer, M Armitage, D Sperry 21.07.2014

③ **Changing Corners** 15m F6b ★★
Climb up for 3m then move along the slab on the right to a short leftward-leaning corner. Pull onto the higher slab then follow the curving corner.
C Downer, W Young 17.05.2018

④ **Turncoat** 15m F6b ★
Follow *Changing Corners* to the short leftward-leaning corner; continue rightwards up a slabby corner until just below a tree root then move left and up to finish.
C Downer, M.Armitage, M Attwood, C Wornham, W Hurford 5.06.2018

⑤ **Pangolin** 15m F6b ★★
Start at a slab just left of a shallow grooveline (*Grand Union*). Climb the slab and the corner to join *Turncoat*. Move up to just below the tree root then move left and up to the lower-off.
C Downer, M Armitage, M Attwood 5.06.2018

⑥ **Grand Union** 30m F6c ★★★
An excellent route - one of the finest in the quarry. Start at a shallow right-facing grooveline in the slab. Follow the groove to a difficult move to pass the first bolt then pull onto a ledge on the right. The corner is climbed with interest to a ledge then powerful moves lead up and rightwards to the lower-off.
L Jones, C Downer, D Sperry, 30.05.2012

⑦ **The Shooting Gallery** 30m F6a ★★★
Brilliant, crossing impressive territory at an amenable grade. Follow the left-leaning diagonal crack past the second bolt. Move up leftwards over blocks to a tree stump then follow a juggy traverse left across the impending wall, ending with a delightful balancy move. Finish by the fine groove above.
C Downer, M Armitage, C Wornham 26.05.2012

⑧ **The Sunshine Gang** 30m F6a+ ★★★
A very fine pitch: long, sustained and deservedly popular. Follow the diagonal left-leaning crack to a steepening. Pull onto a short rib then continue to a ledge. Climb the short wall then follow the fine groove.
C Downer, L Jones, C Fowler, D Sperry 26.05.2012

⑨ **Sunburst Slab** 30m F6a ★
Steady climbing with a difficult finish - especially for shorties. Climb an easy-angled rib bounding the right side of the slabs easily to a bolt. Stand on a large flake left of the bolt then climb the groove above. Follow a rising ramp with an awkward move into the wide crack which leads left.
C Downer, L Jones, D Sperry 2.06.2012

⑩ **The Woodcutter's Lullaby** 30m F6c+ ★
A good route struggling for independence. The central of 3 bolt lines from the ramp on *Sunburst Slab*. Follow the curving fault line leftwards at first then straight up just right of *The Sunshine Gang*. At the last bolt awkward moves lead left to finish.
C Downer, W Young 21.10.2019

⑪ **Stoker** 30m F6c+ ★
The right-hand bolt line from the ramp of *Sunburst Slab*. Difficult climbing leads to a small ledge. Make hard moves into the groove on the left. Up this then right to the lower-off.
L Jones, C Downer, C Fowler 5.06.2012

⑫ **Bring Me Sunshine** 20m F6a
Climb onto the grass ledge and follow the pleasant groove. The slab direct to the first bolt; **F6b**.
C Downer, W Young 30.12.2011

Sunburst Slab | **Bramcrag Quarry** | 225

Limestone

Slate

Micro-Granite

Sandstone

Slaying the Badger F6a+ (page 219) Bill Young — David Simmonite

Promontory Buttress

Fun short routes that dry quickly. The normal arrival point; this sector is the small wall, seamed by grooves, where the narrow grassy ridge meets the crag.

Approach: Cross the grass ridge to arrive at the base of this sector.

① **Yopo** 15m F5b
Step right onto the arête and move up to a ledge. Move left then an awkward move right leads into a groove.
C Downer, L Jones 7.04.2013

② **Benghazi Burner** 15m F6a+
Climb the overhanging crack then pull right onto a ledge; continue more easily up rightwards to the foot of an open groove. Pull directly into this groove which is followed to the top.
C Fowler, C Downer 1.12.2013

③ **Morley Street Mission** 15m F6b ★★
Starts left of a crack below the quartz veins. Strenuous moves lead to a ledge. Swing right round the rib with difficulty (below the second bolt) and climb the face on small holds. Finish up the groove on the left.
C Downer, L Jones, D Sperry 7.04.2013

④ **Last Dash** 15m F6b ★★
Technical varied climbing taking the corner system - an excellent route. Climb the crack then continue up the corner.
C Bainbridge, PJ Kane 7.05.1997

⑤ **Con Artist** 15m F6b+
Climb the rib to join *Last Dash* at its third bolt then traverse left across a slab to finish up the scoop above on the right.
C Fowler, C Downer 30.03.2014

⑥ **Twilight** 15m F5a
Climb the rightward-leaning groove to gain the bottom of a large recess and move diagonally left to a shothole. Climb directly up on big flaky holds.
PJ Kane, C Bainbridge 11.05.1997

Main Wall | **Bramcrag Quarry** | 229

⑦ **Hound-dog**   15m   F6a
Climb into a large recess and move up its right side to gain a niche (crux) then climb directly to the top.
PJ Kane, C Bainbridge 11.05.1997

⑧ **The Quarryman**   15m   F6a
Climb easily to the first bolt. Step right to gain the corner and climb directly to the lower-off.
PJ Kane, C Bainbridge 11.05.1997

⑨ **Luddite**   15m   F5c   ★
Steep climbing which moves through unlikely territory for the grade. Climb an open groove and crack then move right through steep rock; intimidating but on large holds. Follow these up and right in an impressive position then straight up to finish.
W Young, C Downer 1.09.2018

⑩ **Stumbling Block**   15m   F6a+   ★
Steep climbing on big holds - what more can you ask for? From a quartz streak climb directly to the overhang. Move right, via a good crack, to an easing of the angle then up left.
C Downer, W Young 4.09.2018

⑪ **The Wetherby Whaler**   15m   F6a
Named after the best chip shop in the North of England. The climb is on the wall above Promontory Buttress. Climb *The Quarryman* to a belay on the right-hand lower-off or continue in one pitch but beware of rope drag. Pull round the leaning block to gain a slab. Follow a wall and slanting crack.
C Downer, C Fowler 25.06.2014

Main Wall
High quality routes with sustained absorbing climbing. **Main Wall** is the centre piece of the quarry. The left side is quick-drying with little seepage.

⑫ **Director's Cut**   30m   F6b   ★
Start in the corner with a triangular niche at 3m containing a block. Climb up into the niche and pull out with difficulty. Continue up the groove for about 6m before moving left to a rib splitting the grooves. Climb this for 4m until a step left can be made into the left-hand groove above a bulge. Climb the groove over a further bulge to the lower-off.

The lower-off can be reached by following the rib avoiding the move left into the groove. This misses some excellent climbing and the crux.
W Young, C Downer 12.09.2018

TOP ⑬ **The Tipton Slasher**   30m   F6b+   ★★★
William Perry AKA The Tipton Slasher was a British heavyweight prize fighter of the 1850s. Start just left of blocks bounding the left side of the buttress below a slim groove in the arête. The groove leads to an overhang which is climbed into a groove. From the bolt, pull onto the rib then step round right using a quartz vein (tricky). Continue in a fine position up and right onto a large ledge. Step left onto the arête and pull onto a sloping ledge below the overlap. A bold step up leads to the lower-off.

For the full experience, the top arête can be climbed direct without resorting to holds on the right wall.
C Downer, L Jones, C Fowler 20.06.2012

⑭ **Yorkshire Ripper**   30m   F6b+   ★★
Start as for *The Tipton Slasher* and clip the first bolt. Using a dubious-looking flake, pull out rightwards and continue steeply into a recess (crux). Move up and right and pull over a bulge. From the bolt, step out right onto a large detached block and follow the groove above to the large ledge. Climb the wall between the arête and the groove (*Usain Bolt*).
C Downer, M Armitage 20.05.2014

⑮ **Usain Bolt**   30m   F6b+   ★★
This superb route climbs the impressive cleaned corner. Start in the middle of the wall until awkward moves lead into the corner. Climb up the corner with difficulty onto a ledge. Continue until a pull out left leads to a large ledge. The tricky groove on the right leads to a lower-off on the left.
C Fowler, C Downer 10.08.2012

⑯ **Middle East Crisis**   30m   F6b+   ★
The crux is height dependent. Climb the corner. From the second bolt move up and cross the right wall to the edge then over the bulge to easier ground. Continue up a short left-facing corner and then up slightly right until a pull left gains a short left-facing corner; climb to a ledge. Continue straight up heading for a groove capped by a small triangular overlap. Up the groove to the lower-off.
C Downer, J Spencer, J Rigg 15.06.2014

⑰ **Eastern Promise**   35m   F6b   ★★★
An excellent climb up this superb slab. Deservedly very popular. Climb the groove to its top then swing right using a shothole and move up to a small ledge. Continue straight up the wall (crux) to reach an easing in the angle. Climb up for about 5m then trend left below the shallow grooves to reach the headwall.
A Phizacklea, J Holden 14.04.1991

Micro-Granite

(18) **Coup d'Etat** 36m F6b+ ★★
A once serious route tamed by bolt protection. Climb the slab up to the overlap beside a doubtful block. Pull over the overlap using the block to a shothole. Climb the shallow groove to a bolt then embark on a rising traverse to the right aiming for 2 bolts close together beside the next overhang. Make a difficult pull over the overhang to good holds and finish directly up the groove to the lower-off.
A Phizacklea, J Holden 14.04.1991

Coup de Triomphe. An excellent way up the crag which is very quick-drying, **F6a+**. Follow *Coup de d'Etat* to reach the groove of *Arc de Triomphe* and continue up this to the top.

(19) **The History Boys** 30m F6b+ ★★★
Another superb route offering continually interesting climbing taking a direct line up the face. Climb easily to ledges and attain a standing position on the left end of the jammed block. Pull directly over the overhang. Climb the groove and slab to a projecting block. Move right to a bolt then pull out left to a ledge. Finish up the green-speckled groove.
C Downer, G Lee, G Proctor 8.05.2010

(20) **Desperate Dan** 30m F6b+ ★
Sustained and interesting climbing. Starts below an obvious jammed block. Re..a..ch for the base of the block (hard for shorties) and pull up and right to enter a niche. Up two shallow grooves to the overhang. Pull over with difficulty into a hanging groove. Continue more easily to join a slab and continue to a small bay and chain belay.
C Downer, M Armitage, C Wornham 18.05.2014

(21) **Arc-de-Triomphe** 25m F6a+ ★★
A brilliant pitch which sweeps elegantly across Main Wall at an amenable grade. Start at the top left of the scree slope at a large block. Climb onto the large flake and traverse left and then down into a niche. Continue traversing left using the shothole to clip the bolt on *The History Boys*. Move up until it is possible to pull out left onto a ledge (junction with *Eastern Promise*). Climb to the bolt above then finish up the groove on the right.
Photo page 205.
C Downer, C Fowler, M Armitage 13.05.2014

(22) **Bobby Dazzler** 30m F6b ★★
An excellent and very enjoyable route. Start at the top left of the scree slope at a large block. Climb the block and move up through a rock scar - crux. Step left into a fine groove and follow this to its top. Pull out right onto a rib and climb the slab aiming for the large block. Step right and pull into a bay and lower-off.
C Downer, C Higgins, D Ferguson, C Fowler 21.07.2009

(23) **Bon Courage** 20m F6a
Start at a large block as for *Bobby Dazzler*. Climb onto the block then follow the slabby groove rightwards to the upper slab. Follow this, trending rightwards to a small ledge. Climb up to the block overhang then move right into a bay and lower-off.
C Downer, M Nicholson 19.09.2009

(24) **Hell Bender** 30m F6b+ ★
Start 2m right of the block of *Bobby Dazzler* and immediately left of the wet groove. Pull steeply up a bulging wall into a slabby groove and move up left to a bolt at the start of a traverse (a long sling here reduces rope drag). Cross the wall until an awkward move leads to a good side hold on a flake on the arête. Follow this (crux) on small holds in a fine position to a bolt on *Bobby Dazzler*. Climb the slab aiming for the large block. Move round this then step right and pull into a bay and lower-off. Do not remove the maillon on the crux as this is used for protection on *The Girdle Traverse*.
C Downer, T Daly 21.05.2014

(25) **The Quisling** 30m F6b+ ★★
An absorbing route. Technical climbing leads to the overhang. Move left under the overhang then up an easy crack until the wall steepens at a block overhang. Climb the left side of the block to a ledge. Up the steepening slabby groove past a finger pocket until moves right lead to the arête. Easily up this to finish.
C Downer, W Young, D Sperry 29.09.2018

(26) **Mr Angry** 18m F6b ★
Follow the short slab to a difficult pull over an overlap to gain the upper slab. Trend left up a shallow groove. Climb to a block overhang then move right to the bay and lower-off.
C Downer, M Nicholson 19.09.2009

(27) **Bonne Chance** 18m F6c
Climb the short wall. Difficult moves up and left gain a hanging groove. Follow this to a vertical shothole. Intricate moves keeping left of the shothole lead to a bay and chain.
C Downer, M Nicholson 19.09.2009

Main Wall | **Bramcrag Quarry** | 231

10	Stumbling Block	F6a+ ★	
11	The Wetherby Whaler	F6a	
12	Director's Cut	F6b ★	
13	The Tipton Slasher	F6b+ ★★★	
14	Yorkshire Ripper	F6b+ ★★	
15	Usain Bolt	F6b+ ★★	
16	Middle East Crisis	F6b+ ★	
17	Eastern Promise	F6b ★★★	
18	Coup d'Etat	F6b+ ★★	
19	The History Boys	F6b+ ★★★	
20	Desperate Dan	F6b+ ★	
21	Arc-de-Triomphe	F6a+ ★★	
30	Girdle Traverse	F6b+ ★★★	

Micro-Granite

28 Take It or Leave It 20m F6a
A short slab and arête lead to a bulge. Surmount this and go up to a ledge. Gain a crack and lay-back to a ledge.
RJ Kenyon, C King 26.06.1991

29 Welcome to Rio 25m F6a ★
The start to the girdle makes a pleasant pitch. Climb the corner and follow the flake handrail across the slab to join and finish up *Bonne Chance*.
C Downer, D Sperry 25.05.2014

30 Girdle Traverse F6b+ ★★★
A brilliant route taking in some impressive country at a sustained grade. Familiarity with the other routes helps with route finding. Start at the top of a grassy rake by a tree stump.

1 F6b Climb the corner and follow the flake handrail across the slab to join *Bonne Chance*. Continue horizontally to the bolt on *Mr Angry*. Descend *Bon Courage* and follow the traverse of *Hell Bender* to the arête. Difficult moves left lead into the corner of *Bobby Dazzler* and a bolt belay. By threading a sling into the maillon, the second is protected and it is possible to reach back and retrieve the sling.

2 F6b+ Step down and reverse the traverse of *Coup d'Etat* to the bolt on *History Boys*. Pull onto the ledge and cross the wall aiming for a slab low down. A tricky move across a shallow corner gains a ledge and a choice of finishes.
C Downer, D Sperry 25.05.2014

 There have been two rock collapses between Main Wall and Center Parc in recent years. Most recently, Feb 2020, a massive rockfall took place in wet weather. The debris gives pause for thought.

Center Parc

Fun routes in the easier grades make this a popular sector. The central slabs are prone to seepage but the area between *Long Good Friday* and *St John's Ambulance* dries extremely quickly.

Approach: Cross the approach ridge and head rightwards crossing the debris below a line of unstable square cut overhangs.

1 Conflict Zone 25m F6b ★
Undamaged by rockfall but but threatened by unstable rock; use your judgement! Easy slabs lead to exciting moves over an overhang. An easy-angled slabby rib above the blocks is followed to the overhang. Pull over then climb the wall to an easing of the angle. Follow the rightward-slanting groove.
C Downer, W Young 17.06.2018

2 Bambino Bolero 25m VS
The overgrown ramp right of the overhangs. Avoid.
RJ Kenyon, G Baum, G Irvine 26.05.1991

3 On the Edge 23m F5b
Immediately right of the overhangs is a prominent rib which forms the right side of the right-slanting ramp. The wise will use the belay bolt as the ground below the route drops away quickly into the lower quarry. Spaced bolting. Climb just right of the toe of the rib into a scoop then onto the arête. Follow the arête, or the groove.
RJ Kenyon 14.12.1991

4 Tyke's Teeter 23m F6b
Serious. Start at a left-leaning gangway right of a prominent rib. There is a horizontal shothole just above the ground. Follow the gangway to its top. Traverse right (tricky) into a scoop. Move up and left of the shothole. Then right to gain a grassy ledge. Climb the right side of a jutting prow (tricky) to a desperate pull (hidden bolt) onto a slab.
RJ Kenyon, A Davis 28.12.1991

5 Tyke's Teeter Direct 20m F6c
A very precarious sequence of moves leads across the slab away from the groove of *Tyke's Teeter*. Clip the bolts then step right to a conspicuous foothold: move up and right (crux) onto a scoop. Continue up and left onto the arête using a creaking flake and climb to the belay. Beware rope drag.
C Bainbridge, PJ Kane 4.05.1993

6 Gorilla Monsoon 20m F6a+
The crux, passing the first bolt, is slow to dry. Climb the groove through the obvious notch. Follow the rib rightwards to the open groove. Step left to exciting moves over the bulge.
C Downer, M Nicholson 14.04.2014

Micro-Granite

⑦ **Good Luck Mr Blair!** 20m F6b
Ascend the wall just right of the arête to the overlap. Pull directly over this and follow the arête.
RJ Kenyon, P King 1997

⑧ **Botterill's Slab** 20m F6b
Climb to the second bolt on *Good Luck Mr Blair!*. Move left round the arête into *Gorilla Monsoon*. Step left again and follow the slabby rampline to the arête.
P Botterill, A Davis 16.07.2015

⑨ **Farewell to Adventure?** 20m F6a+ ★
Starts at a vertical shothole behind a large block. Tricky moves to start the slab then up to an overlap which is climbed to gain a ledge. Pass the overlap above on the right and finish up a short groove.
RJ Kenyon, J Bardgett 1.02.1992

⑩ **Fringe Benefits** 20m F6c ★
Climb the corner to the ramp. Above is a bulge. Make intricate moves left then over the bulge (crux) to easier ground. Move up then climb the centre of the delicate slab.
W Young, C Downer 24.04.2015

⑪ **Sorry, No Bolts** 25m E2 5a ★
Reach right to clip the bolts on *A Miller's Tale*: F6a. Climb the smooth corner (crux) to a right-trending ramp. Follow this then climb directly up pleasant slabs above. Trend left at the top.
S Miller 1.07.1991

⑫ **A Miller's Tale** 25m F6a ★
Climb the initial groove for 3m to a bolt. Pull directly on to the slab which is followed to the top.
C Downer, C Fowler 2.04.2014

⑬ **Fargo** 25m F5a ★
Pleasant climbing but slow to dry. Climb an easy rib to black-streaked slabs. Follow the black streak then up and right over a small overlap. Continue left across a rib then up and left to the lower-off.
C Downer 27.04.2014

⑭ **Whicker's World** 25m F5c ★
The line up the left side of the slabs. Belay bolt at the base. Start up a slim groove and finish up the fine arête.
C Fowler, C Downer, L Jones 25.06.2013

⑮ **The Rookie** 25m F5b ★
Belay bolt at the base. Climb a short corner capped by a shothole to a ledge. Move right, then pleasant climbing right of *Whicker's World* leads to the lower-off.
C Downer 15.06.2014

⑯ **The Comfort Zone** 25m F5b ★
Start below a large block. Climb directly to a white-coloured rib then continue to the lower-off.
C Downer 15.06.2014

①	**Conflict Zone**	F6b ★ ⚠
②	**Bambino Bolero**	VS ⚠
③	**On the Edge**	F5b
④	**Tyke's Teeter**	F6b
⑤	**Tyke's Teeter Direct**	F6c
⑥	**Gorilla Monsoon**	F6a+

(17) **Blencathra Badger** 27m F5c ★★★
Named after Paul Ross' Parson Jack Russell terrier that was Best of Breed at Crufts in 1991. Delightful climbing - a gem of a pitch which climbs the right side of the water-worn slabs.
A Phizacklea, J Holden 1991

(18) **The Long Good Friday** 27m F5b ★★
Excellent climbing which makes a good alternative when the rest of the slabs are wet. Climb to the second bolt on *Blencathra Badger* and step into the groove in the arête on the right. Climb directly to the large hanging groove then up right and bridge onto a flake to finish. If the final groove is wet; finish up the arête.
C Downer, M Armitage 18.04.2014

(19) **The Good Friday Agreement** 30m F6b
A minor variation with a short hard section. Follow *Blencathra Badger* to a ledge by the second bolt. Climb the mottled-green wall heading rightwards into an open groove to join *The Long Good Friday*.
C Downer, C Wornham 19.04.2014

(20) **Ship of Fools** 27m F6a ★
Climb the black-streaked wall to a grassy ledge then easily to the foot of a black wall. Make a rising traverse across the black wall to a grooved arête which is followed to the top.
C Downer, K Forsythe, A Tilney 27.04.2014

(21) **Brothers in Arms** 30m F6a+
Follow the ramp and rib to the second bolt. Step up and left then climb to the overhang. Over this to reach and finish up the steep cracked slab.
C Bainbridge, S Bainbridge 7.06.1992

(22) **Barrow Boys' Day Out** 30m F6a ★★
Good open climbing. Climb a rounded rib (left of a shothole at 4m) to a bolt. Climb diagonally right to the conspicuous slim ramp. Follow this rightwards and the corner above.
A Phizacklea, J Holden 23.03.1991

(23) **Vale of Secrecy** 30m F6a+ ★
Climb to a rib and continue steeply into a large open groove. Up this and a short groove in the right wall. Continue to the left of a rib to finish.
A Phizacklea, J Holden 14.04.1991

(24) **Ripper Street** 30m F6b
An eliminate with a short hard crux. Climb up to a shothole at 4m. Move up right then left. Climb the slim left-facing groove directly above with difficulty to finish left of a rib.
C Downer, D Sperry 16.11.2013

(25) **Goodbye Mr Major!** 31m F6a ★★
An excellent route at a consistent grade. Starts at the lowest point of the buttress. Gain a ledge at 3m either direct or by a groove on the left. Follow darker-coloured rock to a ramp. Cross the ramp, climb a slab to a groove which leads onto a rib; finish up this.
RJ Kenyon, P King 1997

(26) **Goodfellas** 27m F5b ★
Lovely climbing - most enjoyable. Starts at the lowest point of the buttress. Climb over the bulge (or more easily the groove to its left). Climb the wall and continue up a groove.
P Botterill, A Davis, C Downer, C Fowler 16.07.2013

(27) **St. John's Ambulance** 30m F4+ ★
Climb a sloping groove on the right side of the face to its top, step delicately left and climb the upper corner.
A Phizacklea, J Holden 14.04.1991

(28) **Endgame** 20m F6a
The slabby rib on the right side of the buttress.
M Armitage, W Young 04.2014

Center Parc | Bramcrag Quarry | 237

14	Whicker's World	F5c ★
15	The Rookie	F5b ★
16	The Comfort Zone	F5b ★
17	Blencathra Badger	F5c ★★★
18	The Long Good Friday	F5b ★★
19	The Good Friday Agreement	F6b
20	Ship of Fools	F6a ★
21	Brothers in Arms	F6a+
22	Barrow Boys' Day Out	F6a ★★
23	Vale of Secrecy	F6a+ ★
24	Ripper Street	F6b
25	Goodbye Mr Major!	F6a ★★
26	Goodfellas	F5b ★
27	St. John's Ambulance	F4+ ★
28	Endgame	F6a

Micro-Granite

The Fun Factory

Steep juggy climbing with a distinct character. These routes weave up through bulges on the steep black wall, bristling with overhangs, located beyond a grassy bank right of **Center Parc**.

① **Joy Division** 18m F5c ★
Starts at a large detached pinnacle at the left-hand side of the wall. Climb to the top of the pinnacle. Step right onto the wall and finish up a groove with overlaps. Lower-off on the left
C Downer 5.07.2015

② **The Fun Factory** 20m F6a ★★
Climb the right edge of the pinnacle. Step onto the wall and make a rising traverse rightwards to finish up a slabby groove.
C Downer, W Young 13.05.2015

③ **Tramadol Nights** 18m F6b ★
Steep satisfying climbing through the upper bulges. Start at a crack forming the right side of the pinnacle. Pull onto the wall and take a series of grooves and overlaps.
C Downer, W Young 15.06.2015

④ **Zoom** 20m F6c ★★★
Another great technical offering. Climb the wall via a difficult overlap at 5m to the overhang. Pull round to the right then over the overhang by jammed blocks to the large flakes. Climb the wall right of the arête and a short groove.
C Downer, W Young 3.11.2015

⑤ **The Aphasic Syndrome** F6c ★★★
⑥ **The Spring Offensive** F6b ★★
⑦ **The Crossing** F6a+ ★
⑧ **Greek Exit** F6b+ ★
⑨ **Tunnel Vision** F6a+ ★★

The Fun Factory | **Bramcrag Quarry** | 239

The Aphasic Syndrome F6c (page 240) Colin Downer — David Simmonite

Micro-Granite

⑤ The Aphasic Syndrome 22m F6c ★★★
Brilliant, sustained and varied. Start 5m right of the pinnacle at a white scar in a recess. Climb a slim grooveline to a resting position. Continue up over the overhang via a couple of blocks then follow the steep wall above.
Photo page 239.
C Downer, W Young 14.05.2015

The next five routes share a common start above some debris.

⑥ The Spring Offensive 18m F6b ★★
Climb the flakes then trend left to below a bulge. Rightwards over the bulge then up to a lower-off in a recess.
C Downer, W Young 23.04.2015

⑦ The Crossing 25m F6a+ ★
Climb *The Spring Offensive* to the 5th bolt below the bulge, step left and climb up to and over the overhang via the two jammed blocks. Traverse left along the flakes round the edge and continue in the same line.
C Downer, W Young 15.06.2015

⑧ Greek Exit 18m F6b+ ★
Climb *The Spring Offensive* to the third bolt. Step left under the bulge then pull steeply right climbing the edge of the wall, past a block, to easier ground.
W Young, C Downer 6.07.2015

⑨ Tunnel Vision 18m F6a+ ★★
A very popular route with varied and continuously interesting climbing. Climb the shallow groove right of the first bolt to reach the right-hand side of the overhang. Climb this and the wall above.
C Downer, W Young 26.04.2015

⑩ Double Jeopardy 20m F6b ★★
From the first bolt climb the ramp on the right to a junction with *Dignitas*. Climb straight up to the overlap. Pull over then head up steeply slightly leftwards until moves right lead to the lower-off.
C Downer, W Young 13.04.2017

⑪ Dignitas 20m F6b
Spooky moves through the final blocks. Climb a short black slab over a steepening. Move right then up below an overhang. Pull round this to a crack; finish up the groove.
C Downer, W Hurford 3.06.2015

⑫ The Watchman 10m F6a+
Climb the wall to the first bolt then head up leftwards over bulges to an easing of the angle. Follow the arête up then rightwards to the lower-off. Avoid the groove to the left of the arête.
C Downer, A Davis, P Botterill 6.09.2016

⑬ The Night Watch 10m F6a+ ★★
A delightful little route. Follow the line of bolts through the overlaps on the right by elegant climbing.
W Young, C Downer 14.05.2015

⑭ The Clydebank Kipper 15m F6a ★
Climb up and into a white niche. Move left then up to an easing of the angle.
C Downer, W Young 12.06.2015

⑮ The Vital Spark 15m F6a ★
Climb the left side of the slabby wall and short groove to an intimidating bulge. Climb leftwards through the bulge and up to finish.
W Young, C Downer 9.10.2016

⑯ Glasgow Kiss 20m F6a+ ★★
An excellent route. Climb up into a small niche and step up left over a steepening into a short groove. Climb this then move right following a slab rightwards under the steep wall and up to finish.
C Downer, W Young 14.10.2016

⑰ Sauchiehall Street 20m F5b ★
The right-hand line close to the waterfall. Climb easily to the steeper wall leading into a large niche. Climb out right along the sloping ramp then up until a short traverse left leads to the lower-off.
W Young, C Downer 17.10.2016

242 | Micro-Granite

⑫ **The Watchman** F6a+
⑬ **The Night Watch** F6a+ ★★
⑭ **The Clydebank Kipper** F6a ★
⑮ **The Vital Spark** F6a ★
⑯ **Glasgow Kiss** F6a+ ★★
⑰ **Sauchiehall Street** F5b ★

The Fun Factory | **Bramcrag Quarry** | 243

Limestone

Slate

Micro-Granite

Sandstone

Fire Starter F6c (page 244) Steph Marshall — Chris Cunningham

Micro-Granite

The Amphitheatre
Slow to dry. This area starts just right of the permanent wet streak (or more usually a waterfall). This sector was hard won from its guarding carpet of gorse and bramble which choked the area.

Unfortunately, this sector has suffered rockfalls in the last two winters casting doubt on the stability and safety of the area especially the central section.

Approach: Cross the grassy bridge and head rightwards to the furthest rocks.

① Payday   15m   F6a
The first line of bolts right of the wet area.
W Young, C Downer 23.04.2018

② Swindler's List   15m   F6a
Climb the wall using a thin crack in the drill hole then direct over the bulge. Up the groove in the arête onto a slab. Climb the slab and the short wall.
W Young, C Downer 3.05.2018

③ Loan Shark   15m   F6a   ★
An enjoyable pitch - the best of its grade in this area. Climb the corner then the slab on the left. Move up a short slab and wall then left to finish.
W Young, C Downer 23.04.2018

The steep central area suffered rockfall during winter 2019/20. This altered some routes and remaining unstable rock left by the rockfall was cleared in June 2020. The affected area now appears to be stable.

④ Fire Starter   10m   F6c   ★
Short, steep and technical. Climb direct up the overhanging arête then pull left onto the slab; follow this rightwards.
Photo page 243.
C Downer, W Young, D Sperry 5.05.2018

⑤ Burning Issue   10m   F6b+
The blatantly obvious groove.
C Downer, W Young 27.04.2018

⑥ Crack Addict
The line of bolts indicates a route that fell down!
C Downer 07.06.2018

The Amphitheatre | Bramcrag Quarry

⑦ **The Beast** 10m F6b+ ⚠
The 3-stepped groove. The name gives a clue to the delights which await. Easy rock and a short overhanging wall lead to a sloping ledge in the overhanging corner. Climb the corner to an awkward landing on the ledge above. More easily over the jammed blocks.
C Downer, W Young, A Davis 14.05.2018

⑧ **Power Share** 10m F6c ★
The right-hand groove is the toughest of the three.
C Downer, M Armitage 3.06.2018

⑨ **False Prophet** 12m F6b ★
The crag turns through 90 degrees below a short overhanging wall. Head left then climb the overhanging wall to a sloping ledge. Finish up a groove on the left.
C Downer, W Young 5.05.2018

⑩ **Incendiary Groove** 12m F6b
Climb the short steep groove and exit left. Continue up then step left into a short V-groove which is climbed to an awkward exit.
W Young, C Downer 30.04.2018

⑪ **The Advocate** 10m F6a ★
Delightful and delicate. Climb into the base of the groove; head rightwards then straight up to a niche and trend left.
C Downer, W Young 23.04.2018

⑫ **Gonzo** 10m F6a
W Young 9.04.2018

⑬ **Toll Road** 10m F5c
Start at an overhung niche. At first straight up then trend left.
P Botterill, A Davis 21.04.18

⑭ **The Network** 8m F6a
C Downer, W Young 23.04.2018

⑮ **The Bitter End** 8m F5a
Start at a large drill hole.
W Young, C Downer 14.05.2018

⑯ **A Walk In The Park** 35m F6a
Start up *The Bitter End* then traverse left heading for the short V-groove high on *Incendiary Groove*; finish up this.
W Young, C Downer 11.06. 2018

The Side Circle

Two tiny buttresses provide pleasant warm-ups.

Approach: From the left end of the **Lower Quarry**, climb steeply up a short slope (a knotted rope aids progress) to where it levels off. About 40m left is the first group of climbs below a small tree at the top of the crag. This area can also be accessed easily from the approach to the upper quarry.

① Stage Left 10m F6a
Climb the left-hand groove then rightwards to the tree.
W Young, C Downer, L Jones 1.09.2016

② Centre Stage 10m F6a
Take the shallow central groove.
W Young, C Downer 30.08.2016

③ Stage Right 10m F6a
Move easily rightwards into a short left-facing corner. Pull awkwardly onto a ledge then leftwards up the wall.
C Downer, W Young, L Jones 1.09.2016

About 40m right are the next group of climbs. This is at the point where a ledge system heads right above the drop into the **Lower Quarry**.

④ Footlights 10m F5b
The left-hand groove for 4m then the wall on the left.
C Downer, W Young 17.06.2016

⑤ Encore 10m F5c
Climb the central groove then the left wall.
C Downer, P Wilde 06.2016

⑥ Beyond The Fringe 10m F5b ★
Start at the edge of the ledge system at a slabby gangway. Climb the left edge of the slabby corner to a sloping groove then its continuation.
RJ Kenyon 27.12.1991

⑦ Dress Rehearsal 10m F5b
Climb the slabby corner, using the crack on the right wall, to a ledge. Climb the wall up and rightwards..
A Davis, P Botterill 23.05.2017

⑧ Coming Up For Air 10m F6b+ ★
Climb the slabby corner and move onto its right wall. Climb the wall past a protruding block.
C Downer, A Davis 25.05.2017

⑨ Understudy 10m F4+
Climb the left-facing corner to a lower-off on a tree.
W Young, D Sperry, C Downer 7.05.2017

⑩ State of Play 10m F6a
Start one metre right of the left-facing corner. Climb the slim groove in the wall.
C Downer, W Young 9.05.2017

⑪ Critic's Choice 10m F6a+
Climb the crack in the rib to a ledge. Move onto a slab then right into the corner.
C Downer, W Young 17.05.2017

⑫ Blind Audition 10m F6a
Start at the right-hand end of the ledge below a shallow rightwards-leaning v-groove. Belay bolt. Climb the groove to a steep wall. Climb this on good holds, to the left of the bolts, to an awkward landing and up to the lower-off.
W Young, C Downer 18.05.2017

Lower Quarry | **Bramcrag Quarry**

Lower Quarry

A surprisingly peaceful location with an attractive pond filling its base. It's sheltered, out of the wind and gets afternoon sun. For much of its length, there is a persistent seepage line at 4m. A number of pillars do stay dry and give access to the excellent climbing above.

Approach: Follow the quarry track round the first bend then take a grassy path rightwards into the quarry.

⑬ **Production Line** 20m F6a
Start at the north end of the pond behind a large pine. Climb the quartzy wall to the break then up left to a ledge. Climb the left edge of the slab to where it joins a steep wall. Climb the crack/groove right of the bolts to a ledge.
W Young, C Downer 15.06.2016

⑭ **Synergy** 25m F7a ★★
The left-hand line on the impressive steep wall. Climb up to and pass the overlap on the left. From the top of the blocks climb the leaning wall to a ledge and its technical continuation.
L Jones, C Downer 27.05.2016

TOP ⑮ **Skywalker** 25m F6b+ ★★★
A brilliant route - not to be missed. Climb the wall then a crack through the overlap onto blocks below an overhanging wall. Climb the wall then traverse left to a corner/crack. Climb this then, as it curves left, climb the vertical crack above in a superb position to a lower-off on the right. **Variation Finish: F6c+** From the bottom of the corner/crack climb the wall on the right to the overlap then the tricky arête to a ledge.
C Downer, L Jones; Variation Finish 1.08.2016 T Daly, W Young 10.05.2016

⑯ **Aqua Man Direct** 25m F6b ★
Climb *Waterworld* to the fifth bolt then move left and up to the left-hand side of the overhang. Pull round this then up the wall past a tree stump.
C Downer, W Young 17.05.2016

⑰ **Waterworld**   25m   F6a+   ★★
A fine route with sustained climbing and an exciting bulge. Start below an open groove leading to overhangs. Climb diagonally up right then climb the steep groove with interest. Pull over the left side of the overhang then, just below the top, traverse left past a tree stump to the lower-off.
C Downer, W Young, G Lee 3.09.2015

⑱ **Revenant**   25m   F6b   ★
Climb to a quartzy wall which leads to easier-angled rock. Move up to the large overhang then awkwardly round left into a hanging corner.
C Downer, D Sperry 13.03.2016

⑲ **Katyusha**   25m   F6b+   ★
Climb a short rightward ramp then a short wall to a ledge. Up the impending wall via a faint crackline then easier rock to an overhanging crack. Climb the painful crack and the short corner to the overhang. The lower-off is above this on the right.
W Young, C Downer 22.06.2016

⑳ **Life Begins at Forty**   25m   F6b   ★★
Starts below the obvious V-groove 5m above the ground. Climb to the break then up to a groove. Ascend the groove then follow a crackline leftwards to a cracked corner. Climb this and the short slab.
R J Kenyon, G Baum, A Davis, T Price 5.06.1991

 In June 2020, the large groove to the right of *Endeavour* collapsed.

㉑ **Endeavour**   25m   F6a   ⚠
Climb to the first bolt then awkwardly into the groove on the right. Up this to a ledge. Move up to the left-hand side of the overhang, pull over this rightwards then climb up and left then over an overhang.
C Downer, W Young, D Sperry 26.09.2015

㉒ **Drapolene**   25m   F6a+   ★
From a cracked nose of brown rock (this dries quickly) climb to the break. Continue up the short wall to easier ground. Climb a short shallow groove in the arête to finish up a slab.
W Young, C Downer 22.10.2018

㉓ **Nappyrash**   25m   F6a   ★
Climb the nose to the break. Move up right to a good hold just left of a V-groove. Climb up and left to ledges. Ascend the corner, over an overlap and continue in the same line.
R J Kenyon, G Baum, P Figg 25.04.1991

㉔ **No Country For Old Men**   25m   F6b+
Another technical exercise by the retirement club. Climb the wall (often wet) then the left-facing groove to a large overhang. Move left to a hanging left-facing corner which is climbed to easier rock. Move right then continue up to finish at a lower-off just right of the overhang.
W Young, C Downer, T Daly 4.05.2016

㉕ **Baptismal Vows**   25m   F6a+   ★
The original route on this area of the crag. From a sharp nose, climb to the second bolt and move up left to the base of a groove. Climb this to its top then pull over the left-hand side of a small overlap to gain the final slab.
RJ Kenyon, G Baum, G Irvine 26.05.1991

㉖ **Easter Rising**   25m   F6a+   ★
Climb the nose to the second bolt, move slightly right and gain the slab. Continue via a groove through the overlap and follow the faint crackline.
W Young, C Downer 31.03.2016

The next area, Marine's Slab, lies above a very wet drainage line at 4m. A pillar at the left-hand side stays dry and gives access to these excellent routes.

㉗ **Another Poolside Attraction**   25m   F6a+
Climb the pillar to the second bolt. Step left into a short groove and exit left at the top to the base of a slanting corner. Climb the corner.
W Young, C Downer 22.06.2016

㉘ **Kill Bill**   25m   F6b
Climb the pillar to the second bolt. Step left into a short groove and exit left at the top to the base of a slanting corner. Above is a steep arête climbed utilising the cracks on the left wall. A final difficult move on the front face leads to easy ground.
C Downer, T Daly, S Murphy 15.08.2015

㉙ **Forever Young**   25m   F5c   ★
Climb the pillar to ledges at the base of the corner. Step left and climb the crack in the front of the prow then easy rock.
C Downer, T Daly, S Murphy 15.08.2015

㉚ **Seconds Away**   25m   F5c   ★★
A fine climb up the groove bounding the left edge of the slabs. Climb the pillar to ledges. Trend left to the corner which is followed to the overhang. Move right and then back left.
J Holden, A Phizacklea 14.04.1991

㉛ **The Mutineer** 25m F6b+ ★
Climb the pillar to ledges. Climb the steep slab, right of the corner, by a series of difficult moves to a ledge then more easily in the same line.
C Downer, W Young 16.07.2015

㉜ **Marine's Slab** 25m F6a ★★
Climb the pillar to the second bolt. Move right then up to finish via a thin crack.
A Phizacklea, J Holden 23.03.1991

TOP ㉝ **Captain Pugwash** 25m F6a ★★
Revisited
A gem of a pitch. From the right side of the dry pillar climb to the break. Traverse the lip of the overlap for 3m then climb up to ledges in the centre of the face. Move up and over the left-hand side of the overlap; continue in the same line.
W Young, C Downer 14.09.2015

㉞ **Here's Lookin' at Euclid** 25m F6b+ ★★
If wet, an approach may be possible via *Viagra Falls*. Climb up to ledges then step left and up a short wall just below the corner to a large slab. Climb the slab, left of the corner, then left until above the large ledges in the middle of the slab. Either climb the shallow groove up to the middle of the narrow overlap, over this direct to a ledge. Or, climb to the right of the shallow groove up to the ledge. Continue up then, just below the top, move right to the lower-off.
Photo page 253.
C Downer, W Young 16.07.2015

㉟ **Viagra Falls** 25m F6a ★
Very slow to dry - wait for a drought. Climb the wall up left to enter the main corner. Up this with an interesting move over the overhang; continue in the same line to a lower-off on the left.
W Young, C Downer, G Lee 25.05.2016

㊱ **Priaprism** 25m F6a
Climb the wall over the bulge to easier rock. The start is slow to dry.
C Downer, W Young, G Lee, G Proctor 25.05.2016

㊲ **Scrotal Recall** 25m F6a+ ★★
An excellent route - the best in this area. Climb into the groove. At the first bolt move leftwards up the wall then steeply via a crackline through the overlaps. Continue in the same line to a lower-off. The start is slow to dry but juggy so the route may be climbed in less than perfect conditions.
C Downer, W Young 22.04.2016

㊳ **The Water Boys** 25m F6a ★★
Climb the easy groove for a few metres then the short rib and groove to the overlap. Pull over then climb the groove to a lower-off on the left.
W Young, C Downer 20.04.2016

㊴ **Comedy Shuffle** 20m F6a+ ★
Climb the short easy groove to the first bolt, step right and climb the wall to the overhang. Above is a left-facing corner. Pull directly over into this, climb it, and continue in the same line.
W Young, C Downer, D Sperry 28.10.2018

㊵ **First Footing** 10m F6a
An isolated route on the area of clean rock as one enters the quarry, after crossing the pool outlet. Climb right then more easily up to the overlap. Pull over this then up the short slab.
C Downer 8.06.2017

Micro-Granite

Lower Quarry - Right

- 36 Priaprism — F6a
- 37 Scrotal Recall — F6a+ ★★
- 38 The Water Boys — F6a ★★
- 39 Comedy Shuffle — F6a+ ★
- 40 First Footing — F6a

Here's Lookin' at Euclid F6b+ (page 251) Pete Botterill — 📷 Bill Young

SANDSTONE

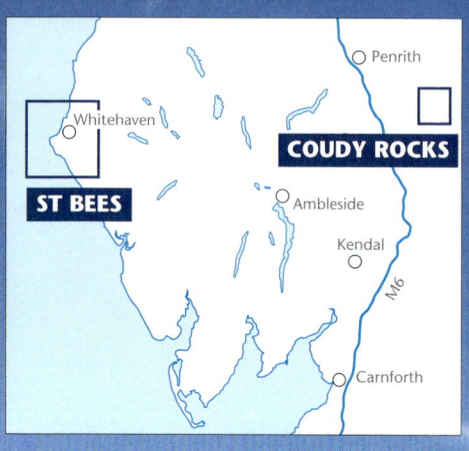

Crags
- **ST BEES HEAD** — Page 256
- **COUDY ROCKS** — Page 274

Fisherman's Friend F5 (page 265) Stephen Coughlan — David Simmonite

ST BEES HEAD

OS Grid Ref: NX 939 145
Altitude: 5m

     Accessible with calm waters

Varied and absorbing climbing on the impressive red sandstone cliffs of St Bees Head make the journey to visit this unique venue worthwhile. The rock aesthetics are out of this world and the coastal setting second to none. The cliffs enjoy seaside weather and sunshine and are a fast drying location, however, even on fine dry days seepage can be persistent for several days after rain.

A programme of re-equipping has been undertaken by the Cumbria Bolt Fund and many lines are now equipped with seaside specific stainless steel bolts and pig's tail lower-offs. These lower-offs require a degree of competence to use safely. Be suspicious of all old gear. Please use the lower-offs and respect the bird restrictions and access agreement avoiding topping out onto the vegetation above.

Climbing here sometimes requires a set of skills not often used at more typical sport venues. Occasionally a level of determination is required to overcome a layer of fine sand that can develop on the less-travelled routes. However, perseverance pays off and a brush with the hand more often than not removes the worst. If redpointing on less frequented lines is your objective, a few minutes spent with a brush will pay dividends.

All routes are accessible at all times in calm weather, although at the south end of **Scabby Back** you can get cut off at high water. Tides, the same as Whitehaven, can be checked using http://www.wired-guides.com/links/?ref=whitehaven-tides.

The rock platform below the crag can be extremely slippery when damp.

All routes south of Scabby Back are restricted from 1st Feb to 31st July to protect sea bird nesting.

Approach: From Whitehaven use the B5345 to St Bees and soon turn right to Sandwith. Through the village take the private farm road. Parking fees are paid in the honesty box by the farmhouse door. Follow the path to the lighthouse and down to the foghorn. Approaches to individual areas are described below.

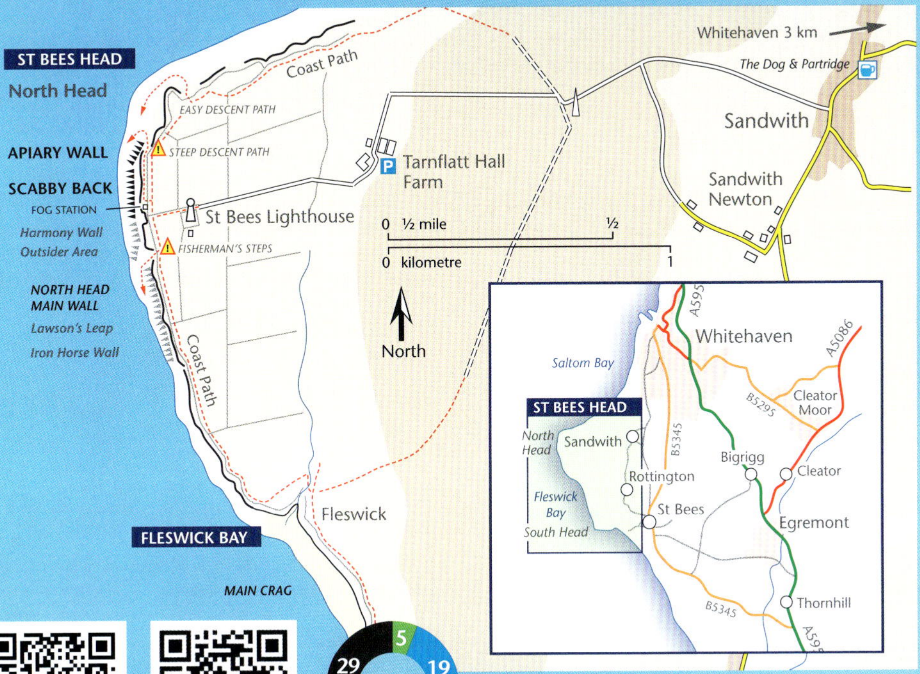
ST BEES HEAD
North Head
APIARY WALL
SCABBY BACK
FOG STATION
Harmony Wall
Outsider Area
NORTH HEAD MAIN WALL
Lawson's Leap
Iron Horse Wall
EASY DESCENT PATH
STEEP DESCENT PATH
FISHERMAN'S STEPS
St Bees Lighthouse
Coast Path
Coast Path
Tarnflatt Hall Farm
Whitehaven 3 km
The Dog & Partridge
Sandwith
Sandwith Newton
0 ½ mile ½
0 kilometre 1
North
Fleswick
FLESWICK BAY
MAIN CRAG
Saltom Bay
Whitehaven
A595
A5086
B5295
Cleator Moor
ST BEES HEAD
North Head
Sandwith
B5345
Bigrigg
Rottington
Cleator
Fleswick Bay
St Bees
Egremont
South Head
B5345
Thornhill
A595

RAD St Bees Head

P GPS 54.515716 -3.626311

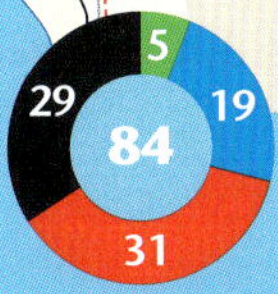
5
19
31
29
84

50m rope

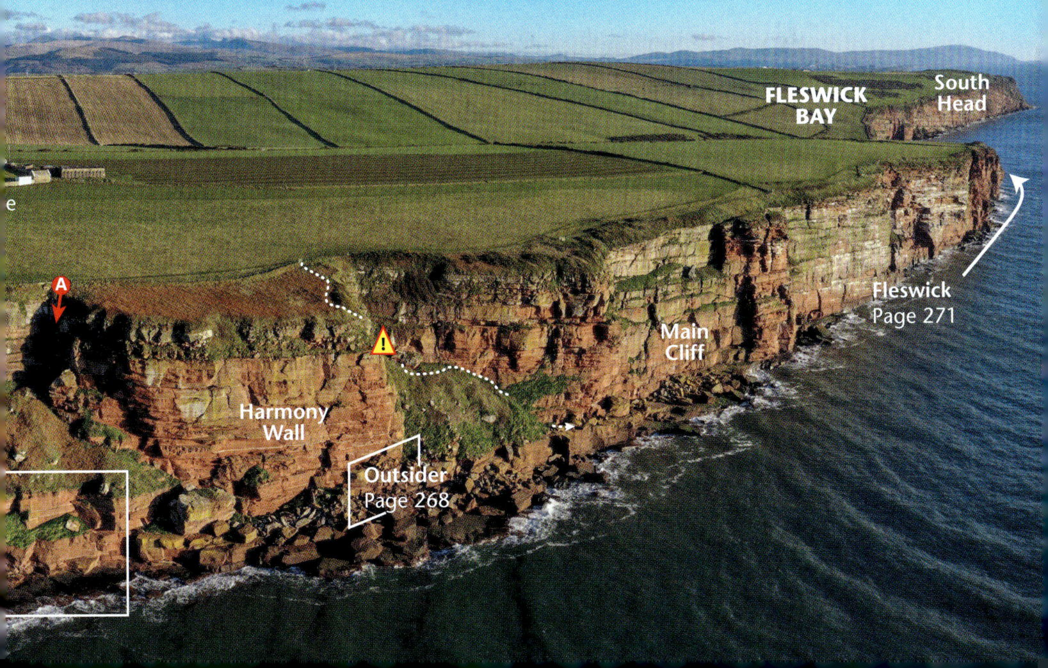
FLESWICK BAY
South Head
Fleswick
Page 271
Main Cliff
Harmony Wall
Outsider
Page 268
A

Apiary Wall

Nectarine rises above massive boulders and the group of routes round the corner are of great quality and give the longest routes on this part of the headland.

The boulders provide a wide variety of world-class problems; see the **Lake District Bouldering** guidebook.

Approach: From the Fog Station turn right and immediately cross the fence to find the descent on the left after 50m. Continue northwards under a small crag then steeply down vegetation and blocks, with some aid from knotted ropes, to reach a bare ledge. 20 mins from the car. The first routes are 15m along the ledge to the south. Drop down towards large boulders to arrive at the left-hand northern end of **Apiary Wall**. Other than at high spring tides, a less steep way from the foghorn is to turn right (north) and follow the landward side of the fence, at the second stile cross the fence and drop down to the sea. Boulder hopping south you arrive at **Apiary Wall**.

① **Absolutely Fabulous** F6b
The top section of this climb has become a sandy beach. Lower-off second from top bolt if you're brave.
C Johnstone 11.1993

② **Kleeneze** F6b
The first good hold is at about 3m, making the start much harder than the rest of the route.
C Johnstone, J Wilson 13.07.1994

③ **Blooming Marvellous** F6c ★★
The square arête with a sting in the tail.
I Williamson 22.11.1993

④ **Just Nice** F6a+
The wall right of the arête. Shared lower-off.
C Johnstone 04.1994

⑤ **Ancient Mariner** F5+ ★
Good climbing up the corner/crack, trying not to disturb the in-situ insect inhabitants.
J Wilson 1993

The next lines start lower down, on the main wall, just above an excellent circuit of boulders.

⑥ **Will's Route** F7a ★
The first line of bolts, left of *Nectarine*, is often covered in a layer of sand. The climbing improves the higher you get.
W Sim

TOP ⑦ **Nectarine** F6c+ ★★★
Mega classic. The impressive left arête of the wall.
J Adams, S Scott 04.1994

⑧ **Drone** F7a+ ★
Start in a leftward-facing corner.
A Jones 1989

⑨ **Virgin Queen** F7a ★★★
Climb up the corner and into the second corner, exiting on the right to the lower-off.
A Jones 1989

⑩ **Royal Jelly** F6b ★
Wobble up the central flakeline, past the first 3 bolts then traverse left along the ledge and follow the bolts up to the lower-off.
J Adams, P Cheung 6.05.1995

⑪ **Honey Pot** F6b+ ★
Start as for *Royal Jelly* but continue all of the way up the central flakeline.
A Jones 1989

⑫ **Beeswax** F6b
Follow *Royal Jelly* past the first 3 bolts to exit up the rampline passing the roof on its right.
A Jones 1989

TOP ⑬ **Swarm** F7a ★★★
A technical start leads to a pumpy and spectacular finale up the open groove.
A Jones 1989

⑭ **Bee Line** F6b+ ★
A short route with a fierce start up to the ledge at 10m. Start at a rightwards-slanting crack with a small upside down V at its base. Climb the crack with difficulty then trend leftwards across the slab to the lower-off .
A Jones, W Hannah 07.1999

⑮ **Bee Hive** F6c
Start up *The Apiarist* then break out left after the second bolt. Follow the bolts to the lower-off.
J Adams, W Hannah 7.05.1995

TOP ⑯ **The Apiarist** F6b+ ★★★
Great sustained climbing with an alternating series of hard moves and good rests, the final layback corner is tackled in a spectacular position. Start just right of a low level roof and climb the series of grooves and corners.
A Jones 1989

⑰ Unfinished Project
The line of bolts between *The Apiarist* and *Bee Sting* marks an unfinished project.

⑱ **Bee Sting** F7a ★★
Below the left-hand end of the large roof on the right-hand side of **Apiary Wall**.
A Jones 1989

⑲ **Foul Brood** F7a+ ★
Directly over the right-hand end of the large roof.
A Jones 1989

Route Two F4 (page 263) Jim Daley — 📷 David Simmonite

Sandstone

Scabby Back

Continuing south, **Scabby Back** offers a huge range of climbing. There is so much to occupy you that the day will just pass in the beat of a gull's wing.

The southern extremity is tidal.

Approach: **Scabby Back** is accessed above the step in the rock platform equipped with a chain.

20 **Promenade Crack**   F7b   ★★
The impressive steep crackline left of *Aurora*
K Murphy, J Adams 1994

21 **Aurora**   F6a+
The wide groove at the start of **Scabby Back**.
C Sice, A Stephenson, N Jowett 1983

22 **Toxic Rock**   F7b   ★★
The bubbly arête starting immediately above the **Scabby Back** access chain. The moves up to and passing the small roofs provide a difficult crux.
SO Miller 1993

23 **Nuclear Seepage**   F7b   ★
The line of bolts just to the right of *Toxic Rock* gives a bouldery challenge on pockets and edges. Finish at the twin bolts before reaching the ledge.
P Cornforth 1993

A series of bolts right of *Nuclear Seepage* highlights an unfinished project.

24 **Scurvy**   F6a
Easy moves up the obvious groove after some wild swinging about to start.
M Greenbank 1993

TOP **25** **Andy's Route**   F6b   ★★★
Start 20m right of the **Scabby Back** access chain. A roof at 5m is followed by delicate slab climbing.
A Jones 1989

26 **Andy's Route - Right Hand Variation**   F6a+   ★
After the steep start of *Andy's Route*, this eases rapidly. After establishing yourself above the roof, follow the flakeline rightwards
J Adams, A King 1995

27 **Quantum Leap**   F6b+
Traverse rightwards underneath the roof and exit up the line of bolts at the right-hand end
M Johnson 1993

Right of *Quantum Leap* is a steep slab; the next three climbs all start up a weakness in its centre.

28 **Route One**   F4   ★
The easy groove on the left to the lower-off.
C Whornham, J Loxham 1980

Scabby Back | **St Bees Head** | 263

㉙ **Recharge** F6a+
The left-hand line up the slab with a hard move for the short to finish.
J Adams 1994

㉚ **Feeling Groovy** F6c ★★★
The central line on the slab has a balancy crux.
S Wood 1992

㉛ **Stage Fright** F6b
The right-hand arête starting direct.
S Scott 1993

㉜ **Route Two** F4
Up the groove on the right with a step left at the top to finish on the same lower-off as *Stage Fright*.
Photo page 259.
E Cleasby 1980

㉝ **Megadrive** F6b+ ★★
Climb the left side of the wild leaning arête.
J Adams, S Scott 1994

TOP ㉞ **Dreaming of Red Rocks** F7a+ ★★★
The St Bees must do! A stunning route up the overhanging right side of the arête. A good test of fitness.
Photo page 267 and 2.
A Hyslop 1992

㉟ **China Syndrome** F6a+
Up to the ledge and continue up the twin cracks.
C Sice, A Stephenson, N Jowett 1983

㊱ **Driller Killer** F6a
The next crackline.
C Sice, A Stephenson 1984

㊲ **Molly Malone** F6c ★★
To the right of the corner, in the middle of the next face, is a thin crack which finishes part way up the wall. Climb to the right of the crack and then to the top.
S Wood, A Hyslop 1993

㊳ **Westworld** F7a+ ★
Follow the line of bolts to the left of the obvious crack; hard to start and hard to finish.
A Hyslop, S Wood 1993

㊴ **Whisky Galore** F7a ★★
The line to the right of the obvious crack; another hard start and finish.
S Wood, A Hyslop Pre-1994

㊵ **Dave's Route** F7a+
Yet another hard start.
D Birkett 1993

Sandstone

㊵ Dave's Route   F7a+
Yet another hard start.
D Birkett 1993

㊶ Pieces of Eight   F6a   ★★
A left-slanting line up the slab left of the overhang.
J Hughes 1993

㊷ Rainbow Warrior   F6b+   ★★
Straight up to the roof then traverse rightwards to finish.
SO Miller 1993

㊸ Scorpion   F6a   ★
Climb to the lower roof, traverse rightwards to the right-facing corner and finish just below the top.
C Sice, A Stephenson 1984

㊹ Screamadelica   F7a+
Climb direct to the lower-off on *Rainbow Warrior*, crossing the roof over *Scorpion* on its right-hand side, to finish with a long reach.
I Turnbull 1993

㊺ Twilight Zone   F3
The easiest bolted route at St Bees. With only two bolts it feels run out but it is possible to supplement the protection with wires. Climb onto a ledge, round the flake, and finish up a crack.
A King 1993

㊻ Northern Lights   F6b+   ★
The overhanging crack left of the prominent nose.
C Sice, A Stephenson 1993

㊼ The Adventures of Pinocchio   F7a   ★
Up the overhanging crack until a delicate traverse rightwards, across the nose, can be made to the lower-off at its end.
SO Miller 1993

㊽ Nasal Passage   F6a   ★
A surprisingly pleasant route, given such a name, but unfortunately often dripping and so only worth picking in a prolonged dry spell. Climb the chimney.
J Adams 1993

㊾ Legend's Friend   F7a   ★
Start below a hanging corner right of the nose. Difficult moves gain access to the corner and thence the top.
C Johnstone 1993

㊿ The Steal   F7a   ★
Aptly named: a purloined old project right of *Legend's Friend*. Start directly below the line of bolts just left of the arête. An awkward start leads to good climbing up the slab.
M Robinson, C Johnstone 1995

(51) **Natural Habitat** F6c ★

A line up the wall right of *Legend's Friend*. Climb to a ledge then left under the roof (when the second bolt has been clipped, unclip the first to avoid rope drag). Traverse left under the line of *The Steal* and up the line of bolts via two small finger pockets.

C Cunningham 1999

(52) **I Wish I Was** F8a ★★

The pockets and thin crack in the overhanging wall provide a bouldery challenge.

D Birkett 1998

(53) **Friggin' in the Riggin'** F6b

The obvious groove; often wet, always awkward.

1993

(54) **Frigging Friends** F6c

A parasitic route that not only lives off bolts from the two adjoining routes, but also uses their names. Start up *Fisherman's Friend*, but step left and climb to gain the top break. Traverse left to lower-off *Friggin' in the Riggin'*.

A Greig, PJ Kane 2000

TOP (55) **Fisherman's Friend** F5 ★★★

The flake and crack right of the corner with a tricky final move.

Photo page 255.

A Stephenson, J Loxham 1982 Later bolted G Bowen

(56) **Elysium** F7b ★★★

Move up to the obvious pocket to the right of *Fisherman's Friend*. Step in the pocket and make a difficult balancy move to a sloping break. Straight up the pocketed wall above to the lower-off. Magnificent.

S Wood 1998

Sandstone

57 Poseidon F7c ★
A good companion route to *Elysium*, similar style, just more difficulty. Take the curving crack to the overlap and a mono. The sloping break above can prove stubborn; pass this and climb the wall.
C Fisher 2001

58 Halloween F4+
Up the obvious line of bolts just left of the big ledge at 3m. Lower off the large boulder on the ledge at the top.
B Davison 1993

59 Happy Friday F5
Climb onto the ledge and make a few moves up to the wall to where a gnarly move is required to finish on the ledge above. Lower off the same boulder as *Halloween*.
C Johnstone 11.1993

60 Sinking in the West F6a+ ★★
Climb up to the overhang and make awkward moves round to the left of it to get established on the wall. The lower-off is at the bottom of the next tier.
J Adams, W Young, A King, B Davison 1993

61 Cutlass F6c+ ★
The roof direct, then up the wall above.
C Johnstone 1994

62 Mr Sandman F6a+ ★
The groove to the right of the overhang.
Photo page 269.
A Stephenson, J Loxham 1982

63 Chimney Route F4+
The straightforward chimney.
Pre-2000

64 Friday 13th F7a+ ★
The difficult wall to the right of *Chimney Route*. Lower-off on *Trick or Treat*.
1984

65 Trick or Treat F6b+ ★★
The awkward left-slanting slabby groove.
J Adams, A King, B Davison 1993

Routes **66** and **67** fell down in 2020.

68 Something for the Weekend F6b+ ★
Some good moves up the wall right of the arête: the arête itself being strictly out of bounds. The lower-off is just back from the edge.
C Cunningham 1999

69 Slash and Grab F6b
A one bolt wonder right of *Something for the Weekend*. From the good ledge at 2m go direct up the wall. The lower-off is just back from the edge.
J Wilson 1999

52	I Wish I Was	F8a ★★
53	Friggin' in the Riggin'	F6b
54	Frigging Friends	F6c
55	Fisherman's Friend	F5 ★★★
56	Elysium	F7b ★★★

Dreaming of Red Rocks F7a+ (page 263) Will Sim — Johnathan Griffith

Sandstone

Outsider

A smaller area, also known as **Fishermans' Steps**, below the impressive but loose **Harmony Wall**. There is excellent bouldering to be found in abundance at the base.

Approach: Continue south from **Scabby Back** up a short wall and through a rock archway. Once around the next boulder, the climbs can be reached by scrambling. At this point the crag is tidal and has a bird restriction.

Siren Wall

Rock of exceptional quality, in an out there position.

Approach: 100m south from the fog station, follow a low wall that borders the edge of the cliff until a gully is reached where a small headland forms a right angle. A stake at the top (may have a piece of wire attached to aid location) allows an abseil down the gully to a bramble-strewn ledge in a great position above the sea.

70 Outsider F6a+ ★
Ten metres left of a blocky gully is a crackline with a small hanging left-facing corner at the bottom which changes into a right-facing corner at the top. Start just left of the crackline and trend rightwards to finish up the right-facing corner; no lower-off.
J Wilson 2000

71 Rank Outsider F6b+ ★
Just right of the blocky gully is a small slab topped by a V-groove. Climb the slab with difficulty and then up the groove with a tricky finish, easier for the tall; no lower-off.
J Wilson 2000

1 Song to the Siren 20m F7a+ ★★★
An excellent climb as good as any at St Bees; the sandstone is of immaculate quality. The short wall then awkward moves right in to a groove. Exiting the groove to the break is the crux. From the break, follow pockets up an overhanging honey-combed wall. Technical moves up the off-vertical wall lead to the lower-off.
K Phizacklea, I Cooksey

2 Moist Meaty Chunks 18m F7b+ ★★
The easy looking crack is much tougher than it looks! A series of laybacks and poor jams may lead to success. Shared lower-off with *Ebb and Flow*.
M Chunks, K Phizacklea

3 Ebb and Flow 18m F6c ★★
A short wall/crack to gain a curving flake. Pull out of the flake (crux) and climb the blocky edge into a crack that leads to a final short corner and the lower-off.
I Cooksey

From **Scabby Back**

Mr Sandman F6a+ (page 266) Stephen Coughlan — David Simmonite

Bertie Basset F6c (opposite) Keith Phizacklea — 📷 Alan Steele

Fleswick Bay | St Bees Head

Fleswick Bay

Impressive and inspiring lines, all are worthwhile including a couple of easier climbs with friendly bolting; there is something for everyone. However, the challenging *Sea of Sands* wall is particularly striking. Calm seas or neap tides are required - it's best avoided when the sea is high. Morning dampness disappears as the sun passes the yard arm.

Approach: From the farm, follow the track towards the lighthouse to reach the coastal path which is followed south to Fleswick Bay. The gully, with a muddy path and stream, is used to descend to the shingle beach. The routes are to the right. It is best to check the tide is going out as climbing the routes furthest from the Fleswick Bay shingle beach may result in being cut off.

① **Castaway** F7c ★★★
The line of bolts on the larger seaward wall 200m north of *Bertie Basset*.
C Fisher 08.2011

② **Bertie Basset** 20m F6c ★★
The slab and groove to the half-height break. Scamper up the wall to finish.
Photo opposite.
P Ibbinson

③ **Cockle Shell Hero** 20m F6b+ ★
A crack leads to the half-height break. A steep scoop tops the final wall.
P Ibbinson

④ **Sea of Sand** F7c ★★★
A very fine route indeed. Up and over two roofs, leading into the technical crux on the wall above.
Photo page 273.
K Phizacklea 2010

⑤ **The Long Voyage Home** F7a ★★
Another long and varied route with sustained interest.
A Steele

⑥ **The Sea Shall Not Have Them** F6c+ ★★
A long and varied route. Adventure sport climbing at its best!
A Steele 2010

⑦ **Sink The Bismark** F7b+ ★★★
Takes the eye-catching arete. Stunning climbing all the way gives one of the best routes of its grade at **St Bees**.
K Phizacklea 2010

⑧ **Up Periscope** F6b+ ★
The wall and stepped overlaps gives an interesting route not to be overlooked.
P Ibbinson 2010

⑨ **Unfinished Business** 20m F5+
Wander into the open groove from the stepped grooves on the right. Rarely dry.
P Ibbinson 2010

⑩ **Z Climb** F7a ★★
The stepped grooves lead to the roof. Launch across to reach the break and swagger up the wall above.
K Phizacklea 2010

About 75m south is the cave of *Cave Route RH*.

⑪ **Cave Route RH** F7a ★★
The right wall of the cave. The shingle beach advances and recedes so a clipstick may be useful. Slow to dry but worth the wait.
A Steele 2010

⑧	**Up Periscope**	F6b+ ★
⑨	**Unfinished Business**	F5+
⑩	**Z Climb**	F7a ★★
⑪	**Cave Route RH**	F7a ★★

Sea of Sand F7c (page 271) Keith Phizacklea — Alan Steele

COUDY ROCKS

OS Grid Ref: NY 687 200
Altitude: 160m

An impressive sandstone wall in an extremely attractive setting located in the centre of Appleby, on the east side of the River Eden.

The crag lies on private land and access has been granted on the understanding that:

- Only bone fide climbers.
- Any livestock should not be disturbed.
- The gate is always left closed.
- No litter.
- No damage to property.
- No dogs in the field below the crag.

Approach: From near the Royal Oak on the B6542 follow Mill Hill, on the opposite side of the road, down to the car park next to the River Eden.

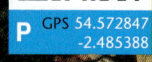

GPS 54.572847 -2.485388

RAD Coudy Rocks

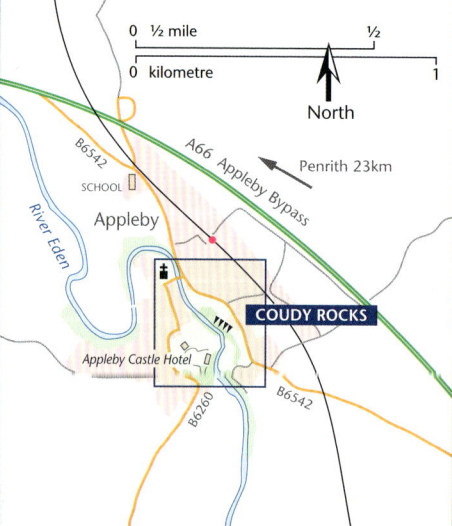
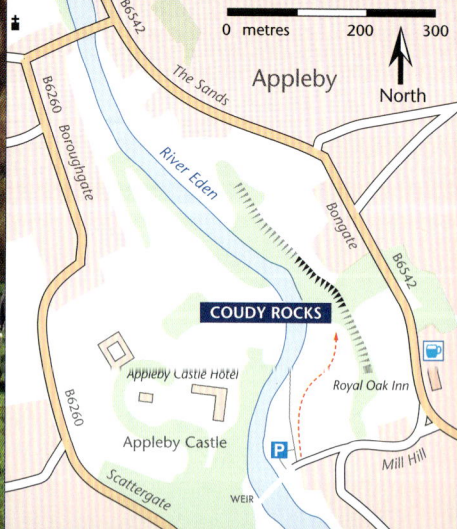

Megamoose Area

① The Wider Sea 5m F6b+
Climb the slab and rib using a crucial small vertical edge on the slab to move left to the finishing ledge.
A Davis, Ms MG Brown, RJ Kenyon 3.07.2010

② The Places in Between 6m F6c
A short corner and battle up the continuing crackline.
Rockrat 2010

③ El Presidento Robbo 6m F6a+
Climb the shield of rock and finish up the fine arête above, making use of holds on the right of the arête.
JH Robinson, RJ Kenyon 3.07.2010

④ Megamoose 7m F6c+ ★
An absorbing route following the crackline slanting up from left to right. Gain the arête on the left and following the crackline with sustained interest to gain a short groove and finish at belay on the right.
D Pattinson 14.04.2010

⑤ Open Project
Wall left of *The Witness* finishing at the *Megamoose* lower-off.

⑥ The Witness 5m F7b+
Climb direct up the thin wall to the *Megamoose* lower-off.
D Campbell, S Marshall 5.04.2016

Perfect Weather to Fly F7a (page 278) Jonah Monks — Ron Kenyon

Sandstone

Main Wall

⑦ **Perfect Weather to Fly** 9m F7a ★★
Start behind the large tree and overcome the overhung base to gain the wall above then ascend leftwards by the arête.
Photo page 277.
D Bush 2.03.2010

⑧ **Tenuous Fly** 10m F7b ★
Start up *Perfect Weather to Fly* then move right and finish up *Flying Low*.
S Leahy 29.05.2018

⑨ **Flying Low** 9m F7b
Start up the corner to the roof on good holds. A big reach up and a hard pull with poor feet bring better holds towards the top.
W Harris 2017

⑩ **Occupational Hazard** 9m F7b ★
Start below the right of the overlap and use widely-spaced holds to gain the upper wall and continue with much interest.
D Varian 2013

⑪ **Periculo 'D' Sinister** 9m F7a+ ★
   Manus
Line of bolts left of *Dangerous Davies* avoiding holds on that route.
N Davies, S Leahy 6.08.2017

⑫ **Periculo 'D' Sinister** 11m F7b
   Manus Direct
Start as for *Periculo 'D' Sinister Manus* and after the 2nd bolt only use holds to the left of the bolt line - this extends the crux sequence, and makes the route slightly harder, but less wandering.
N Davies 6.08.2017

⑬ **Dangerous Davies** 9m F7b+ ★★
Technically interesting climbing starting just left of *Big in Japan*. The middle band of rock is a bit friable and may result in the grade changing over time. The line should be maintained direct and avoid deviation to *Big in Japan* until the shared lower-off.
N Davies 12.07.2017

⑭ **Big in Japan** 9m F7a ★★
Sustained climbing up the wall leads to an obtuse finish.
J Hughes, T Dixon 29.10.2009

⑮ **Resisting a Chippy Tea** 9m F7a ★
The slab in between *Resisting Chiptation* and *Big in Japan* with thin start, fingery middle and thuggy finish. It's not ticked until the holds above the lower-off!
D Allen, N.Davies 10.05.2018

⑯ **Resisting Chiptation** 9m F6c+ ★
Interesting climbing leads to a crucial traverse left on crimps to finish.
D Robinson, MF Kenyon 27.06.2009

⑰ **Brown Eyed Girl** 10m F6b ★
In between *Chiptation* and *Two Pints*. On the first ascent a flake, from which the third bolt is clipped, broke away but has now been glued back into place.
N Davies, D Allen 19.10.2018

⑱ **Two Pints and a** 9m F6b+ ★
   Packet of Crisps
Weave up the wall before or after refreshment in the Royal Oak.
E Parker, MF Kenyon, RJ Kenyon, D Robinson, J Farnworth 27.06.2009

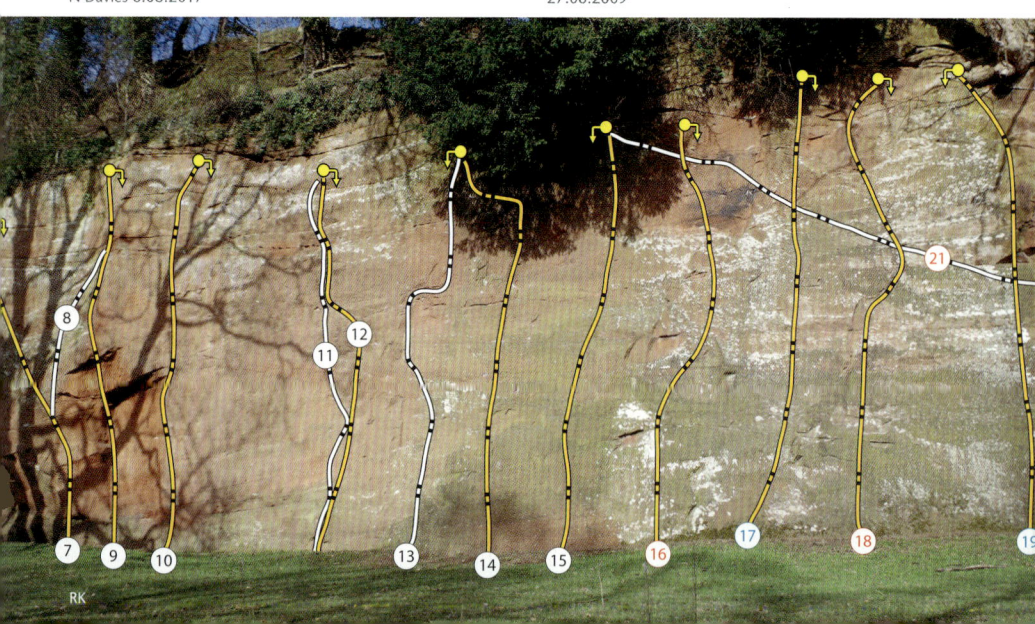

Main Wall | Coudy Rocks

19. The Sands of Time 9m F6a+ ★
Climb the vague arête to finish slightly left of a tree.
RJ Kenyon, D Robinson, E Parker, MF Kenyon, J Farnworth 27.06.2009

20. Trust in Mu 9m F6b ★
An interesting and delicate climb.
N Davies, D Allen 4.05.2018

21. The Line of Least Resistance 16m F6b+ ★
Start at the bottom ledge of *Headbutt the Bed* and ascend leftwards, getting a bolt higher, as one passes each route, to end at the lower-off of *Resisting a ChippyTea*.
N Davies, D Allen 18.10.2018

22. Headbutt the Bed 9m F6c+ ★
Climb rightwards up a groove then climb with interest up the wall to finish.
D Bush, L Bush 10.04.2010

23. Sequence Dance 9m F7b ★
Climb gymnastically up and with difficulty to gain the obvious finishing crack.
M Magus 9.05.2010

24. Big Trouble in Little China 9m F7b
Easy start then a long reach to flat hold then it gets interesting.
A Hocking 16.07.2017

25. Open Project
Wall between *Big Trouble* and *Buffalo Bill* making full use of two pockets.

26. Sandy Ripple-dithers 25m F6c ★
(in a Sea of Forgetfulness)
A slightly rising right-to-left traverse, starting as for *Buffalo Bill* and finishing at *The Sands of Time*. Quite intense in places!
C Cunningham 4.08.2017

27. Buffalo Bill 6m F6a ★
Climb the right arête.
J Farnworth, E Parker, RJ Kenyon 11.10.2009

28. New Fair Invasion 5m F6b
Climb a short corner or wall on the right then finish up the wall above.
A Davis, E Parker 5.07.2010

29. Here's to the Coalition 6m F5c
Awkward moves gain the large ledge then the slabby wall above and move up leftward to lower-off.
A Davis, E Parker 5.07.2010

30. Bongate Boogy 5m F5c
Gain the large ledge and continue up the steep wall, keeping away from the corner/crack on the left.
A Davis, E Parker 5.07.2010

31. Hooray for Harold 6m F6a+
Start up carved steps to gain the end of the large ledge. Overcome the steep wall, with difficulty, to gain and climb a crack.
A Davis, E Parker 5.07.2010

32. Helm Bar 4m F5a
A short wall to the right of *Hooray for Harold* gives this route - unfortunately getting somewhat vegetated.
RJ Kenyon, E Parker 7.07.2010

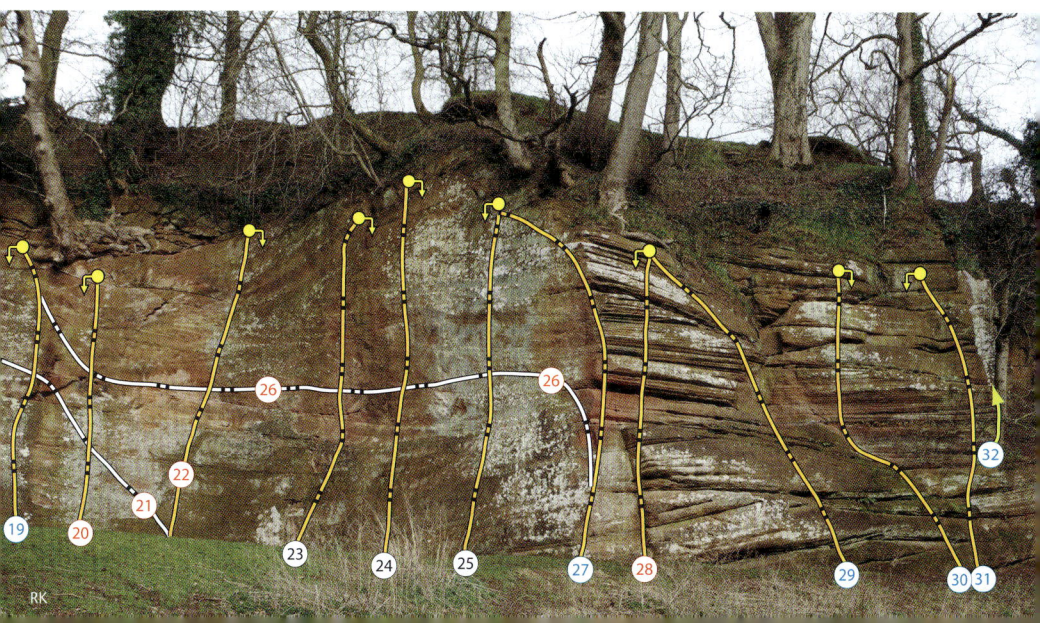

Steve's Corner M6 (page 147) John Hartley — 📷 Jonathan Doyle

Index

Symbols

3-2-1   20m   E2 5b   74
9½ Weeks   12m   F7a ★   65
!!!!!!!!!!!   10m   E3 (F7a) ★   110
21st Century Schizoid Man   25m   E3 5b   85
62 War Trick   47
62 West Wallaby Street   27m   F7a+ ★   47
300 Spartans, The   25m   F6b   103
??????   E3 (F7a) ★   110

A

Absolutely Fabulous   F6b   258
Acrachnophobia   15m   VS 4c   166
Act of Contrition   21m   E5 5c   169
Adela   18m   F6c   79
Adventures of Pinocchio, The   F7a ★   264
Advocate, The   10m   F6a ★   245
A Fistful of Steroids   24m   F6b+ ★★★   68
Agent Provocateur   F7c+ ★   51
All Weather Gym, The   114
Al's Slab   F5+   202
A Meeting with Don Juan   F6c ★   166
A Miller's Tale   25m   F6a ★   234
Amphibian   60m   F7a ★★   126
Amphitheatre, The   244
An Alabuse   32m   E2 5c   187
Ancient Mariner   F5+ ★   258
Andy's Route   F6b ★★★   262
Andy's Route - Right Hand Var   F6a+ ★   262
An Oasis of Tranquility   30m   E4 6b   137
Another Poolside Attraction   25m   F6a+   249
Antiques Roadshow   25m   F6a ★   217
Anvil Arête   12m   F6b ★★   162
Aphasic Syndrome, The   22m   F6c ★★★   240
Apiarist, The   F6b+ ★★★   258
Apiary Wall   258
Aqua Man Direct   25m   F6b ★247
Arcade Fire   25m   F6a+ ★★★   219
Arc-de-Triomphe   25m   F6a+ ★★   230
Arm & Hammer Slab   12m   F6c   127
Arnold Rimmer   17m   E3 6a   178
Arthur Dolphin isn't Dead, I've Seen Him in News World   10m   HVS 4c   172
A Slight Slate Escapade   20m   F4+   103
A Sorry Affair   24m   F6c+ ★   139
A Spate of Slate   10m   F6a   114
Aurora   F6a+   262
Autan   28m   F6c   138
A Vision of Things Gone Wild   16m   F7b+ ★★   68
A Walk In The Park   35m   F6a   245

B

Backfire   F6b   201
Back to the Future   11m   F7c+ ★   76
Bad Moon Rising   16m   F6b ★   99
Bakestone Quarry   150
Bambino Bolero   25m   VS   232
Banana Slide   F6a   138
Baptismal Vows   25m   F6a+ ★   249
Barbi Junior   10m   F6c   190
Barnes Big Day Out   F6a   166
Barney Rubble   25m   F6c ★★   50
Barrow Boys' Day Out   30m   F6a ★★   235
Barrowfield Buttress   71
Barrow Scout Cove   90
Bar Six   16m   F7b   68
Basilica   45m   F7a ★★★   190
Bat out of Hell (a.k.a Mac's Crack)   HVS 5a   201
Bay of Pigs   40m   E4 6a   112
Baywatch   F6b   202
Beast, The   10m   F6b+   245
Beaver Patrol   32m   F7b ★   134
Beef Jerky   40m   F7a ★★   127
Bee Hive   F6c   258
Bee Line   F6b+ ★   258
Beers for Fears   16m   F7a+ ★   68
Bee Sting   F7a ★★   258
Beeswax   F6b   258
Behind the Lines   33m   HVS 5a ★★★   129
Belay Bunny   20m   F6b ★★   169
Belly Button Slab   13m   HVS 5a ★   177
Benghazi Burner   15m   F6a+   228
Bertie Basset   20m   F6c ★★   271
Best Western   25m   F6a+ ★★★   218
Better Red than Dead   F5+   202
Betty Rubble   25m   F6c ★★   50
Beyond The Fringe   10m   F5b ★   246
Big Crack   160
Big Dipper   46m   E1 5b ★★   127
Big Gym   10m   F5+   114
Big in Japan   9m   F7a ★★   278
Big Link, The   50m   E6 6b   116
Big Mirror   E2 5b ★★★   127
Big Tree Corner   13m   E1 5b ★   162
Big Tree Corner Sector   162
Big Trouble in Little China   9m   F7b   279
Bishop and the Actress, The   30m   E3 5c   187
Bitter End, The   8m   F5a   245
Black Hole Boys, The   30m   E3 6a   187
Black Mamba   19m   F6a   193
Blank Expression   33m   E5 6a ★   129
Blank on the Map   20m   F6c ★★   212
Bleep and Booster   27m   F6c ★★   44
Blencathra Badger   27m   F5c ★★★   235
Blind Audition   10m   F6a   246
Blinkered   15m   F6c ★   88
Blood Donor   15m   M9+   146
Bloodline   20m   M10   146
Blooming Marvellous   F6c ★★   258
Blue Bayou   20m   F5   103
Blue Moon   25m   F6b ★★   103
Blue Movie   24m   E2 5c   103
Blue Oyster Cult   F6a ★   202
Blue Remembered Hills   25m   F6c ★   103
Blue Riband   10m   E1 5b   103
Blue Screw   18m   F6c+ ★   71
Blue Steel   22m   E2 5c ★   103
Bobby Dazzler   30m   F6b ★★   230
Boiling Point   12m   F5   88
Bolt from the Blue   20m   F6b ★★   212
Bon Courage   20m   F6a   230
Bongate Boogy   5m   F5c   279
Bonne Chance   18m   F6c ★   230
Boob Tube   17m   F6c+ ★   193
Borg, The   25m   F7a+ ★★   50
Born Again   26m   F6a+ ★★   66
Born Free   F6a ★★★   66
Born to Run   24m   F6c ★★★   66
Bornville   12m   F6a   66
Borrowdale Lad's Day Out   XS 5c   154
Botterill's Slab   20m   F6b   234
Bramcrag Corner   20m   F6a ★219
Bramcrag Quarry   208
Bramcrag Wall   212
Bramcrag Wall   19m   F6c+ ★★212
Breakthrough   15m   F6b   88
Bright Eyes n' Blue   55m   E4 6a ★   131
Brilliant Disguise   16m   E2 5c ★   194
Bring Me Sunshine   20m   F6a   224
Broken Pelvis   10m   F6a   114
Broken Zipper   71
Brothers in Arms   30m   F6a+   235
Brown Eyed Girl   10m   F6b ★   278
Buffalo Bill   F6a ★   279
Burkini   10m   F5b ★   44
Burly Dudes   22m   F7b ★★   189
Burning Issue   10m   F6b+   244
Burning, The   10m   F6a+ ★   177
Bury my Heart   F3   202
Bus Pass   VS 5a   88

C

Cable Wall, The   139
Cadillac   24m   F6c ★★★   59
Café Boys do their Thong   10m   F5+ ★   110
Calling Mr Hall   21m   F8a ★★   51
Calling the Shots   27m   F7a ★★   108
Camaro   F6c+   59
Captain Pugwash   16m   HVS 5a ★   165
Captain Pugwash Revisited   25m   F6a ★★   251
Carpe Diem   18m   F7a+   116
Caspian   15m   F5b   172
Castaway   F7c ★★★   271
Cathedral Quarry   180
Caveman   22m   F8b+   182
Cave Route RH   F7a ★★   271
Celestial Cyclone   25m   E3 5c   85
Celica Groove   12m   F5+   137
Cellar Dwellers   10m   F6b   114
Cement Head   25m   F7a+ ★★   44
Center Parc   232
Central Area   66
Central Gully Wall   42
Centre Stage   10m   F6a   246
Chance Encounter   VS 4b   110
Changing Corners   15m   F6b ★★   224
Chapel Head Scar   38
Charcoal Burner's Buttress, The   218
Charcoal Burner, The   25m   F6b ★★★   219
Charm Offensive   13m   F6b+ ★★★   217
Chestnut Mare   15m   F7b ★   119
Chickenhawk   F5+ ★   202
Chimney Route   F4+   266
China Crisis   20m   F7a+ ★★   189
China Syndrome   263
Christmas Cracker   10m   HS ★160
Cleaver, The   41m   E4 6a ★   134
Clone Wars   F7b S1 ★★★   113

Index | 283

Close Call 42m E4 6a ★ 131
Close Encounters 12m F5 88
Close Encounters 174m E5 6a ★ 135
Clutching at Straws 13m F6a+ ★ 176
Clydebank Kipper, The 15m F6a ★ 240
Cockle Shell Hero 20m F6b+ 271
Cold Fusion 18m F6c 193
Cold Turkey 10m E4 6b ★ 189
Combat Plumber 25m F7a ★ 44
Combi 12m F5b 212
Comedy Show 15m F6b 42
Comedy Shuffle 20m F6a+ ★251
Comfort Zone, The 25m F5b ★ 234
Coming Up For Air 10m F6b+ ★ 246
Command Performance 47m E6 6b ★ 125
Common Wood Quarry 192
Con Artist 15m F6b+ 228
Conflict Zone 25m F6b ★ 232
Contagion 10m F6b 178
Contorted Creations 14m E5 6b ★ 119
Cool Hand Luke 25m F6b+ ★★ 217
Cool Your Jets Mum 12m F6c+ 42
Corbyn 12m F4 ★ 64
Corona Nightmare 15m F6a+ ★ 178
Cosmic Dancer F7b ★★ 57
Coudy Rocks 274
Countach 23m F7b ★★ 59
Coup de Grace 16m F7b+ ★★75
Coup-de-Grace 20m F6b+ ★★★ 224
Coup d'Etat 36m F6b+ ★★ 230
Coye Dog 10m F6a 176
Crack Addict 10m F6c+ 244
Creative Contortions 15m F7b+ ★★ 119
Crimes of Passion 15m F7a ★★ 68
Critic's Choice 10m F6a+ 246
Crossed Lorraine F5+ ★★ 71
Crossing, The 25m F6a+ ★ 240
Crumblefoot 18m F6a+ 71
Crunchy Kibble 30m F7a ★★ 86
Cryptic Contortions 137
Crystal Maze F7b S0 ★★★ 113
Culling, The 20m F6c ★★ 219
Cup and Lip 13m F6b 137
Curtain Call 40m F7a+ ★ 129
Curver, The 12m E2 5b 163
Cutlass F6c+ ★ 266
Cyborg 21m E2 5c ★ 50

D

Dalt Loch Chimney F5 202
Dalt Loch Monster F6a 202
Dalt Quarry 198
Dancing in the Danger Zone! 35m F6b+ ★★★ 217
Dan Dare 39m VS 4c 131
Dangerous Davies 9m F7b+ ★★ 278
Dark Angel F7b+ 201
Darklands 38m F6b ★★★ 189
Darkness Beckons, The 25m F6b ★★ 217
Dark Side, The 216
Dave's Route F7a+ 263

Dave's Route F7a+ 264
Daytime Blues 32m F6b ★ 134
Dead Calm 16m E1 5c 194
Dead Head 14m HS 194
Death Warrant 20m E5 6b ★★ 169
Deceptive Bends E1 5b 84
Descent Route M 64
Desperate Dan 30m F6b+ ★ 230
Desperate Dan the Dyno Man 22m F6c+ ★ 138
Deviant Direct, The 25m F7a+ ★ 219
Deviant, The 25m F6c+ ★ 219
Dibdab M7 151
Dick Tatoes 14m F5+ 194
Diet of Worms E6 6b 189
Dignitas 20m F6b 240
Director's Cut 30m F6b ★ 229
Direct Variation F7c+ 76
Doctor Evil 24m F7c+ ★★★ 54
Doctor's Dilemma 7m F6c+ 57
Dogfight at Virgin Massacre Creek 20m F7c+ ★★ 110
Double Jeopardy 20m F6b ★★ 240
Double Time 9m M6 142
Douglas 13m F6b ★ 66
Drapolene 25m F6a+ ★ 249
Dreaming of Red Rocks F7a+ ★★★ 263
Dress Rehearsal 10m F5b 246
Driller Killer 30m F7a+ ★ 57
Driller Killer F6a 263
Drone F7a+ ★ 258

E

Eastern Promise 35m F6b ★★★ 229
Easter Rising 25m F6a+ ★ 249
Easy Rider F5+ 131
Ebb and Flow 18m F6c ★★ 268
Edgar's Arch 76
Electric Warrior 21m F7b ★★★51
Elicit Scenes of Sex and Violence F8a ★ 168
El Presidento Robbo 6m F6a+ 276
Elysium F7b ★★★ 265
Encore 10m F5c 246
Endeavour 25m F6a 249
Endgame 20m F6a 235
End Walls 86
Englebert Humphreding 8m F7b 76
Enoc 10m F6b ★ 110
Entertainer, The F6a+ ★ 126
Entertainment Value F6c 126
Eraser Head 25m F7b+ ★★★ 50

F

Face Life 25m F7b 108
Face the Music 24m F6c+ 108
Face the Times 20m F6c 108
Fallen Roof M6+ 147
Fall From Grace 17m F6b ★ 193
False Prophet 12m F6b 245
Fancy a Jump 10m F6b 174
Fang, The 10m E3 (F6c) 110
Fang, The 15m M8 150
Farage 9m F5 ★ 64
Far Crag Foot 91
Farewell to Adventure? 20m F6a+ ★ 234
Fargo 25m F5a ★ 234
Far Out 12m E5 6a 137

Far Right Buttress 71
Fatal Attraction 43m F7b 134
Fat Guy goes Nutzoid 18m E6 6b ★★ 168
Feeling Groovy F6c ★★★ 263
Feral 11m F6c ★ 65
Final Act, The 44m E6 6b ★ 125
Finger-tips of Civilisation F6b+172
Firebird 20m F7a+ ★★ 59
Fire Starter 10m F6c ★ 244
Firing Squad, The 19m F7b ★★ 74
First Blood 14m F7a+ ★ 65
First Blood M9+ 146
First Footing 10m F6a 251
First Footing 13m VS 4b 119
First Night Nerves 55m E5 6b ★★★ 116
First Order, The F6c+ S0 ★ 113
Fisherman's Friend F5 ★★★ 265
Flake and Corner 13m HVS 5a 163
Fleswick Bay 271
Fly By Wire 17m F6a+ 194
Flying Dutchman, The 25m F6b+ ★★ 216
Flying Low 9m F7b 278
Foghorn Leghorn 16m VS 4c 165
Footlights 10m F5b 246
Forever Young 25m F5c ★ 249
Forgotten Walls 79
Forphil 17m F6a ★ 88
For When The Tree Goes F7b+ ★ 54
Fossil Crack 12m F6b 59
Fossil Groove 9m F6a 59
Foul Brood F7a+ ★ 258
Friday 13th F7a+ ★ 266
Frigging Friends F6c 265
Friggin' in the Riggin' F6b 265
Fringe Benefits 20m F6c 234
Fuel My Fire 8m F7a+ 91
Fun Factory, The 238
Fun Factory, The 20m F6a ★★ 238
Fusion 17m F6c 74

G

Gallery, The 174
Gambler, The 12m F6c 137
Gandalf 13m F6b+ ★ 172
G.F.I. 13m F6b 137
Gilbert Cardigan 20m F7a+ ★ 51
Girdle Traverse F6b+ ★★★ 232
Glasgow Kiss 20m F6a+ ★ 240
Going Ballistic 14m F7b ★ 138
Going for a Swing 15m M9+ 143
Going Underground 40m F6b ★★ 187
Gollum's Gully 12m VD 172
Gone Surfin' 42m E2 5c 134
Gonzo 10m F6a 245
Goodbye Mr Major! 31m F6a ★★ 235
Goodfellas 27m F5b ★ 235
Good Friday Agreement, The 30m F6b 235
Good Luck Mr Blair! 20m F6b 234
Good Medicine 20m F5+ ★★ 66
Gorilla Groove 30m F6a+ ★ 138
Gorilla Monsoon 20m F6a+ 232
Grand Design 9m M7 ★ 142
Grand Designs 25m F6c ★ 222
Grand Union 30m F6c ★★★ 224
Grand Wall 222
Gratuitous Violence 52m F7a ★ 139

Index

Grave New World 13m F7b ★★ 68
Gravity Blade 17m F7a+ ★★ 193
Gravy Bones 50m F6b+ ★★★ 84
Gray Race, The 9m F6b 91
Greasing My Teapot 10m F6a ★ 177
Great Buttress 50
Great Expectations 42m F7a ★★★ 125
Greek Exit 18m F6b+ ★ 240
Green Route, The 20m F7c 59
Groove, The 137
G-Spot, The 113
Guardian of the Underworld 30m M12 146
Gully Wall 16m F6b 42
Gully Wall Direct F6c ★ 42
Guloot Kalagna 21m F7c ★ 51

H

Haggis 42m E6 6a 127
Half-Life 27m F6b+ ★ 50
Halloween F4+ 266
Hammerlock 22m E4 5c 74
Hang 'em High 49m F7a+ ★★ 138
Hang Like a Hound 10m F7a+ ★ 176
Happy Friday F5 266
Hats Off Direct 10m F6b 177
Hats Off to Linten Miller 10m F6a ★ 177
Headbutt the Bed 9m F6c+ ★ 279
Head Like a Hole 15m F8b+ 76
Heart of Glass F6b 202
Heaven Can Wait 25m F5c ★★ 222
Heaven Sent 25m F6a 222
Heinous Penis 21m F6c 44
Hell Bender 30m F6b+ ★ 230
Hello Helen 10m F7b+ ★★ 196
Hell's Mouth 17m F6b+ 194
Helm Bar 4m F5a 279
Helter Skelter 25m F6b+ ★★ 217
Here's Lookin' at Euclid 25m F6b+ ★★ 251
Here's to the Coalition 6m F5c 279
High Blue Quarry 100
High Heels 16m F6c+ ★★ 71
Histocompatable Hanger 15m F7b ★ 163
History Boys, The 30m F6b+ ★★★ 230
Hodge Close Quarry 104
Hodgetastic 18m F6c 126
Hollow Lands 12m F6c ★ 76
Homeward Bound 26m F7a 99
Honey Pot F6b+ ★ 258
Hoof Hearted 40m E4 6b 134
Hooray for Harold 6m F6a+ 279
Hothouse F6b+ 201
Hot Tuna 13m E2 6a 189
Hound Dog 9m F5+ ★★ 193
Hound-dog 15m F6a 229
House of Correction 10m F7a+ ★ 139
Humphrey Bogart 16m F7a+ ★ 75
Humphrey Cushion F7a+ «« 75
Humphrey Dumphrey 8m F6a ★ 76
Humphrey Dumphrey Buttress 76
Humphrey Head 72
Humphrey Hymen (Met a Sly Man) 16m F7b+ ★★ 75
Hunter Returns, The 35m E5 6b 187
Hurt Locker, The 20m F6c ★★★ 212

I

Ian's Day Off HVS 5a 202
Icicle HVS 71
Idaho Connection Wave, The 9m F7b+ ★ 119
Idle Times 15m F7a ★ 68
I Got Horribly Drunk 10m F6c+ 182
I Got Horribly Sober 40m F8b ★★★ 189
Impoverished Pioneers 23m E2 5c 103
Incendiary Groove 12m F6b 245
Industrial Sector 142
Ingham's Route 16m F7c ★★163
Integrali 22m F7a+ ★★ 59
Interstellar Overdrive 24m F6c ★★★ 44
I Sold my Soul for Whisky and Mushrooms 20m E3 6a 169
It's Moi Land 12m F6a 176
Ivy League 16m F7a+ ★★★ 68
Ivy League Buttress 68
I Wish I Was F8a ★★ 265

J

Jack the Dripper 25m F6b+ ★218
January 22m F6a ★ 79
Jelly Head 25m F7a ★ 44
Jim of Shadows 32m E3 5c 138
Jitterbug 12m E3 6a ★★ 165
Johnny No Mates F6c+ 42
Johnson 9m F4+ 64
Joie de Vivre 57m F6b+ ★★★ 116
Joy Division 18m F5c ★ 238
Juggler's Crack 12m HVS 5a ★★ 162
Just Nice F6a+ 258

K

Kathleen 16m F6b+ 68
Kathleen's Nightmare 13m F7a ★ 68
Katyusha 25m F6b+ ★ 249
Keep On Keeping On 9m F8a+ ★★ 196
Keep the Car Running 27m F6a+ ★ 219
Kept Woman F7c+ 196
Kick Off 10m HVS 5a ★★ 160
Kick Off Sector 160
Kill Bill 25m F6b 249
Kleeneze F6b 258
Kryten Corner 17m F6b ★ 178
Kyber Crystal F6b+ S0 ★★ 113

L

Laguna Verde F5+ ★ 202
Lakes Ethics 25m M9+ 143
La Mangoustine Scatouflange 22m F7b+ ★★★ 54
Last Dash 15m F6b ★★ 228
Latex Generation 15m F7a+ ★ 163
Leather Pets 16m F6c+ ★ 68
Le Flange en Decomposition 15m F6b+ 42

Left Hand Cave 143
Left-Hand Line 9m F6c ★ 196
Left Route M4 144
Left Slip 10m M4 150
Legend's Friend F7a ★ 264
Legless in Gaza F6c ★ 202
Le Grand Traverse 85m F7c ★★ 57
Leicester Tit Lab 20m E3 5b 110
Leo's Hard Traverse F7b S1 113
Leo's Traverse F6c+ S1 113
Let there be Light 30m M10+ 146
Licking The Wounds 15m VS 4b 194
Life Begins at Forty 25m F6a ★★ 249
Life in the Bus Lane 5b 161
Life in the Fast Lane 45m E5 6b ★★ 126
Like a Dick Only Smaller 10m F6a+ ★ 91
Limited Edition 33m E4 6a 127
Line of Least Resistance, The 16m F6b+ ★ 279
Lister 16m E3 5b 178
Little Sydney F5 202
Live Rounds 20m F7a+ ★ 75
Loan Shark 15m F6a ★ 244
Lobsters' Quadrille, The 30m F6a 134
Lockdown 10m F6a+ 178
Long Good Friday, The 27m F5b ★★ 235
Long Voyage Home, The 17m F7a ★★ 271
Look Sharp 19m E2 5c ★★ 168
Look Sharp Sector 168
Looper 15m F6b+ ★ 212
Lorna's Orifices 12m E3 6a ★ 166
Lower Quarry 172, 247
Low level Traverse M4 151
Lucid Dreams 16m F6b ★★ 178
Luddite 15m F5c ★ 229
Luna Prick 47
Lunatic 25m F6c ★ 47
Lynn-er Motion 10m E1 5b 174

M

Maboulisme Merveilleux 16m F7c+ ★★ 47
Mad Alice 30m F6a+ ★★ 134
Magenta De Vine 14m F7a+ 137
Main Crag 74
Main Event, The 70m E5 6a ★★ 116
Main Wall 84, 229
Main Wall, The 116
Major Misdemeanor 20m F7c+ ★ 169
Making Peace With God HVS 4b 166
Malice in Wonderland 43m E4 6a ★★★ 129
Marginal Gains 20m F6b ★★214
Marine's Slab 25m F6a ★★ 251
Meet the Wife 12m F7b+ ★★ 65
Megabyte 15m E5 6a ★★ 183
Megadrive F6b+ ★★ 263
Megamoose 7m F6c+ ★★★ 276
Meltdown 18m F6c 193
Melting Point 12m F5 ★ 88
Michael Angelo 11m F6c ★ 138
Michelangelo 16m F6c ★ 212
Micro-Granite 204

Index | 285

Mid-Air Collision 25m   F7b   ★★★   50
Middle Earth   16m   F7b   212
Middle East Crisis   30m   F6b+   ★   229
Middle Quarry   176
Middle Route   M4   144
Middle Way   17m   F6a   88
Midgebite   10m   F6c+   108
Mighty Fly   30m   E5 6b   ★★★   86
Mill Side Scar   58
Mindfields   15m   F7a+   ★   76
Mirror Image   40m   F7b+ E5 6c   131
Mirrormere   52m   E2 5b   ★   127
Mirror Mirror   131
Misplaced   12m   F6a   88
Mission, The   25m   F6b   ★★★   222
Model, The   13m   F5+   137
Modern Man   8m   F3   91
Modern Times   26m   HVS   ★   85
Modern Wall   85
Modern World, The   8m   F3   91
Moist Meaty Chunks   18m   F7b+   ★★   268
Molly Malone   F6c   ★★   263
Monster Dog   10m   F7a   ★   172
Moonchild   24m   F6c+   ★★   44
Moonchild Buttress   44
Moonlight Sonata   30m   F6a   134
Moonshine   22m   F6a   ★★   87
More Banana Related Japery   32m   F7a   ★★   187
Morecambe and Wise   9m   E3 5c   ★★   161
More Come and Rise   11m   E4 6b   ★   161
More Foaming Ales   10m   F6b+ 187
More Games   9m   F7c   ★   54
Morley Street Mission   15m   F6b   ★★★   228
Moss Rigg Quarry   152
Movement   22m   E3 6a   119
Mowing the Lawn   25m   F6c+   ★ 110
Mr Angry   18m   F6b   ★   230
Mr Sandman   F6a+   ★   266
Mr Self-Destruct   12m   F7b   76
Mr T   11m   F6a+   ★★   64
Murder in the Cathedral   40m   E4 6a   189
Mustang   21m   F6b   ★★   59
Mutineer, The   25m   F6b+   ★   251

N

Nameless   F5   201
Nappyrash   25m   F6a   ★   249
Narrow Land, The   F5c   172
Nasal Passage   F6a   ★   264
Natural Habitat   F6c   ★   265
Nebbie   20m   E3 6a   ★   169
Nectarine   F6c+   ★★★   258
Network, The   8m   F6a   245
Newbie   M7   143
New Booties   10m   F6b   172
New Fair Invasion   5m   F6b   279
Nice View, Petunia   13m   F6a   176
Night of the Hot Pies   30m   E1 5b   ★★   187
Night Watch, The   10m   F6a+   ★★ 240
Nirbhaya   18m   F6b+   178
Nisbet Memorial Link   M6+   151
No Country for Old Men   25m   F6b+   249
Nocturnal Emissions   38m   F7c 127
Noda   16m   E1 5a   75

No Face for Dwarfs   13m   F7a+   ★ 190
No Line   15m   F5+   88
Northern Lights   F6b+   ★   264
Northern Soul   20m   F6b+   ★★★ 212
Northumbrian VS   10m   F7a+   114
Not the Full Shilling   18m   F8a   ★★★   47
Nuclear Seepage   F7b   ★   262

O

OAP's Sport Climb Too   11m   F5+   114
Occupational Hazard   9m   F7b   ★   278
Oddbods   15m   F6b+   42
Off the Sneck   15m   F4   88
Oiling the Lawnmower   30m   F6a   ★★   110
Omega Factor   18m   F6c   ★   50
One Arm Bandit   12m   F5+   137
On the Edge   23m   F5b   232
Orifice Fish   40m   E4 5c   ★★   182
Oswald Moseley   37m   F6b E3 6a   134
Outfield   20m   M6+   151
Out of the Ice   71
Outside Leg   12m   M5   151
Outsider   268
Outsider   F6a+   ★   268
Overtime   9m   M6   ★   142

P

Palmer's Performance   22m   F5+   ★   103
Pangolin   15m   F6b   ★★   224
Panzerfaust   F6c+   202
Parrock Quarry   136
Pathfinder   18m   F6b+   ★   59
Payday   15m   F6a   244
Peapod   15m   HVS 5a   ★   161
Pedestal Corner   E2 5b   162
People's Slab, The   144
Perfect Drug, The   F6c   91
Perfect Weather to Fly   9m   F7a   ★★   278
Periculo 'D' Sinister Manus   9m   F7a+   ★   278
Periculo 'D' Sinister Manus Direct   11m   F7b   278
Permitted Development   13m   F7a+   ★   138
Perverse Pépère   25m   F7b+   ★★   54
Perverted Start   12m   F7b+   ★   54
Phantom Arête   V3   174
Phantom Zone   25m   F7b+   ★★★ 44
Picture This   8m   F4   91
Pieces of Eight   F6a   ★★   264
Pigs in Space   33m   F6c   112
Pincher   8m   F4   91
Pioneer Meets His Match   10m   F6b   114
Pioneers' Cave   59
Places in Between, The   6m   F6c   276
Plastic Wall   11m   F4   88
Pleasantly Slobbish   10m   F6c   139
Plunger, The   15m   F6b+   ★★   119
Poetry in Commotion   12m   F7b   ★   71
Poetry in Motion   12m   F6b+   ★71
Polish Direct   35m   M12   143

Polo   22m   F4   ★   88
Pool Wall, The   112
Pork Pie   16m   F6a+   «   75
Poseidon   F7c   ★   266
Powerdab   20m   M13   151
Power of Sila   F5a   172
Power Share   10m   F6c   ★   245
Power Transmission   40m   E5 6c   ★★   126
Pressure Drop   11m   F7a+   160
Priaprism   25m   F6a   251
Prime Evil   24m   F7c+   ★★★   54
Production Line   20m   F6a   247
Promenade Crack   F7b   ★★   262
Promontory Buttress   228
Proton   8   F6c   ★   59
Provocateur, The   12m   F6c+   193
Publish And Be Damned   12m   F6a+   193
Punchy Patterson   12m   E4 6a   ★   162

Q

Quantum Leap   F6b+   262
Quarrymen, The   15m   F6a   229
Quarry Slaves   9m   F7b+   114
Quick Release   15m   M11   146
Quisling, The   30m   F6b+   ★★ 230

R

Rabbithole Redemption   20m   HVS 4b   169
Rainbow Warrior   F6b+   ★★   264
Rainey Park   23m   F6c+   99
Randolph Scott   39m   E1 5b   ★127
Rank Outsider   F6b+   ★   268
Ray of Hope   17m   F6a   88
Rebel Alliance   F7b S0   ★★★   113
Rebel Yell   20m   F6a+   222
Recharge   F6a+   263
Red Bush   19m   F6a   ★   88
Reefer Madness   9m   F6c+   57
Remainer Buttress   64
Resisting a Chippy Tea   9m   F7a   ★   278
Resisting Chiptation   9m   F6c+   ★   278
Return of the Jedi   15m   F5+   ★ 88
Return to Year Zero   29m   E4 6b   126
Revenant   25m   F6b   ★   249
Rhode Island Red   14m   E3 5c   ★★   165
Rhode Island Red Sector   165
Rib, The   166
Riding on Air   22m   F5   ★   88
Right Hand Cave   146
Right Route   M4   144
Rim Fisher   33m   E3 5c   ★   187
Rim Fisher - Left-hand Finish   E2 5c   ★   187
Ring of Fire   52   F6c+   218
Ringpiece Activist   35m   F6c+   ★   187
Ripper Street   30m   F6b   235
Ripping Yarns   25m   F6a+   ★   219
Rookie, The   25m   F5b   ★   234
Ropearse   16m   F6b   68
Roughnecks   20m   F6a+   ★   214
Route of All Evil Direct, The   26m   F7b   ★★★   50
Route of All Evil, The   30m   F7a+   ★★   50
Route of All Evil Wall   50

Index

Route One   F4 ★   262
Route Two   F4   263
Royal Jelly   F6b ★   258
Rubble Wall   50
Runestone Cowboy   10m   F5b ★   177
Runestone Cross   F5b   177
Runestone Quarry   170
Rust Bucket   10m   F5a   177
Rusty Wall   18m   E3 6a   160

S

Sad But True   27m   F6c+   50
Saddlestone Quarry   98
Sam's Day   14m   F4   88
Sands of Time, The   9m   F6a+ ★   279
Sandy Ripple-dithers (In a Sea of Forgetfulness)   25m   F6c ★   279
Sasquatch   38m   HVS 5a ★★   134
Sauchiehall Street   20m   F5b ★   240
Scabby Back   262
Scallywag Slab   30m   F6b ★   103
Scared Rabbit   12m   F7a+ ★★   196
Scarfoot Chimney   8m   F3   64
Scarfoot Wall   8m   F4+   64
Scorpion   F6a ★   264
Scouse   8m   F4   91
Scout Post   15m   F6b   71
Scout Scar   60
Screamadelica   F7a+   264
Scrotal Recall   25m   F6a+ ★★   251
Scurvy   F6a   262
Seam, The   F6a   202
Sea of Sand   F7c ★★★   271
Sea Shall Not Have Them, The   F6c+ ★★   271
Second Coming   55m   F6c+ ★★★   116
Second Order   F6c   113
Seconds Away   25m   F5c ★★   249
Self Isolation   11m   F6a ★   177
Sequence Dance   9m   F7b ★   279
Serial Thrilla   8m   F7b+ ★   91
Shades of Mediocrity   20m   F7a ★   51
Shadow Warrior   F7c   201
Shattered Image   41m   F7a+ E4 6b   131
Sheepwrecked   11m   F6b ★   64
Shining, The   29m   F7a   99
Ship of Fools   27m   F6a ★   235
Shock Treatment   F6c S1 ★★   113
Shooting Gallery, The   30m   F6a ★★★   224
Shooting the Load   20m   F7a ★75
Shot by Both Sides   8m   F7a ★   74
Shot in the Dark   20m   F6b ★★   212
Showroom Dummy   15m   F4+   137
Side Circle, The   246
Sideshow   116
Silicone Crack   15m   F6c   219
Silly Mid On   10m   M5   150
Sinking Feeling   F6a+ S0   113
Sinking in the West   F6a+ ★★   266
Sink The Bismark   F7b+ ★★★   271
Siren Wall   268
Ska Train   12m   F6b ★   172
Skegness is so Bracing   F6a+   201
Sky   47m   F6b+ ★★★   125
Skyline Direct Start   F7a   108
Skyline   F6b+   108
Skywalker   25m   F6b+ ★★★   247
Slash and Grab   F6b   266
Slate Dancer   12m   F7b   163
Slaying the Badger   25m   F6a+ ★★   219
Sleeping Sickness   10m   F6a+ ★91
Slightly Shoddy   11m   F7a   76
Slip of the Tongue   10m   VS 5a ★   161
Slobodan Zhivovinovics   12m   F6a   138
Slobs, The   137
Slobs, The   16m   F6a ★   138
Slow and Easy   10m   5b   161
Smile at the End of the Rainbow   10m   F6a+ ★   177
Sniffing the Saddle   18m   F6a+   74
Sniffin' the Saddle Direct   21m   F6a+   74
Soap Opera   32m   F7a   134
Solitaire   15m   5b ★   161
Something for the Weekend   F6b+ ★   266
Song for Europe   23m   F7b+ ★★★   54
Song to the Siren   20m   F7a+ ★★★   268
Sorry, No Bolts   25m   E2 5a ★234
Spare Wall   15m   F6a+ ★   166
Spare Wall Sector   166
Spectral Wizard   16m   F7b ★★   68
Spectre   22m   F6a ★   222
Speed of Light   13m   F7a+ ★   137
Split Wet Beaver   F6b ★★   168
Spook   30m   F6a+ ★   222
Sport for All   12m   F4   114
Spring Offensive, The   18m   F6b ★★   240
Spycatcher   13m   E5 6b ★   162
Stage Fright   50m   E6 6b ★★★125
Stage Fright   F6b   263
Stage Left   10m   F6a   246
Stage Right   10m   F6a   246
Standing Ovation   157m   E4 6b ★   135
Stan Pulsar   25m   F7b+ ★   44
Starshine   F6b   44
Star Trek   16m   F6a ★★   88
Star Wars   36m   F5+ ★★   88
State of Play   10m   F6a   246
St Bees Head   256
Steal, The   F7a ★   264
Stein Pull   M6 ★   142
Steve's Corner   15m   M6   147
Stiff Little Fingers   116
Stinky Dinks   45m   E2 6a ★   127
St. John's Ambulance   30m   F4+ ★   235
Stoker   30m   F6c+ ★★   224
Straight-8   19m   F8a ★★   59
Straight Tach   F7a+ ★   59
Stretchy Perineum   10m   F7b+ ★★   54
Strongbow   15m   F6b   42
Stumbling Block   15m   F6a ★   229
Stump Flake Wall   HS 4b ★   166
Stymen   16m   F6c ★   75
Sunbeam Talbot   20m   F6b   219
Sunburst Slab   224
Sunburst Slab   30m   F6a ★   224
Sunflake   15m   HVS 5a   75
Sun God   25m   F6a+ ★   44
Sunshine Gang, The   30m   F6a+ ★★★   224
Super Duper DuPont   24m   F7c ★★★   54
Super DuPont   22m   F7b+ ★★★54

Surfing with the Alien   25m   F8a ★   44
Swarm   F7a ★★★   258
Swindler's List   15m   F6a   244
Swingers Extension   25m   M11   143
Swinson   9m   F4+   64
Sylvester Strange   12m   F7c ★   65
Synergy   25m   F7a ★★   247

T

Take It or Leave It   20m   F6a   232
Telegraph Road   15m   F6c+ ★★65
Ten in 2010   9m   F6a ★   91
Tenuous Fly   10m   F7b ★   278
Ten Years After   45m   E5 6a ★★★   125
Terrace Wall   88
The Black Beast Returns, Bottom Line Creeping with the Crypt Trip Boys   70m   E4 6b ★   190
Their Law   8m   F7a   91
There's Nae Fat on me Taties   12m   F6a+ ★   177
The Works   140
This Charming Man   15m   F6a+216
Thrang Quarry   196
Through the Looking Glass   42m   E2 5c ★★★   131
Tiger, Tiger   34m   E3 6a   187
Tilberthwaite Quarry   156
Tilney's Shovel   9m   E2 5c ★★   161
Tilney's Shovel Sector   161
Time and a Half   9m   M5   142
Timeless Flight   12m   F7b ★   131
Tin Can Alley   20m   F6a ★★   224
Tipton Slasher, The   30m   F6b+ ★★★   229
Titanic Arête   50m   F6c+   154
Titbits   12m   F6b+   119
Toirdealbach   18m   F6b   71
Toll Road   10m   F5c   245
Tommy Knockers, The   F6a   135
Top Shot   15m   VS 4b   165
Tormentor, The   16m   F6c   193
Torture Garden, The   30m   E6 6b ★★★   86
Toulouse Sausage, The   14m   F5   194
Toxic Rock   F7b ★★   262
Train Crazy Boys   45m   F6b+   154
Tramadol Nights   18m   F6b ★238
Transfusion   15m   M8   147
Treacle Slab   20m   E3 5c ★★   169
Treacle Slab Sector   169
Trick or Treat   F6b+ ★★   266
Tricky Lunatic   47
Tricky Prick Ears   27m   F7b ★★★   47
Tricky War   47
Trigger Finger   F6c ★★   74
Trivia   13m   HVS 5a   131
True Path   50
Trust in Mu   9m   F6b ★   279
Tufa King Far Finish   15m   F8a ★★   57
Tufa King Hard   11m   F6c ★★   57
Tunnel Vision   18m   F6a+ ★★   240
Turbulent Beast, The   33m   E5 6b ★★★   189
Turncoat   15m   F6b ★   224
Tuxedo Junction   16m   VS 4b ★   161
TV Fan   8m   F4   91
Twilight   15m   F5a   228
Twilight Zone   F3   264
Twisted Wheel, The   15m   F6b ★   219

Index | 287

Two Pints and a Packet of
    Crisps 9m F6b+ ★   278
Tyke's Teeter 23m F6b   232
Tyke's Teeter Direct 20m F6c ★★   232

U

Undercut Buttress   64
Understudy 10m F4+   246
Underworld, The 16m F7a   138
Unfinished Business 20m F5+   271
Unrighteous Doctors 24m F7c+ ★★★   54
Up Periscope F6b+ ★   271
Upper Right Tier   59
Up Town 27m F6c ★★   50
Usain Bolt 30m F6b+ ★★   229

V

Valdez is Coming F6b+   201
Vale of Secrecy 30m F6a+ ★   235
Vanished Times 15m F6b ★   217
Vexed Question, The 10m F6c+   165
Viagra Falls 25m F6a ★   251
Videodrome 26m F7c ★   57
Viennese Oyster 33m E4 6b ★★   129
Violation 16m F6c ★   163
Violation Variation 17m F6c   165
Viral Visions 15m F6a+ ★   178
Virgin Queen F7a ★★★   258
Virility 24m E1 5b   75
Visionary, The 20m F6a+ ★   216
Vital Spark, The 15m F6a ★   240

W

Wai Lord 19m F7b+   212
Walking on Sunshine 13m F5 ★   88
Wargames 24m F7b ★★★   51
War Hero 26m F7a ★★   47
Warm Push 8m F6b+   57
War of the Pulsars   47
War of the Worlds 37m F6c+ ★★   47
Warton Main Quarry   80
War Trick   47
Watchman, The 10m F6a+   240
Water Boys, The 25m F6a ★★   251
Waterworld 25m F6a+ ★★   249
Way of the Wyrd 42m E6 6b   126
Welcome to Rio 25m F6a ★   232
West Wall, The   108
Westworld F7a+ ★   263

Wetherby Whaler, The 15m F6a   229
Wheelbarrow 18m F6c+   71
Where Bolters Fear to Tread 23m F6a ★   79
Whicker's World 25m F5c ★   234
Whisky Galore F7a ★★   263
Wicked Willie 45m E5 6b ★★★   125
Wide Open 11m F5a   177
Wider Sea, The 5m F6b+   276
Wild Garlic 17m F6a   193
Will's Route F7a ★   258
Wings 42m E4 5c   125
Winter is Coming 10m M7   149
Winter Pincher 15m F6b+   42
Witherslack Alice 26m F6c+   51
Witness, The 5m F7b+   276
Woodcutter's Lullaby, The 30m F6c+   224
Wounded Knee F5   202
Wrecking Crew, The 28m F6a ★★   222

Y

Yashmak F6c   44
Yazidi 10m F6a+   212
Year of the Cat, The 34m E2 5a   85
Yodelling in the Canyon 11m F4   177
Yo! Pick Poe! 10m HVS 5b   174
Yopo 15m F5b   228
Yorkshire Ripper 30m F6b+ ★★   229

Z

Zantom Phone 25m F7c+ ★★   44
Z Climb F7a ★★   271
Zero Tolerance 26m F6a+ ★   85
Zima Junction F6a+   201
Zipcode F5+   202
Zoom 20m F6c ★★★   238

Great Gable, the FRCC's gift to the National Trust and site of the FRCC Great War Memorial — Roy Austin

Threlkeld Quarry and Mining Museum

'The Home of Lakeland's Industrial Heritage'

Our narrow-gauge railway, using steam and diesel locomotives, runs daily and offers a grandstand view of the machinery collection and of the local fells.
Steam Gala held in July

On site there is the largest collection of Vintage Excavators in Europe. Oldest Surviving Steam Navvy Demonstration Days.
Excavator Demonstration Weekends in May and September

Experience 'coffin' levels, candlelight and total **DARKNESS** on a 45 minute guided tour of our replica mine (*not suitable for under 7s and booking recommended*). There is also our museum which covers over 400 years of mining and quarrying in the Lake District.

Threlkeld Quarry and Mining Museum, Keswick, CA12 4TT
threlkeldquarrymuseum@btconnect.com
017687 79747 Open daily Easter – October, 10am – 5pm
www.threlkeldquarryandminingmuseum.com